IMAGES
of America

St. Louis Arsenal

Armory of the West

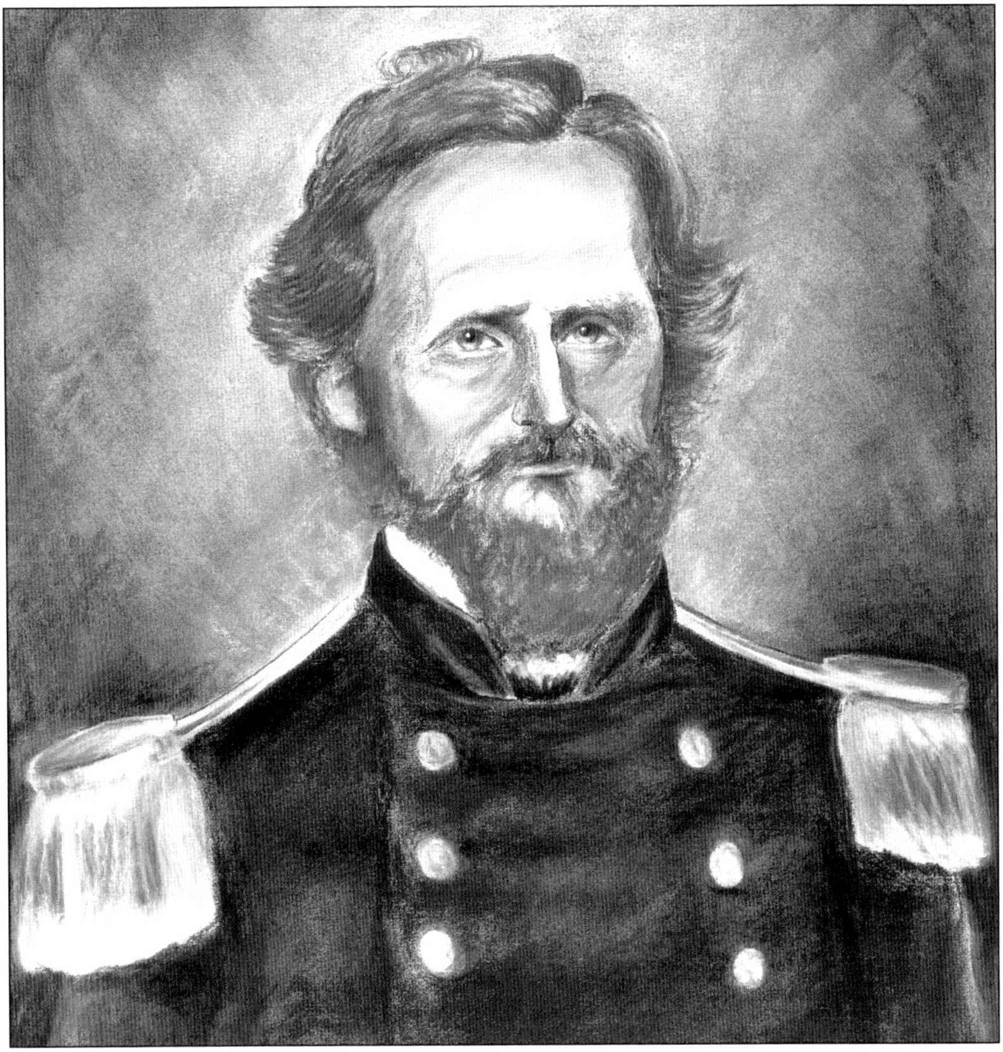

Brevet Brigadier General Nathaniel Lyon. (Courtesy of Jane Wilkinson, NIMA) Although a legion of distinguished Army officers saw service at the St. Louis Arsenal, no name has been more permanently etched in the fabric of this "Armory of the West" than that of Nathaniel Lyon. When Captain Lyon reported for duty at the arsenal in the chaotic winter of 1861, he would remain for a scant six months before leading his troops to glory—and becoming the first general to die in the Civil War—at Wilson's Creek. Yet the impact he made in those six short months, on both the St. Louis community and on the strategic military balance of the West, was nothing less than phenomenal. The fiery-eyed harbinger of a self-dictated justice, whose presence still permeates the atmosphere of the old arsenal, is pictured here in this perceptive portrait by Jane Wilkinson, who works today on the very grounds where Lyon fortified the arsenal against its Confederate foe.

Cover Photo: The three-story main arsenal building rises high on a bluff overlooking the Mississippi in this 1866 Emil Boehl photograph. The arsenal had excelled at equipping the armies of the West under the relentless pressure of four years of civil war. Now it would have to refocus its mission to become a primary collecting point for the return of ordnance as these armies rapidly demobilized for peacetime. (Courtesy of Missouri Historical Society)

IMAGES
of America

ST. LOUIS ARSENAL

ARMORY OF THE WEST

Randy R. McGuire, Ph.D.

ARCADIA
PUBLISHING

ISBN 978-0-7385-0780-4

Published by Arcadia Publishing
Charleston, South Carolina

Printed in the United States of America

Library of Congress Catalog Card Number: 2001090093

For all general information contact Arcadia Publishing at:
Telephone 843-853-2070
Fax 843-853-0044
E-mail sales@arcadiapublishing.com
For customer service and orders:
Toll-Free 1-888-313-2665

Visit us on the Internet at www.arcadiapublishing.com

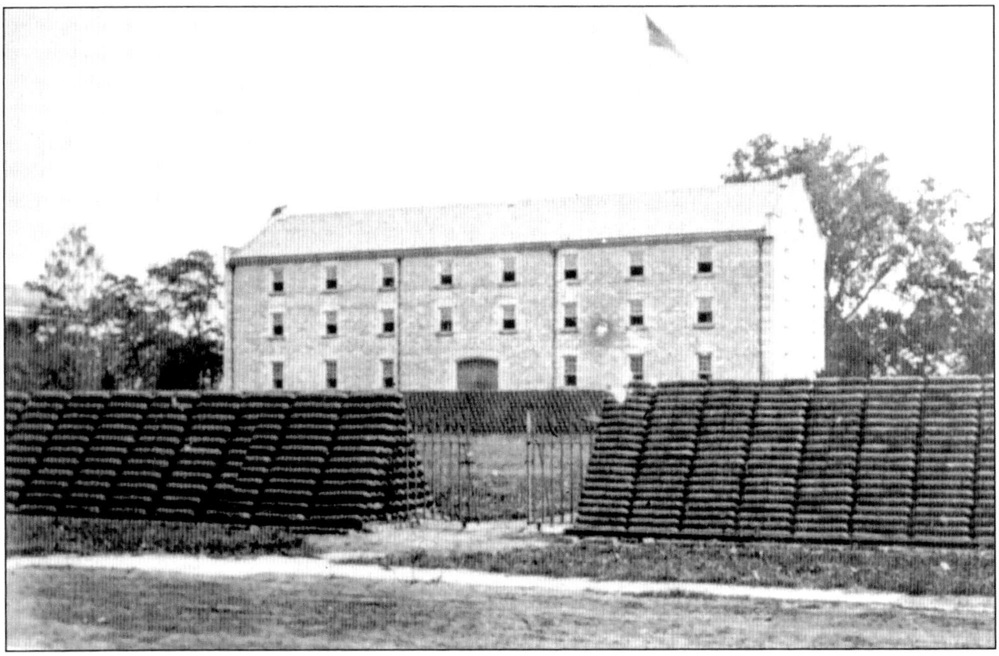

THE MAIN ARSENAL BUILDING EARLY IN THE CIVIL WAR. (Courtesy of Missouri Historical Society) This view of the west side of the main arsenal building illustrates how every foot of ground at the installation was used for the storage of arms and ammunition. Even pigs of lead, as seen here, wait to be melted into bullets. This became a common sight on the arsenal grounds within a year of the beginning of the war. During the war this building was used primarily for the storage of small arms. This image is thought to date from 1862 and, as such, would be the oldest known photograph of the St. Louis Arsenal.

CONTENTS

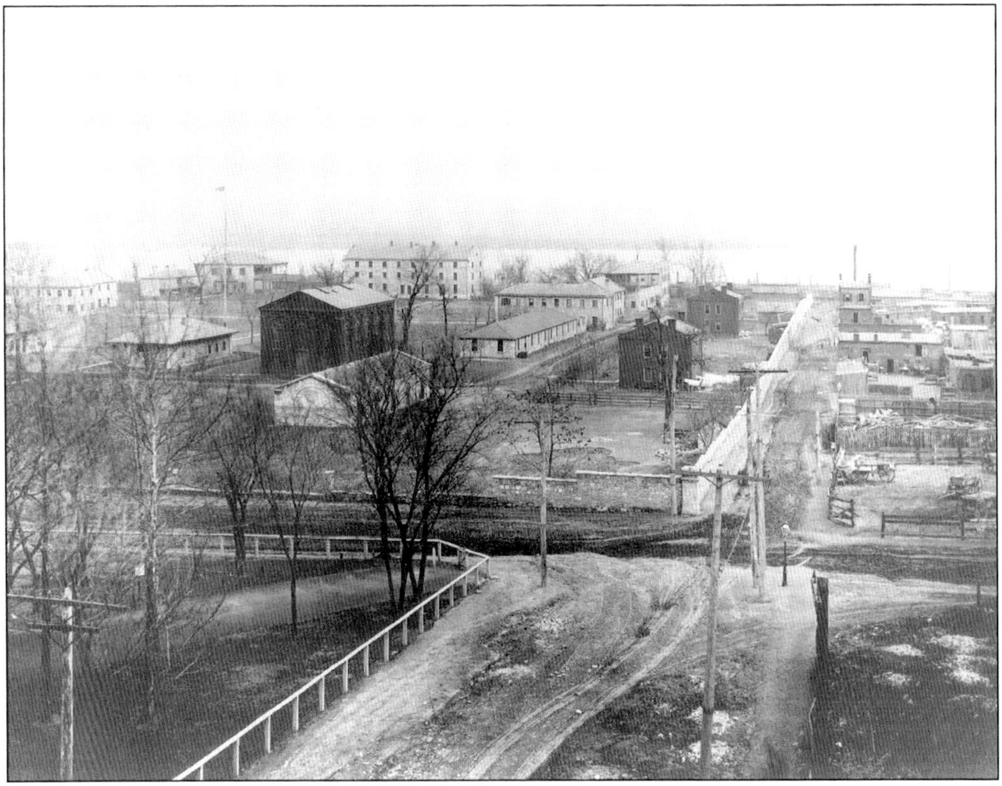

VIEW OF THE ARSENAL BUILDINGS FROM THE WEST. Professional photographer George Stark took this photograph of the arsenal in 1905. It represents a good perspective on the basic layout of the installation from the 1870s to the end of World War I. Various versions of this picture were used for postcards printed around 1910. (Courtesy of Missouri Historical Society)

INTRODUCTION

On the afternoon of May 10, 1861, Army Captain Nathaniel Lyon marched out of the St. Louis Arsenal at the head of 6,000 Union Volunteers to capture an encampment of some 700 reputed Confederate sympathizers at Camp Jackson on the western outskirts of St. Louis. It probably did not occur to him that he was embarking on a mission that would forever enshrine his name, and that of the arsenal, in the annals of Civil War history.

The St. Louis Arsenal's encounter with glory came after 34 years of unheralded but significant contributions to the development of the American West. The arsenal provided the material means by which the West would be won. It armed the militias of the newly developing territories and states and supplied explorers, settlers, traders, and other frontiersmen with the means to protect and establish themselves in this vast wilderness. When the Indian Wars of the 1830s, the Mexican War of the 1840s, the "Mormon Wars" of the 1850s, and the Civil War of the 1860s erupted, the arsenal served its key role of providing arms and ammunition for U.S. forces involved in these conflicts. During the Civil War, in particular, it played a crucial role as an outpost of Union presence in a sea of Confederate sympathies and its security was rarely guaranteed.

The first Civil War conflict on the soil of Missouri was fought for the control of this installation. Had it been lost to the rebels in the opening days of the war, the duration and outcome of the conflict might have been vastly different. One of the key factors in the Confederate loss of the war was its relative disadvantage at matching the North in the production and distribution of arms and ammunition. Because the North held most of the significant arsenals at the outbreak of the war, they held a two-to-one advantage over the South in access to weapons and ammunition. But if southern sympathizers had captured this rich St. Louis repository of war materiel, the South would have assumed a much stronger position in the opening days of the war. Given the chronic shortage of weapons suffered by the Confederacy throughout the war, who can tell the difference that such a situation might have created?

In words and images, this book relates the story of the arsenal, from its founding in 1827, through its transition to Cavalry post in 1872, to its new life and changing fortunes as the installation adapts its mission to meet the ever-changing needs of the US military. The early chapters depict the process by which St. Louis was chosen for the arsenal, the construction of its buildings and fortifications, and the significant service it provided to US troops and citizens establishing themselves in the hostile reaches of the American West. Other sections describe the ordnance stored, assembled, and manufactured at the arsenal. But foremost in the saga are the stories of personalities who served there over the years. Many notable officers had dealings with the arsenal during their years of service: William Beaumont (frontier surgeon), Robert E. Lee (Army engineer), John Fremont (explorer and Civil War general), Robert Anderson (later commander at Ft. Sumter), Ulysses S. Grant, William Sherman, Nathaniel Lyon, Daniel Frost, and many others who would claim a place in the annals of American military history.

A series of maps and drawings will illustrate the physical development of the installation, decade by decade, supplemented with information on the buildings, to illuminate the arsenal's expanding role in American life in the nineteenth century. No other published source draws together so much information on the installation's structures through the close of the arsenal in 1872 and developments at the installation in the years following. I hope this volume will serve as a guide for those who visit the arsenal grounds today, where 11 buildings remain from the Civil War period and earlier, and that it will provide a fitting testimonial to those who struggled to win the West and to preserve the Union.

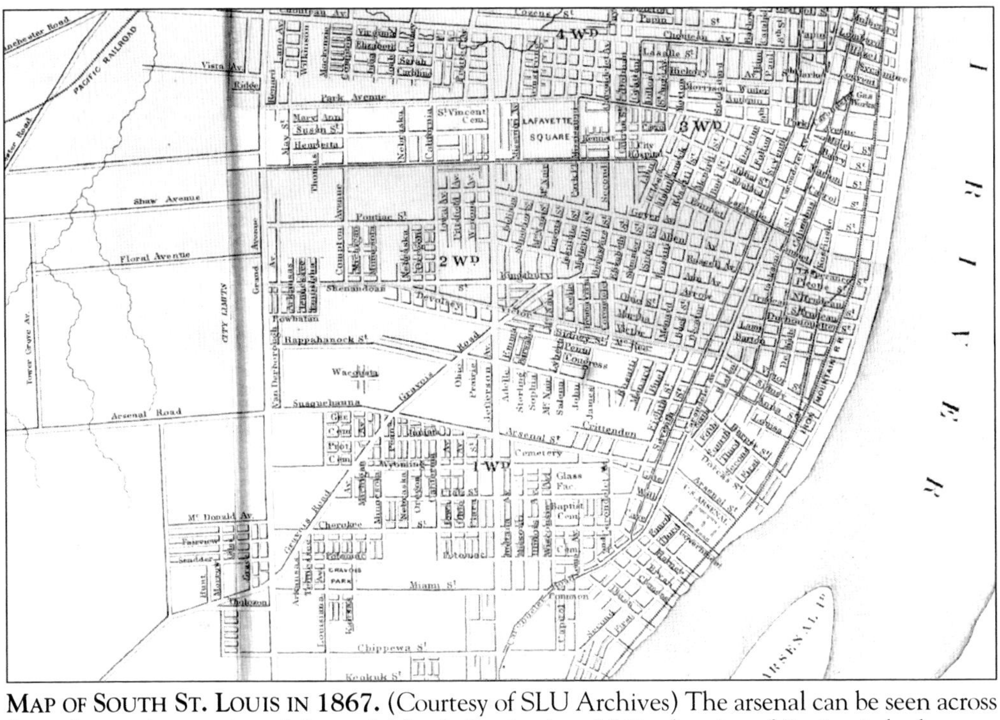

Map of South St. Louis in 1867. (Courtesy of SLU Archives) The arsenal can be seen across from the northern point of Arsenal Island. By the late 1860s the city of St. Louis had grown beyond its early southern border to encompass the entire arsenal area. This map depicts the streets and highways of St. Louis much as they would have appeared during the Civil War.

One

LIFE BEFORE THE ARSENAL

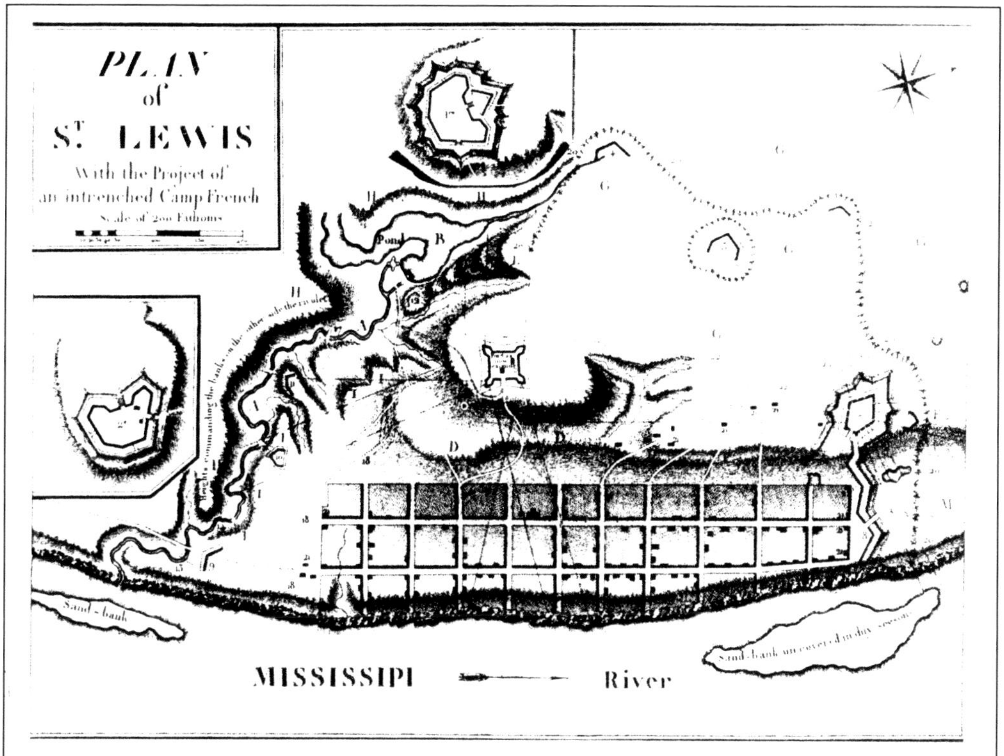

EARLY PLAN FOR ST. LOUIS AND ITS DEFENSES. (Courtesy of SLU Archives) This fanciful design for the protection of eighteenth century St. Louis already recognized the strategic significance of the location of this city on the western American frontier. Although the specific fortifications depicted here may never have been built, many other forts and military structures would dot the landscape of St. Louis and its environs in coming decades, most significantly including the St. Louis Arsenal.

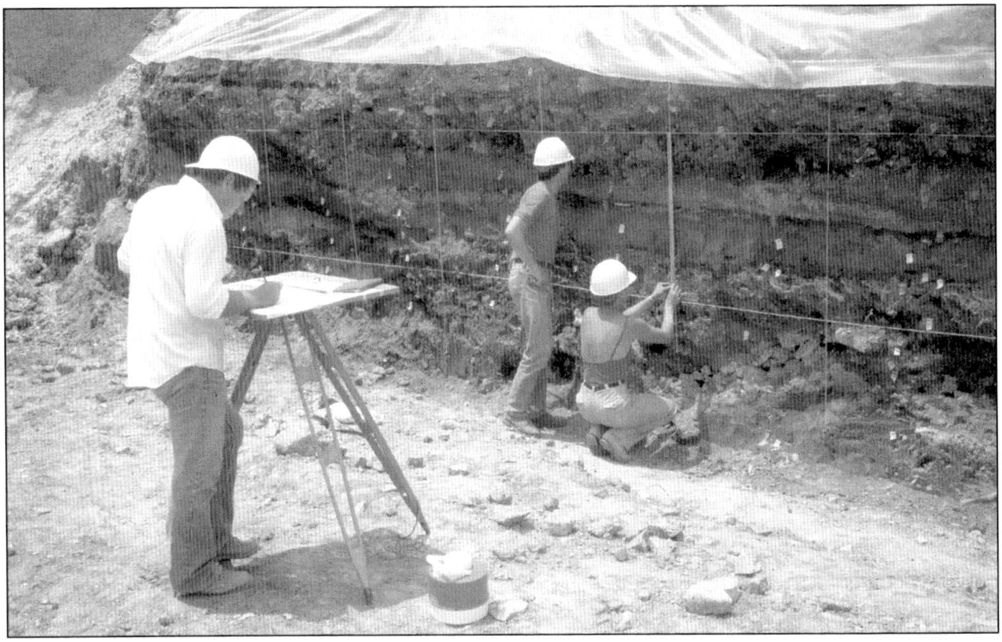

EXCAVATIONS AT THE ARSENAL SITE PRODUCE EARLY NATIVE AMERICAN ARTIFACTS. (Courtesy of William Woods) Portions of the old arsenal site were excavated in connection with construction projects between 1981 and 1984 by Dr. William Woods and a team from Southern Illinois University, Edwardsville. In the above image, Dr. Woods and two assistants create a grid on an excavated surface to aid in drawing an accurate elevation of the site. The projectile points illustrated below, found on the lowest habitation level of the profile seen here, provide evidence for the occupation of this site as early as the Middle to Late Archaic eras (*c.* 3000–1000 B.C.).

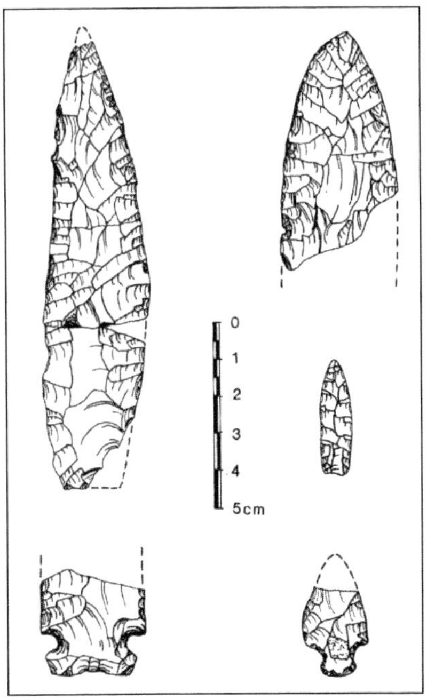

EVIDENCE OF "MOUND BUILDERS" IN THE ARSENAL AREA. (Courtesy of William Woods) Evidence of the later Mississippian culture was also found at the site. Prior to the coming of Europeans, this influential culture, popularly known as the "Mound Builders," had flourished in the region from A.D. 900 to 1400. The outlying settlements reached the future St. Louis area and dominated the central Mississippi region until its decline in the 13th and 14th centuries. Shortly before white explorers and traders arrived in the Mississippi Valley in the 17th century, the Osage and Siouan peoples dominated the region.

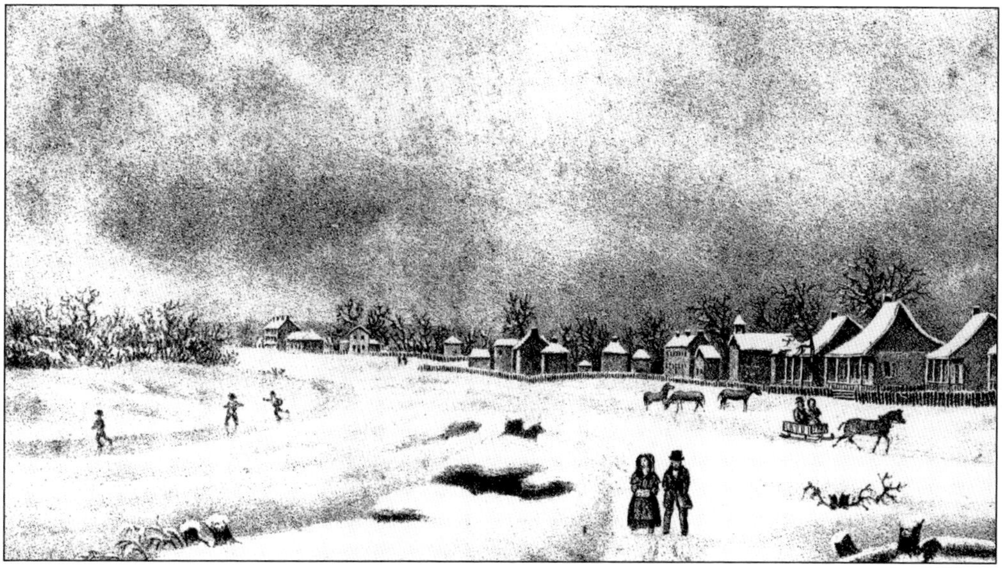

AN IDYLLIC SCENE OF CAHOKIA, ILLINOIS, IN WINTER, BY J.C. WILD, 1841. (Courtesy of SLU Archives) The French explored western Illinois and Missouri for a century before putting down roots in the region. Their earliest settlement in the St. Louis area was at Cahokia, in 1699, across the Mississippi and five miles southeast of the future metropolis. The 142-year-old village that J.C. Wild visited in 1841 still retained "the manners, customs, and the language of old France," whose inhabitants comprised 90 percent of the population.

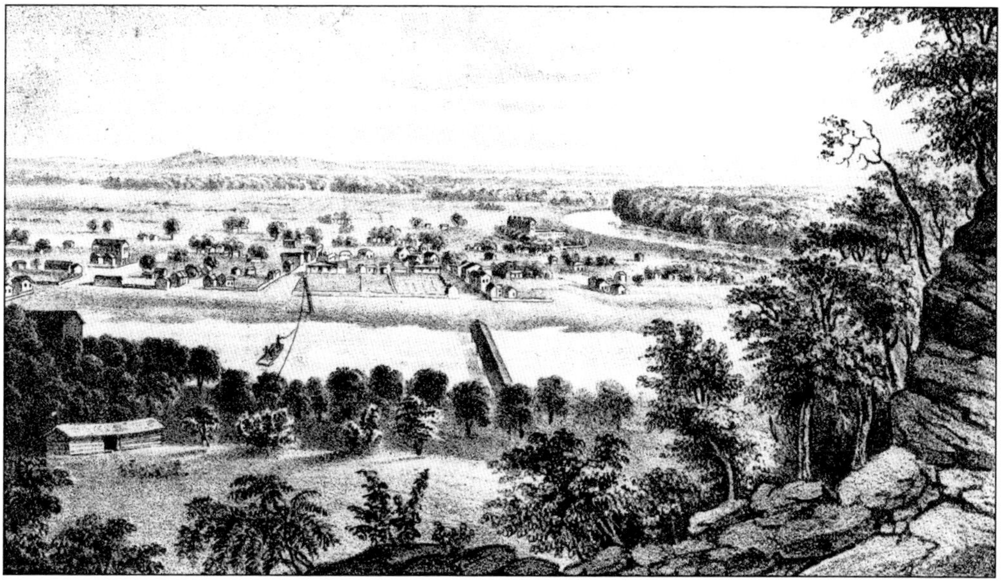

A VIEW OF KASKASKIA, BY J.C. WILD, 1841. (Courtesy of SLU Archives) Some 60 miles southeast of Cahokia and 3 miles east of the Mississippi, on the Kaskaskia River, the French built a fort and a trading settlement in 1700 and named it Kaskaskia. Here the first Catholic Church in Illinois was established. The picturesque village that greeted Wild on his 1841 excursion once boasted 7,000 inhabitants when it served as the first territorial capital of Illinois and the center of trade in the mid-Mississippi region. Its significance would later be eclipsed by the growth of St. Louis.

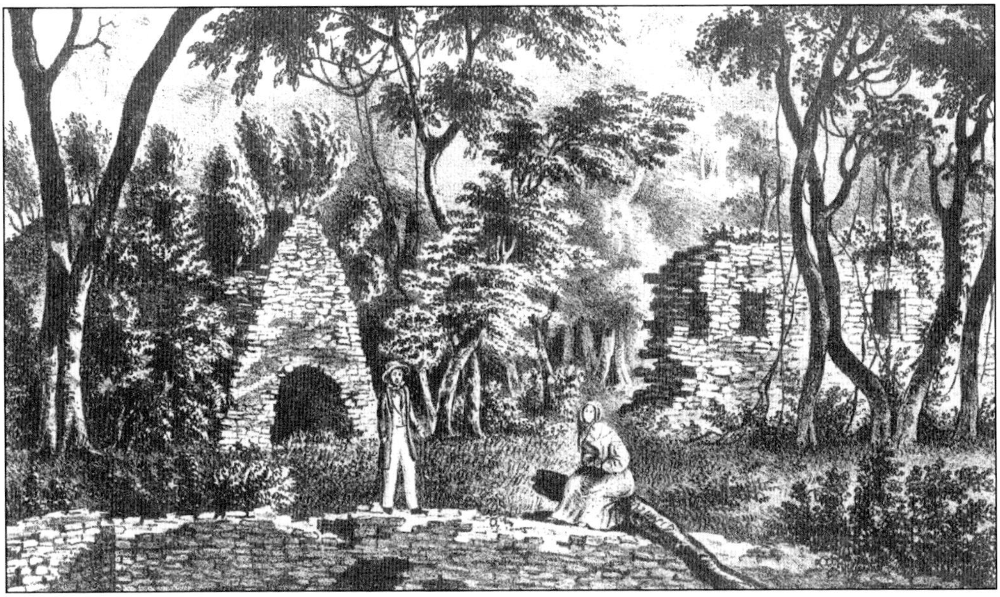

RUINS OF FORT DE CHARTRES AS OBSERVED BY J.C. WILD IN 1841. (Courtesy of SLU Archives) In 1720 Fort de Chartres was established by the French about 15 miles north of Kaskaskia to serve as capital of the Illinois Country (then known as Upper Louisiana). By the time of Wild's visit in 1841 the old fort had fallen into ruin and no one remained to inhabit the site.

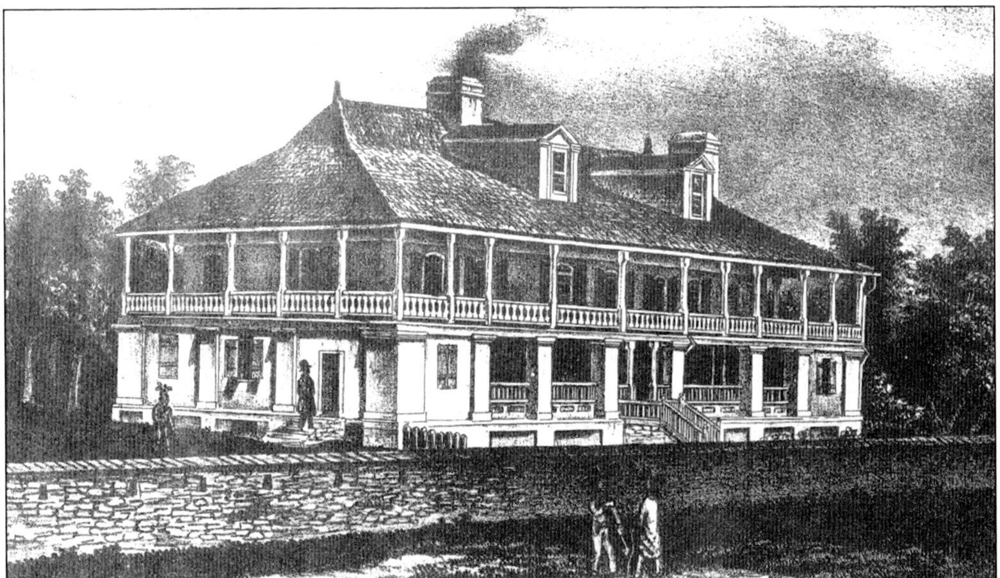

OLD CHOUTEAU MANSION IN ST. LOUIS, J.C. WILD, 1841. (Courtesy of SLU Archives) In February 1764, young Auguste Chouteau of New Orleans was sent by his step-father, Pierre de Laclede, to clear ground on a site in Spanish territory on the west bank of the Mississippi, a few miles south of its confluence with the Missouri River. Laclede named the settlement St. Louis in honor of the French king's patron saint, Louis IX. Here he built a trading post which would establish St. Louis as a center in the fur business and as an embarkation point for western explorers, traders, and settlers.

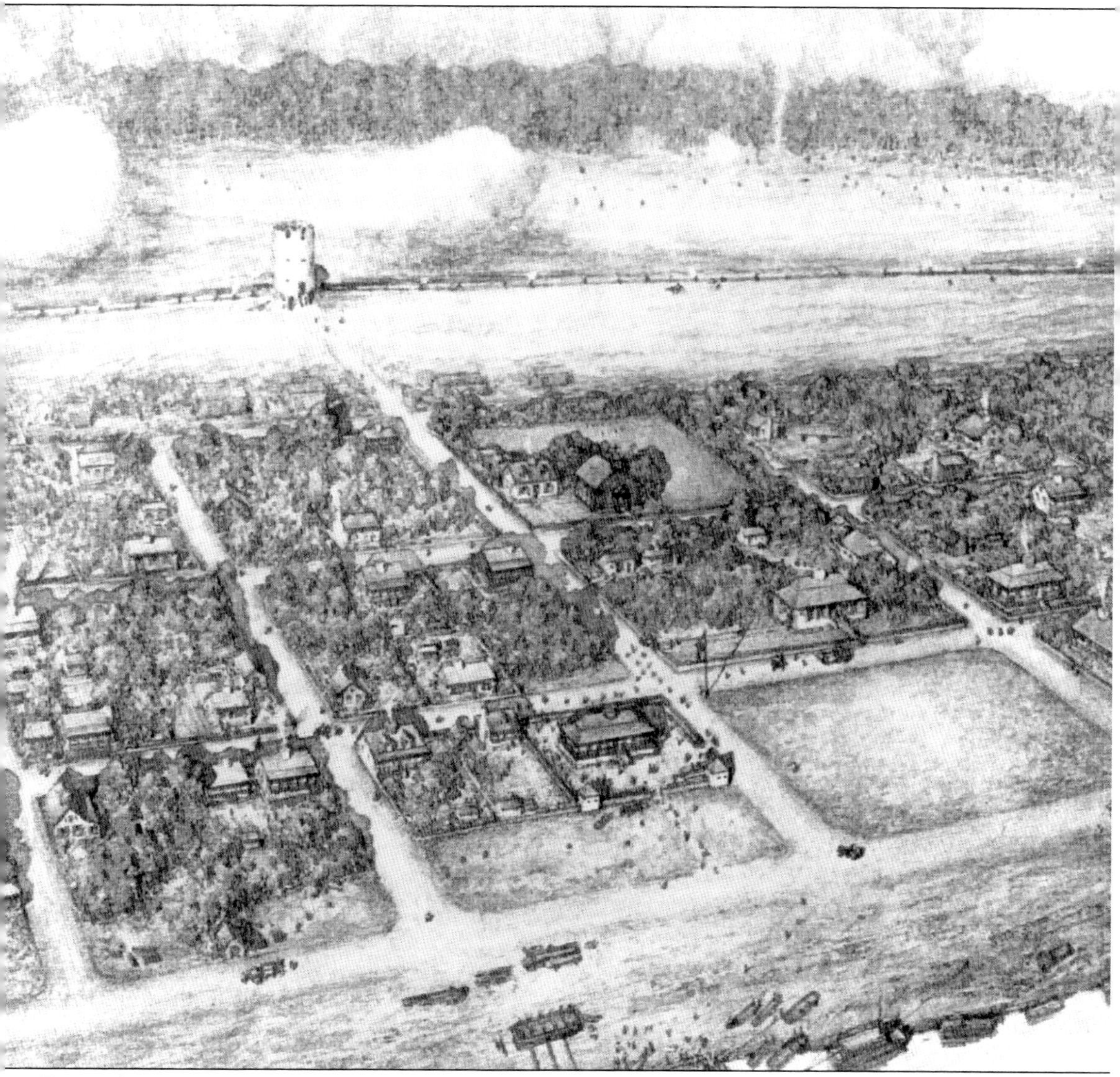

Early St. Louis Arranged in French Urban Style. (Courtesy of NIMA) The village of St. Louis was laid out in a typical French gridiron pattern, with three major streets running northeast and southwest, parallel to the river. The main streets were approximately 38 feet wide, with east-west cross streets 30 feet wide. Each of the first 49 blocks measured 240 by 300 feet, except for the three central blocks dedicated to public purposes, which were 300 by 300 feet. There were generally four lots to a block, but as time passed, the lots would be subdivided and homes and businesses would fill the old town area. The entire old village was situated below a high ridge that backed up the settlement. Through the first decades of its existence, the village grew slowly; in 1772, its population, including slaves, was 577. The above image represents St. Louis a few years later, during the closing days of the American Revolution. After the Louisiana Purchase of 1803, Americans poured into Missouri, taking up residence in St. Louis and nearby settlements. Despite a slowdown during the War of 1812, immigration picked up after 1815 and by 1820 the federal census revealed a robust population of 4,598 in the town of St. Louis, while the surrounding county numbered nearly 10,000. The town grew rapidly in all directions from the river front.

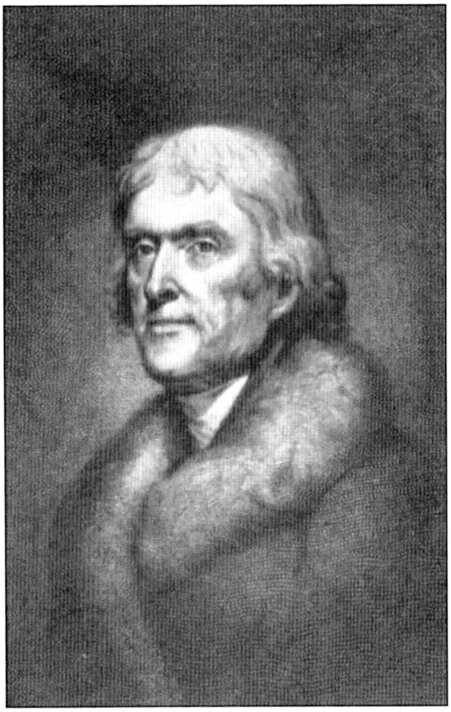

THOMAS JEFFERSON, PRESIDENT OF THE UNITED STATES (1801–1809) AND BROKER OF THE "GREATEST LAND DEAL IN HISTORY." (Courtesy of SLU Archives) The fledgling settlement of St. Louis was under Spanish Imperial control at its inception, though its inhabitants were mostly French, with a smattering of native-born "Americans," Indians, blacks, and a few other nationalities. When French power rebounded, Napoleon induced the Spanish King, Charles IV, to cede Louisiana back to France. But three years later, burdened by war expenses, Napoleon agreed to sell the vast territory to the U.S., and President Thomas Jefferson presided over what many call "the greatest land deal in history."

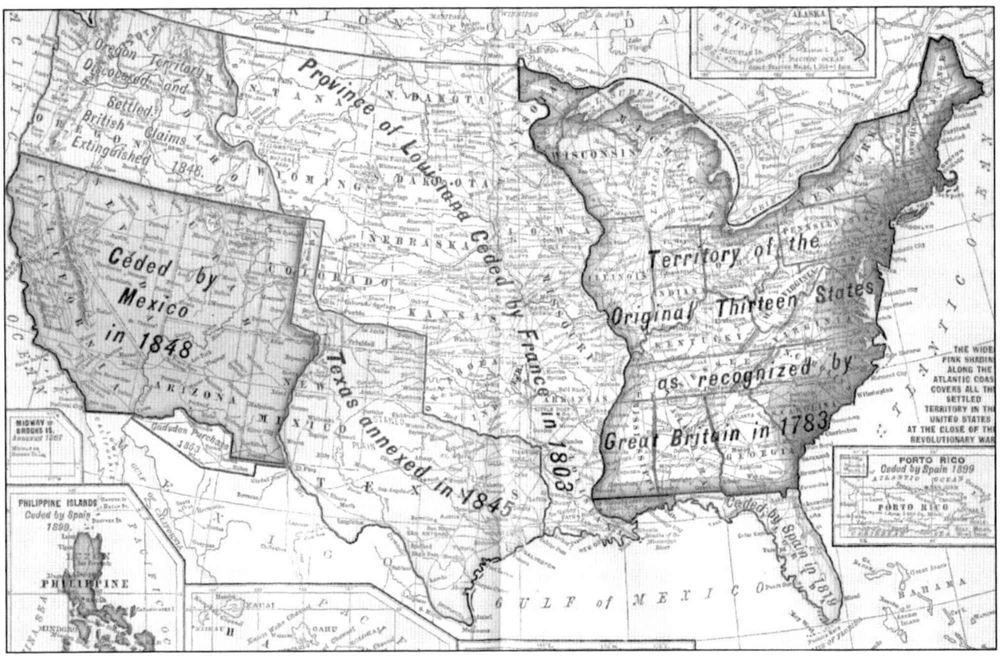

THE LOUISIANA PURCHASE OF 1803. (Courtesy of SLU Archives) For some $27.3 million, America's newest acquisition amounted to 828,000 square miles of pristine wilderness at less than 3¢ an acre. The Louisiana Purchase nearly doubled the size of the United States and significantly strengthened the nation. It fueled a continuing westward movement, which sparked a sense of "manifest destiny" for many Americans. From this point on, St. Louis was an American city, taking on the trappings of a classic western boomtown.

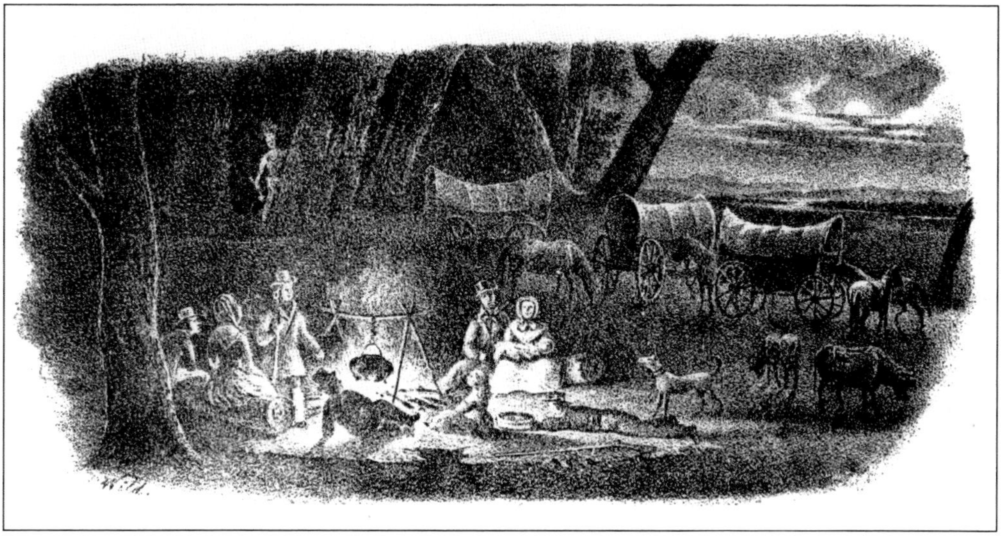

THE JOYS AND DANGERS OF WESTERN TRAVEL AS DEPICTED BY J.C. WILD, 1841. (Courtesy of SLU Archives) With the opening of the Louisiana Territory, thousands of Americans sought their destinies in the wide-open spaces of the West. To protect the settlers and to prevent harm to the Indians, the U.S. government established forts throughout the territory, particularly in the watershed of the Missouri River. To supply the forts with their basic needs and with ordnance for soldiers and militias, supply posts and arsenals were established to provide this materiel.

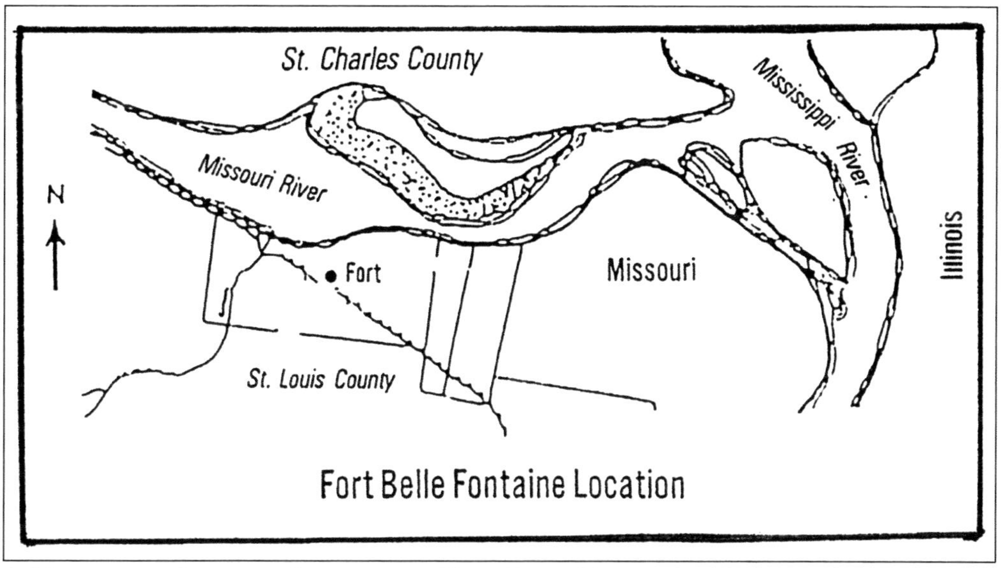

A MAP OF THE ORIGINAL LOCATION OF FORT BELLE FONTAINE. (Courtesy of NIMA) North of St. Louis, some 15 miles distant by primitive road, and 5 miles west of the confluence of the Missouri and Mississippi Rivers, a fort was built in 1805 on the south bank of the Missouri, to serve as the major source of supply for the western installations. In reference to the abundant springs in the area, it was called Belle Fontaine, "beautiful fountain."

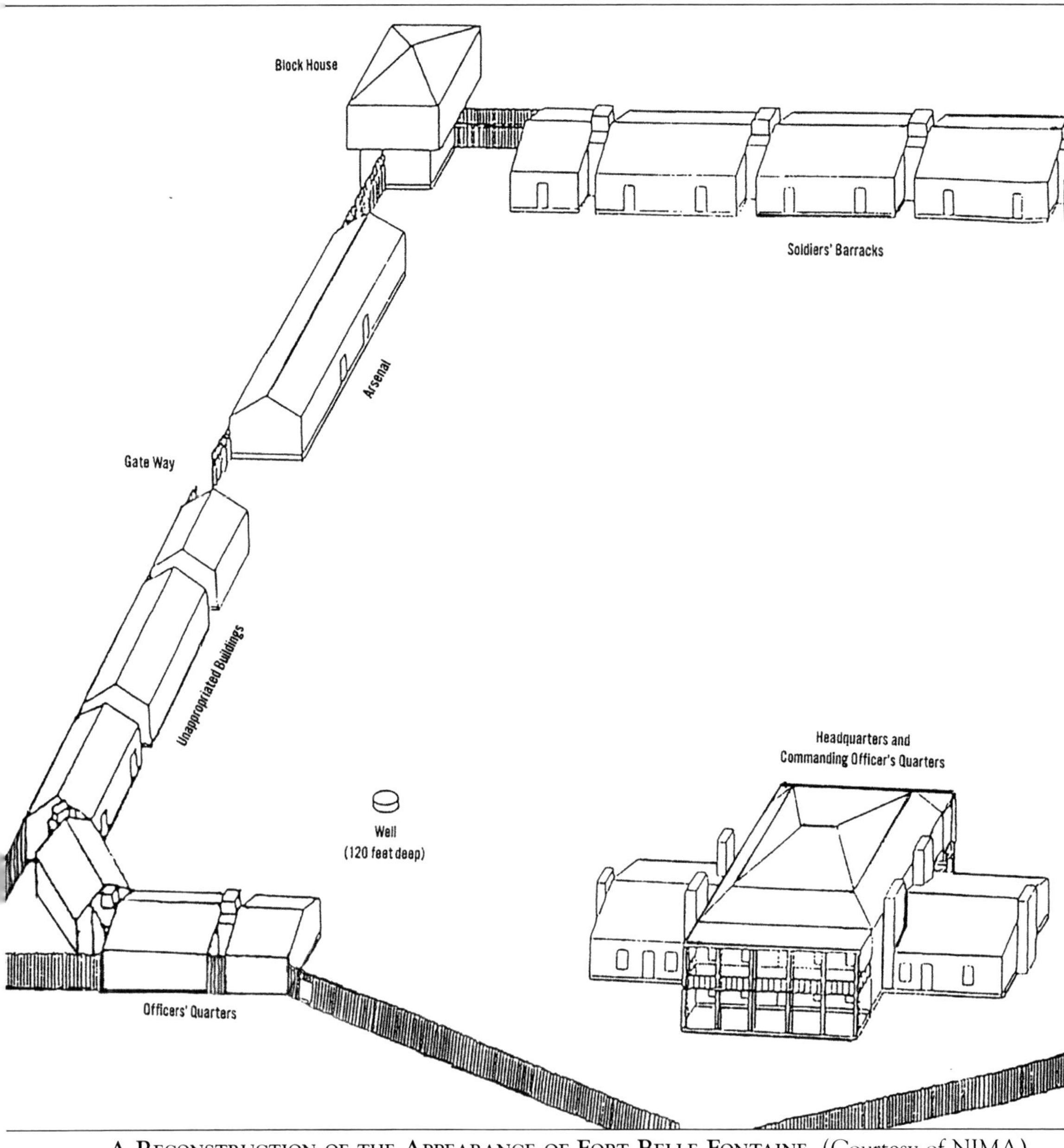

A Reconstruction of the Appearance of Fort Belle Fontaine. (Courtesy of NIMA) Ft. Belle Fontaine quartered a regiment of U.S. troops to respond to emergencies in eastern Missouri and southern Illinois. The post consisted of a wooden stockade, surrounding about 25 buildings, all constructed of timber. The elegance of the fort's name, however, belied its disappointing history. Due to haste and command ineptitude, construction of the post was deficient. The soldiers themselves provided the labor, but most were inexperienced in the building trades. Consequently, non-seasoned timbers were used as the primary building material. Within ten years, many buildings and the stockade fell into decay; within 20, few buildings were fit for use as storehouses and fewer still were habitable. Commanders and inspectors continually requested financial assistance to repair the installation, but the government, seeking to cut military spending in the wake of the War of 1812, ignored the entreaties.

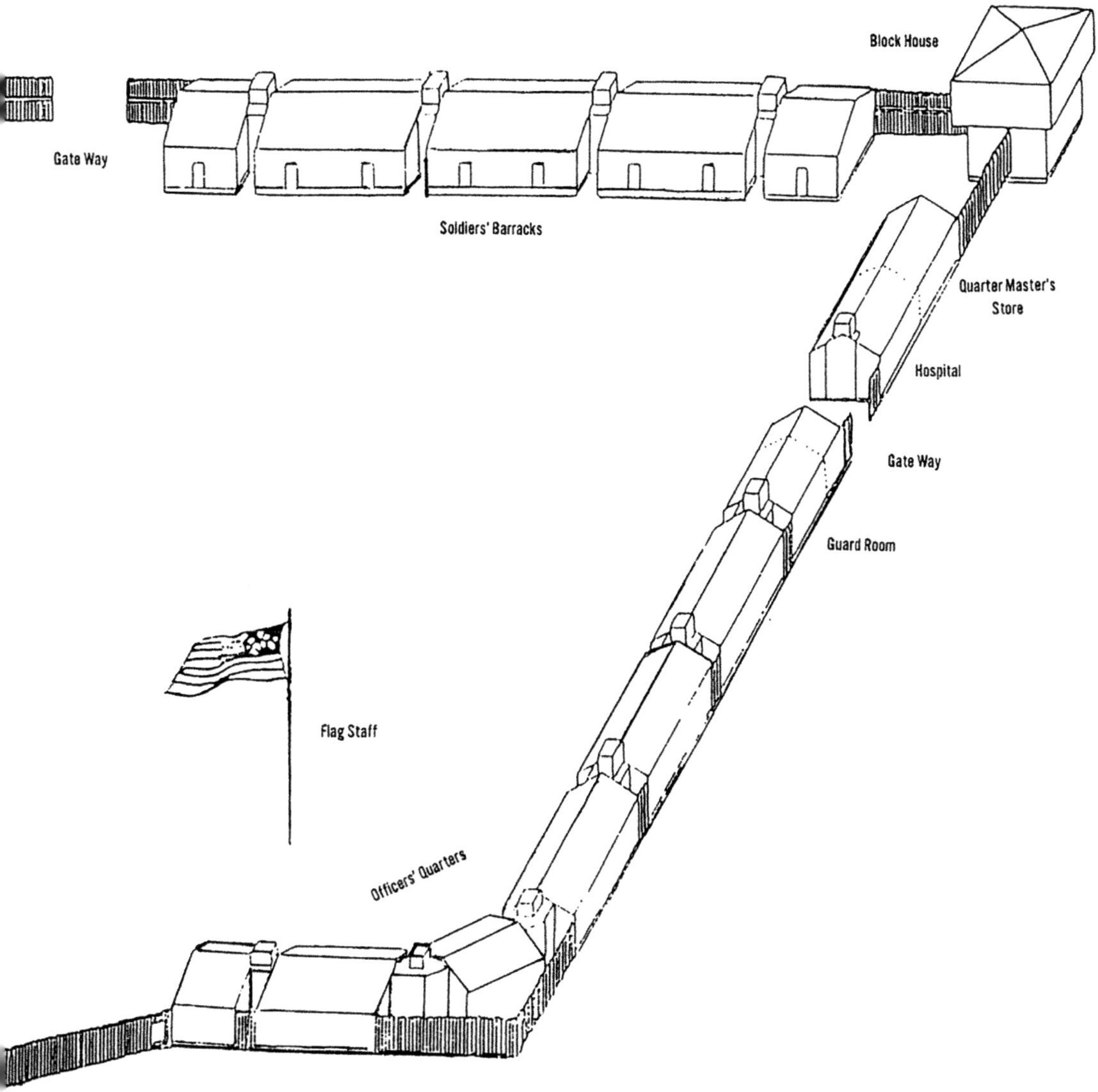

Eventually political pressure led to an inquiry on the establishment of a permanent arsenal at St. Louis. In 1825, the House Committee on Military Affairs conducted a six-month study; its 1826 report was graphic. "The log buildings at Belle Fontaine have become so much decayed that a part of them have recently fallen down, and the remainder are so rotten that they can be kept up but a little longer. There is a considerable quantity of arms and other military stores now at Belle Fontaine, which are so insecurely sheltered in these log buildings that it is feared they will suffer material injury if not soon better provided for." In May 1826, Congress authorized the secretary of war to purchase land for an arsenal at or near St. Louis and to construct the facility. The task of finding property on which to build the arsenal was delegated to Lieutenant Martin Thomas, superintendent of U.S. lead mines in Illinois and Missouri.

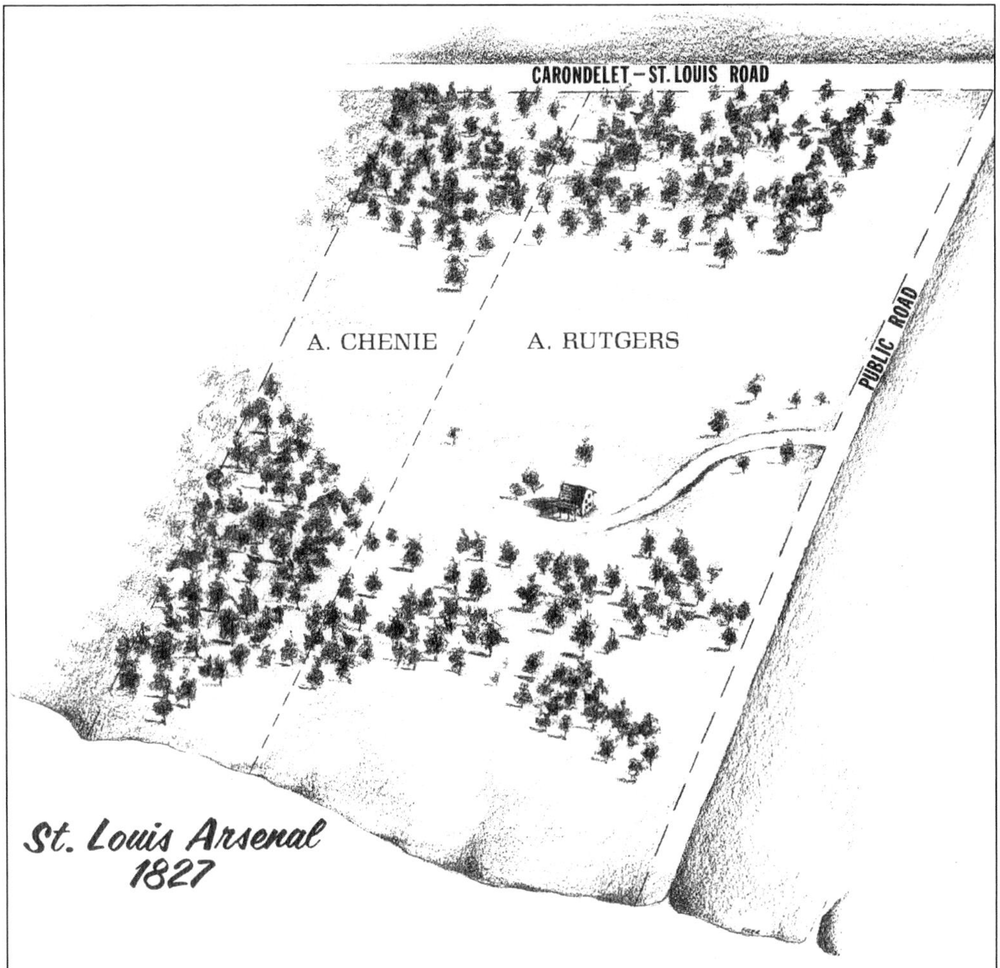

IDEALIZED VIEW OF THE ARSENAL PROPERTY IN 1827. (Courtesy of NIMA) Lieutenant Thomas explored the St. Louis vicinity for a site accessible to the Mississippi, on high ground, well drained, and defensible. In April 1827, he concluded the best "scite" was the Arend Rutgers property 3 miles south of the city. Rutgers had purchased 31 arpents in 1819 and built a spacious dwelling for his sizable family and servants. Thomas wrote: "This is by far the cheapest and best scite, taking every thing into consideration, it is more in the immediate route of transportation, as perhaps twenty steam boats pass it where one passes the scites above the town, in addition to which, there is a fractional quarter section of public land in the rear of it which can be reserved from sale, and attached to the scite, which will make it about 150 acres." He also noted that local contractors said the rock quarried south of St. Louis was of better quality than that found at or above the city and that "disinterested persons" had observed that the grounds north of the city tended to be lower and given to flooding and swampiness, with their "accompanying fevers," whereas the land south of town was higher, and considered healthy. In June, Colonel Bomford approved the purchase of the adjoining properties of Arend Rutgers and August Chenie. The transaction was completed by Lieutenant Thomas on August 2, with the acquisition of 31 arpents from Rutgers and 13 arpents from Chenie, for a total of 44 arpents (36.96 acres). The property was a mix of timbered and cultivated land, mostly undeveloped. Thomas urged headquarters to let him hire laborers as soon as possible, for the building season was far spent and there would be little time to complete a structure before winter.

Two

STONE FORT RISING (1827–1833)

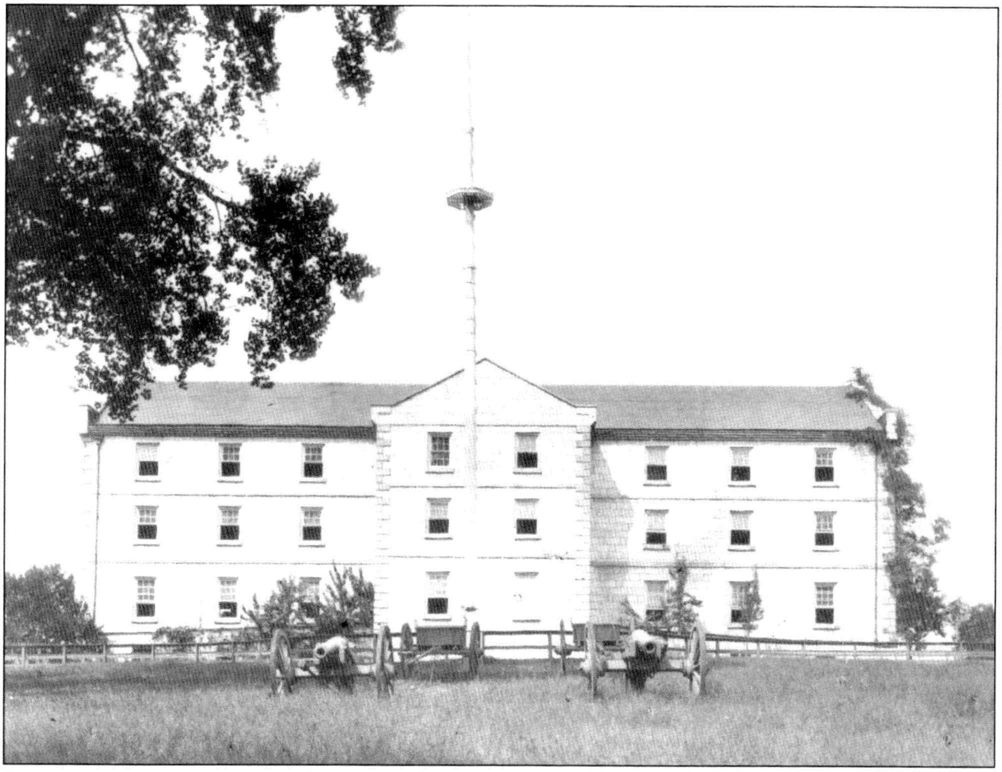

ST. LOUIS ARSENAL MAIN BUILDING, PHOTOGRAPHED BY EMIL BOEHL, 1866. (Courtesy of Missouri Historical Society) Lieutenant Thomas designed the initial layout of the arsenal facility. It would consist of several buildings, arranged in a traditional military manner as a quadrangle surrounding a parade field. The installation was laid out perpendicular to the river, and since the Mississippi flowed from northeast to southwest as it passed the property, the fort had a southeast-to-northwesterly orientation. In the 1820s the river provided the main avenue of approach to the site and this became Thomas's reference point, for the side of the compound facing the Mississippi was considered the "front" of the installation. From this vantage point the three story main arsenal building would rise high above the bluffs, like a sentinel keeping watch over the river.

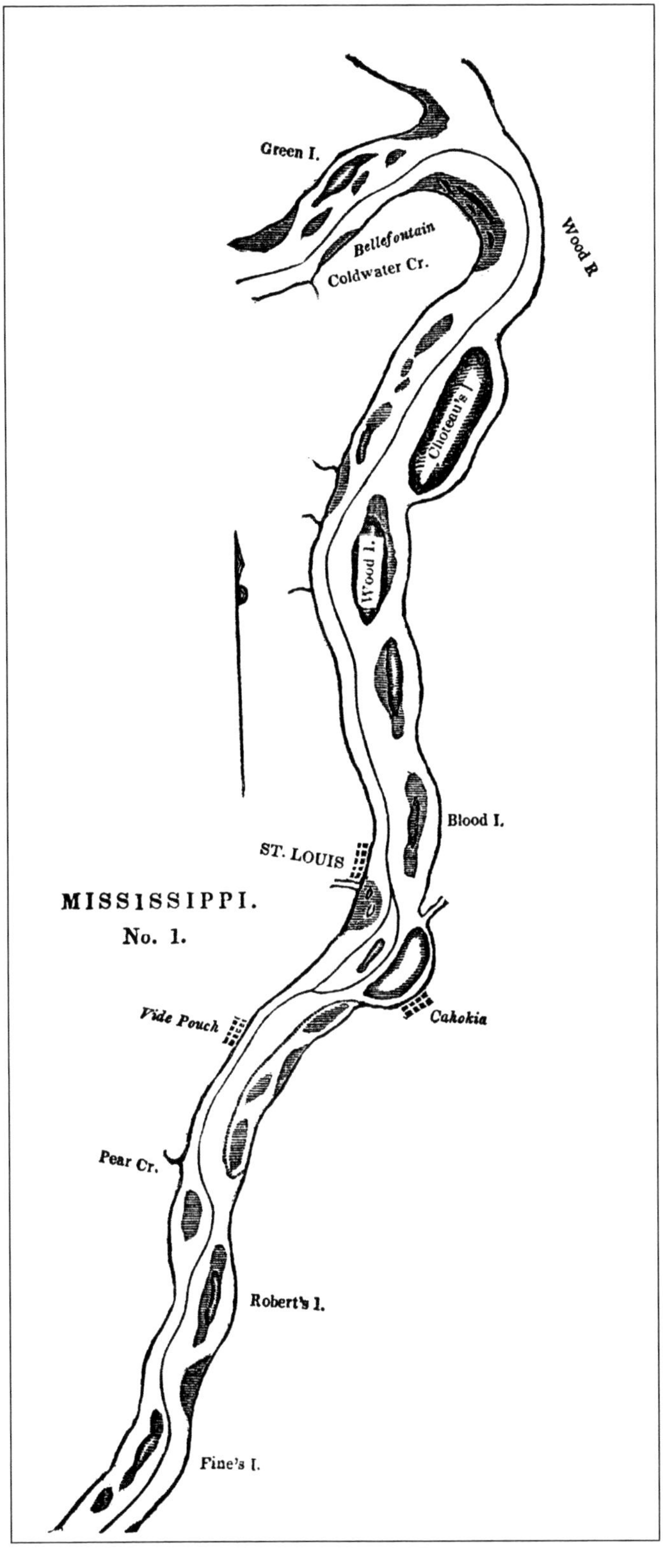

MAP OF THE MISSISSIPPI NEAR ST. LOUIS, 1850. (Courtesy of SLU Archives) This map of a section of the Mississippi near St. Louis was extracted from a mid-nineteenth century travelers' guide to the "western rivers." At the top of the sketch is the confluence with the Missouri River, near which Fort Belle Fontaine was located. Several islands, usually expanded sand bars, broke up the river as it flowed past St. Louis. The city can be seen in the center of this view, with Vide Pouch the next settlement down river. Vide Pouch would later be called Carondelet. The U.S. Arsenal was placed approximately half way between St. Louis and Vide Pouch in 1827, but the City of St. Louis would grow along the river over the next half century until both the arsenal and Carondelet were enveloped within its boundaries.

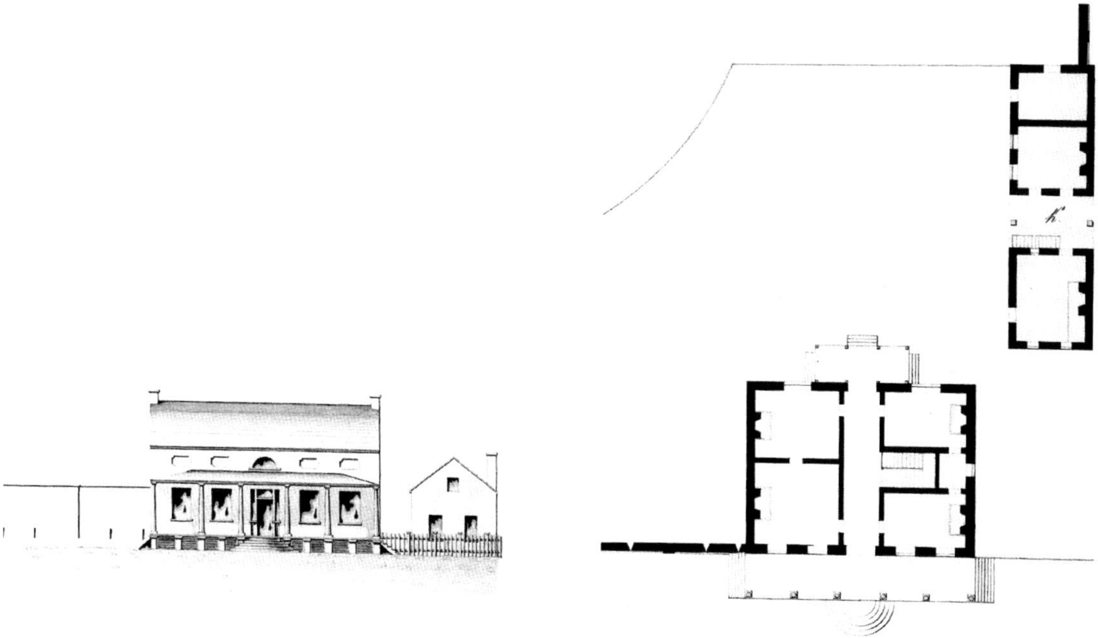

FORMER RUTGERS HOME USED AS OFFICERS' QUARTERS, DRAWN BY LOUIS WINKELMAIER, 1840. (Courtesy of National Archives) When Lieutenant Thomas concluded his purchase of the Rutgers and Chenie properties, there was a bonus in the deal. The former home of the Rutgers family was located on the bluff overlooking the river near the north side of the property. The Chenie tract had apparently been undeveloped, for there is no record of a structure on their land. But the Rutgers home would serve as convenient quarters for officers soon to be stationed at the arsenal. It was eight years old in 1827 when it came into the possession of the government. Lieutenant Richard Bland Lee noted on his 1831 site plan, "This building is much out of repair and requires a new roof and an additional half story." But it must have been basically sound, for it remained in use as officers' (and later civilian) quarters until 1919 when it was razed at a hundred years of age. The house itself consisted of four spacious rooms on the first floor and would later have a second story added with an additional four rooms. A wide verandah graced the front of the home providing an excellent vista of the river for evening relaxation. In back of the home, on the northwest side, was a detached structure that apparently served Rutgers as a kitchen and servants' quarters. The government continued using it as a kitchen and officers' mess. The above drawing and others in chapters two and three are excerpted from building plans rendered in 1840 by draftsman Louis Winkelmaier. In many cases, these are the only surviving images of the buildings.

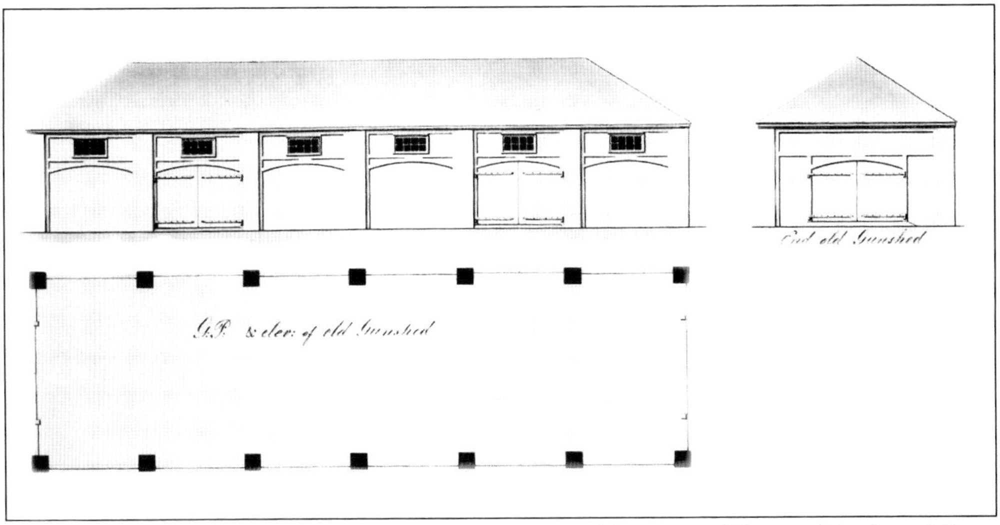

OLD GUN CARRIAGE HOUSE, BY WINKELMAIER, 1840. (Courtesy of National Archives) Soon after closing on the arsenal property, Lieutenant Thomas ran an ad in the *Missouri Republican* calling for bids to erect the first structure on the post, a "gun carriage house." Designed to hold the first shipments of ordnance from Fort Belle Fontaine, specifications called for a building 80 feet long by 40 feet wide, standing 1.5 stories high. Thomas signed a contract with builders Joel Finch and John Whitehall on September 15, 1827. The government agreed to supply all building materials, and Finch and Whitehall would complete the construction for $1,150. The above drawing of the finished building indicates that it ended up being 17 feet narrower than originally called for, and only one story high. There were two sets of double doors on each long side of the structure and one set of double doors on each end. The gun carriage house was located on the northeast edge of the installation, abutting Arsenal Street, halfway between the river and Carondelet Road, and was completed by the end of the year.

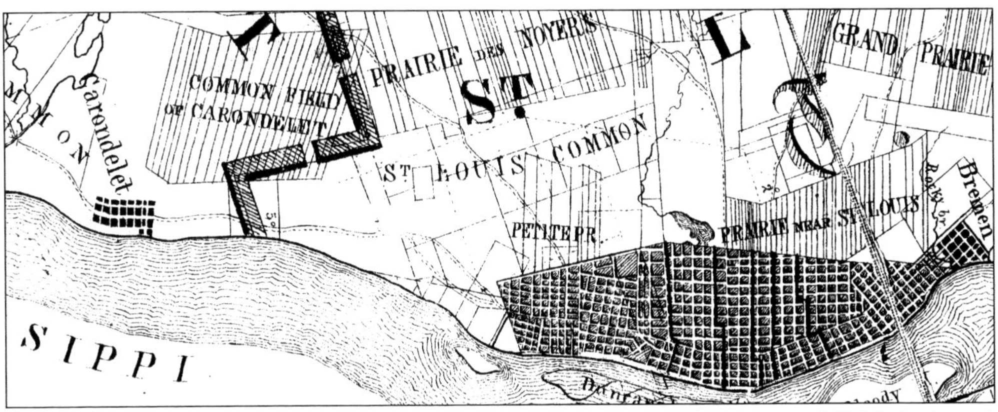

THE ARSENAL SEEKS TO EXPAND INTO ST. LOUIS COMMONS. (Courtesy of SLU Archives) Lieutenant Thomas believed that it would be in the best interests of the U.S. government to purchase more land surrounding the arsenal. He also urged the purchase of Mr. Leduc's land immediately adjoining the southwest side of the arsenal site, which contained valuable limestone quarries and upon which a powder magazine could be built. Thomas feared that otherwise it would "become the property of some person who may be an annoyance of this depot and it will enable us to place the magazine further from the other buildings."

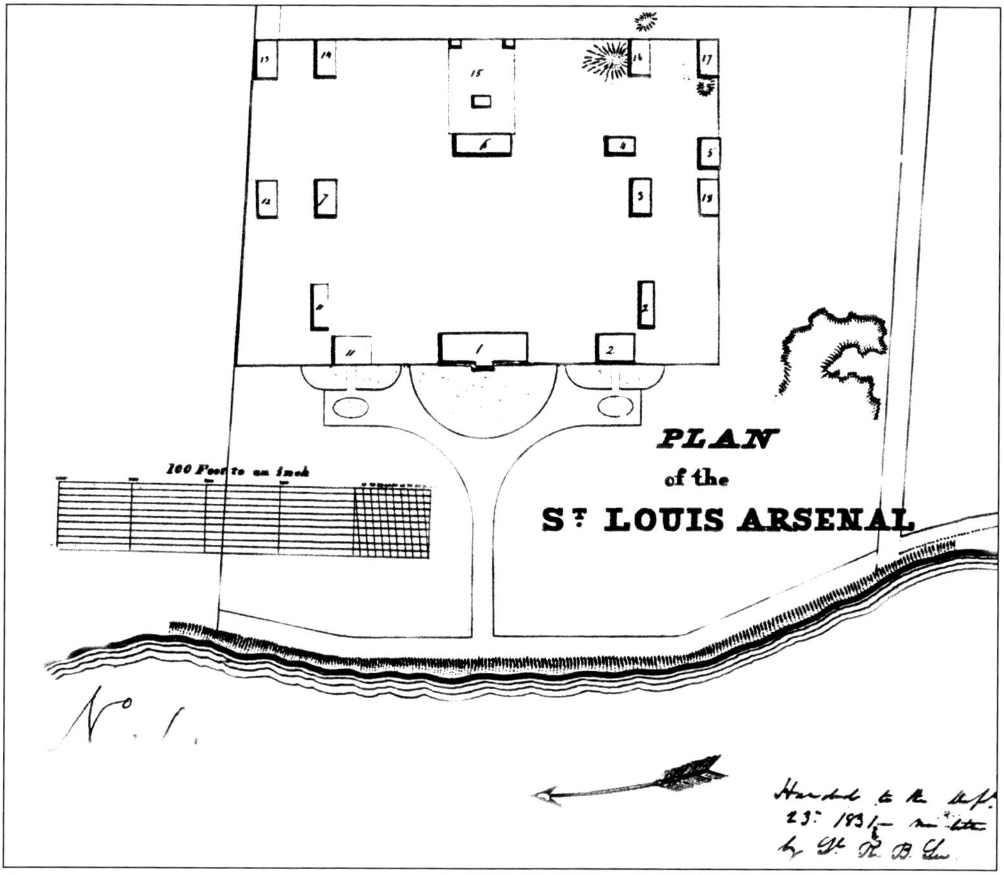

PROPOSED ARSENAL SITE PLAN, 1831. (Courtesy of National Archives) In 1828 Lieutenant Thomas submitted an installation site plan to headquarters showing the positions he proposed for placement of the arsenal buildings. Although his plan has apparently not survived to the present, a similar plan was submitted three years later by Lieutenant R.B. Lee, which reflected Thomas's earlier intentions. Thomas designed a rectangle of buildings keyed on the former Rutgers dwelling (designated #2 on Lee's map), in the northeast corner of the property. To the south of the dwelling he set the main arsenal building (#1), and south of there, he planned the commander's quarters (#11). West of the Rutgers home would be a carriage shop (#3), and a little further west a small, temporary blacksmith shop (#4). North of that would be the first stable (#5) and south of the blacksmith shop. Thomas planned to locate a soldiers' barracks (#6) in the center of the quadrangle. West of the commanders' quarters he foresaw an armorer's shop (#7). He also proposed locating the first powder magazine at the extreme northwestern corner of the property, some 800 feet away from the closest buildings (off the site plan). This would be called the "small magazine," and would stand near the intersection of the Carondelet Road (now Broadway) and Arsenal Street. Three small laboratories were to be located just east of the magazine. The carriage shed would abut Arsenal Street on its north end and lie about 300 feet northwest of the stable. All of these buildings were constructed by Thomas.

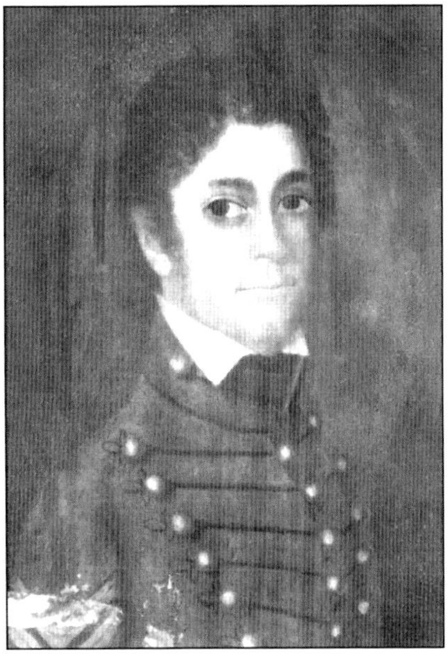

SECOND LIEUTENANT WASHINGTON WHEELWRIGHT. (Courtesy of West Point) Early in 1828, the Ordnance Department sent the first relief to the St. Louis Arsenal in the person of Second Lieutenant Washington Wheelwright, bringing the arsenal's personnel count to two. Wheelwright had been on ordnance duty for two years since serving as an artillery officer at Fort Monroe, Virginia and at Fort Wolcott, Rhode Island. With Wheelwright's assistance, it was now possible for Lieutenant Thomas to travel in pursuit of arsenal business. Wheelwright would serve several short tours of duty at the arsenal between 1826 and 1833.

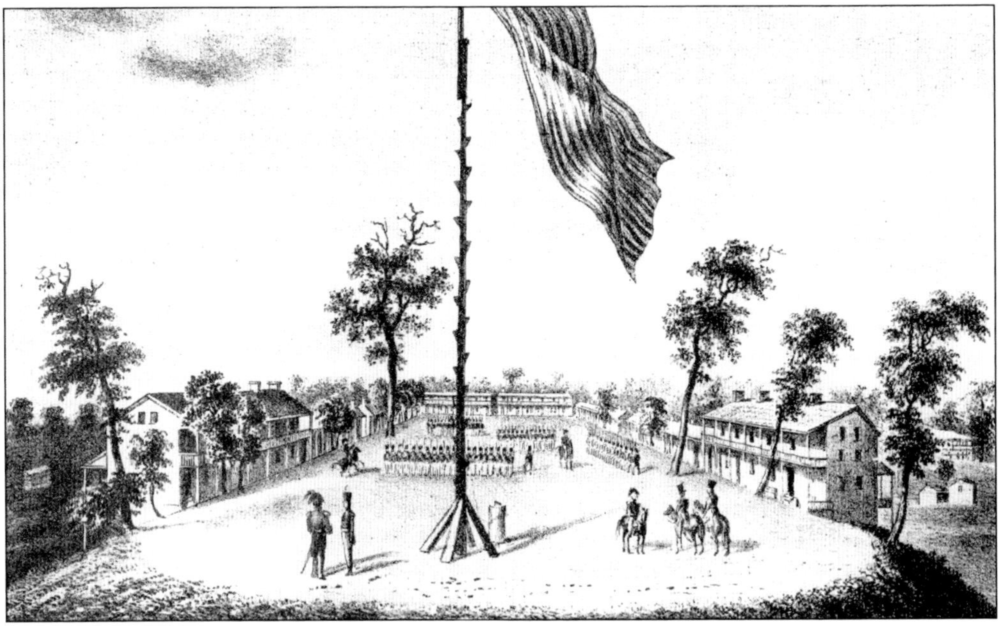

DEVELOPMENT OF JEFFERSON BARRACKS A FEW MILES SOUTH OF THE ARSENAL, J.C. WILD, 1841. (Wild, SLU Archives) Jefferson Barracks was established in 1826 as a cantonment for training and stationing infantry and dragoons (cavalry) in the western theatre. The troops stationed at Fort Belle Fontaine had moved to the site of Jefferson Barracks and had begun construction of the post immediately. In fact, the barracks and the arsenal competed for craftsmen to build their stone structures and this competition helped drive construction prices high in the St. Louis region. A certain Major Whistler remained at Belle Fontaine superintending the diminishing supplies and appealing monthly for relief. In June 1828, Jefferson Barracks was still receiving its supply of gunpowder and munitions from Belle Fontaine, but that function would soon be handled by the arsenal. At that time Whistler reported having only $109.53 in his accounts after selling a batch of gunpowder to Jefferson Barracks.

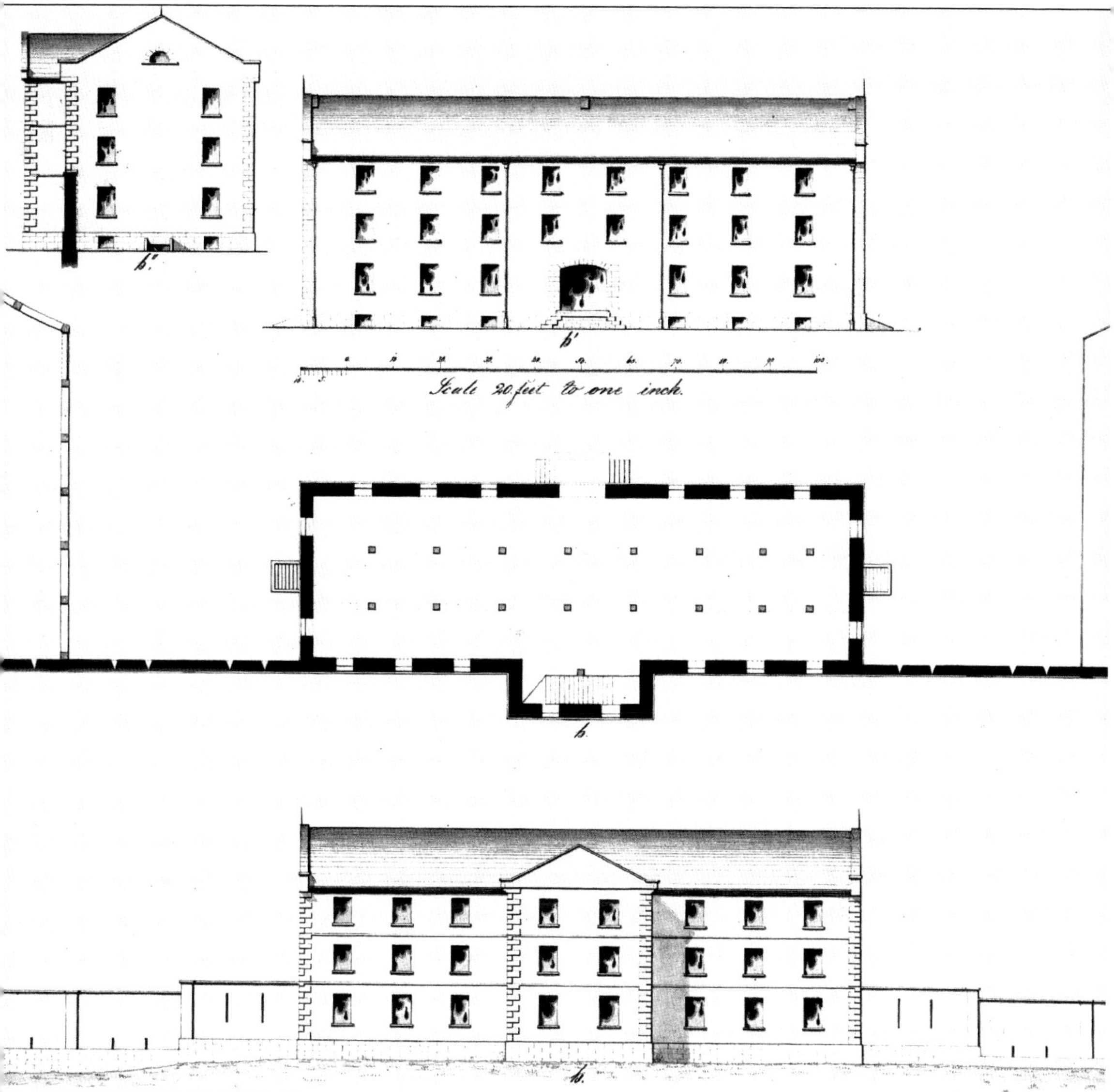

BUILDING PLANS FOR THE MAIN ARSENAL BUILDING, WINKELMAIER, 1840. (Courtesy of National Archives) In February 1828, Lieutenant Thomas had accepted a low bid of $10,460 by Wilder and Cannon for construction of the main arsenal building (later in the century to be designated #14), to be centered at the crest of the bluff overlooking the Mississippi. The contractors came highly recommended by Captain Brandt of Jefferson Barracks for work they had done recently at that installation. Thomas noted that construction prices in the St. Louis area had risen by 20 percent over the past two years and that they would probably continue their sharp ascent. "This is owing to the increased prosperity of St. Louis and the consequent improvements, public and private, together with the United States cantonment [at Jefferson Barracks], which buildings engage nearly all the mechanics in the country." Thomas estimated that the funds remaining from the last appropriation would be exhausted with the construction of the main arsenal building and reminded his superior that he had not yet been informed of the appropriation for the present year. With the season being so far advanced, construction of the arsenal must begin immediately, he asserted.

Fig. 237.

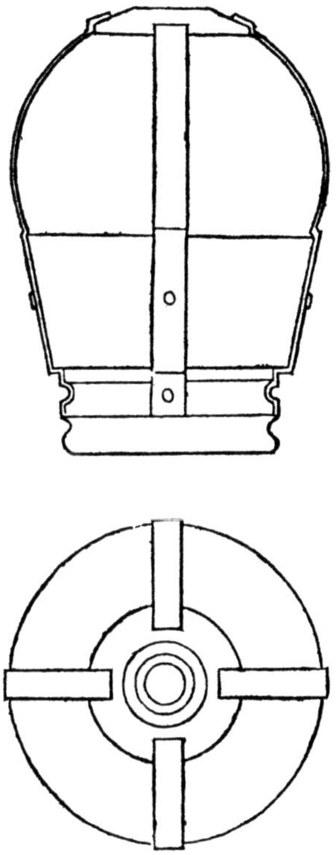

12-pd. Howitzer Shell or Spherical Case.

Fig. 238.

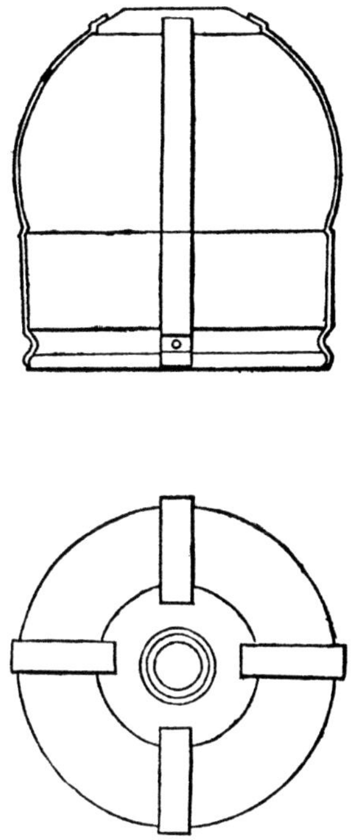

6 and 12-pd. Guns Spherical Case.

FIRST ORDER FOR CANNON BALLS. (Gibbon, SLU Archives) In September 1828, Lieutenant Thomas signed a contract with John Perry and a "Mr. Deering" of Potosi, Missouri, to produce 12,000 6-pounder and 3,000 12-pounder cannon balls for the arsenal, at a cost of $7,590. This represented the first contract for munitions executed at the new facility. Delivery of the cannonballs was expected to take place over the next six months. The arsenal was not involved in the actual production of artillery or its ammunition, so contracts were let to civilian or government factories for the provision of such ordnance. At the local level, the arsenal assembled and distributed small arms, artillery, artillery shells, and various accouterments, but they only manufactured or repaired small arms ammunition and gun carriages.

A year after the cannon balls were ordered, in September 1829, enough progress had been made on the arsenal buildings to permit the final transfer of ordnance and supplies from Fort Belle Fontaine to St. Louis. Captain J.B. Brandt, assistant quartermaster at St. Louis headquarters, let the contract for the shipment of 100 tons of materiel "at the rate of $3 for every 20 hundred pound weight." Thereafter, Belle Fontaine ceased to exist as an active military post and its last officer, Major Whistler, moved to St. Louis, where he died a few months later. In 1829 one enlisted man was assigned to the arsenal to assist with the multitude of tasks. Perhaps he was a clerk that Thomas had requested earlier for "$15 and a ration and a half per month." During the next year five civilians would be hired as the arsenal commenced its regular functions.

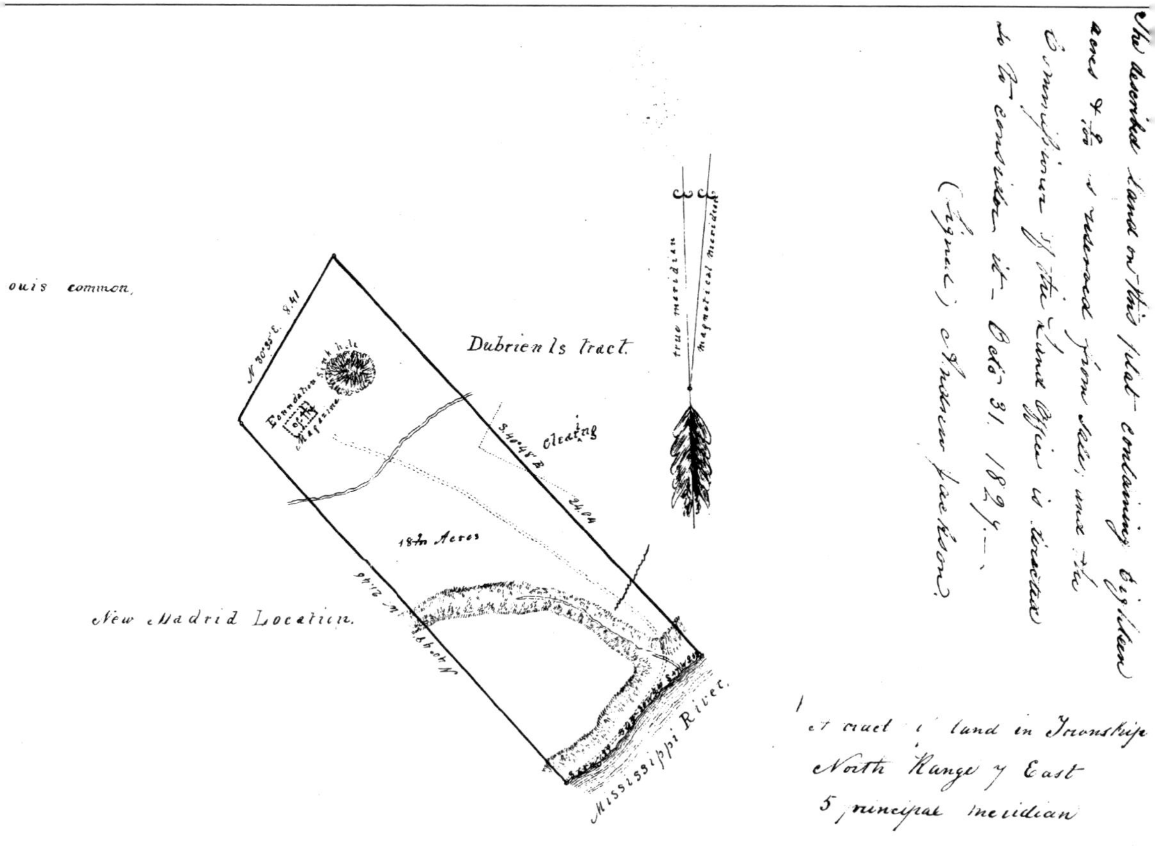

Sketch of Proposed Magazine Site. (Courtesy of National Archives) In April 1829, Lieutenant Thomas requested permission of the U.S. Land Office to grant the arsenal a site for the erection of a powder magazine. The desired site was located about a half mile south of the arsenal tract, overlooking the Mississippi River and adjoining, on the north, the tract of Susanna Dubriel. This site stretched "from the river at low tide," to the Carondelet Road on the west. Thomas included a sketch of the proposed site and estimated that it would be 10 to 15 acres in size. The following month, Thomas had the county register of deeds, William Christy, set the tract aside for government purposes. It took about nine months to get the necessary approval of the president of the U.S. in order to designate the land for government use. But eventually a copy of the plat with President Andrew Jackson's signature on it was submitted to the land office and the tract was turned over to Lieutenant Thomas by the end of the year. Thomas was anxious to proceed with the construction of the powder magazine. As indicated in the above drawing, the only access route to the site was by the river and then up a winding path to the site of the magazine, which was located precariously near a large sink hole. Soon, however, the site was connected to the Carondelet Road and access became much more convenient.

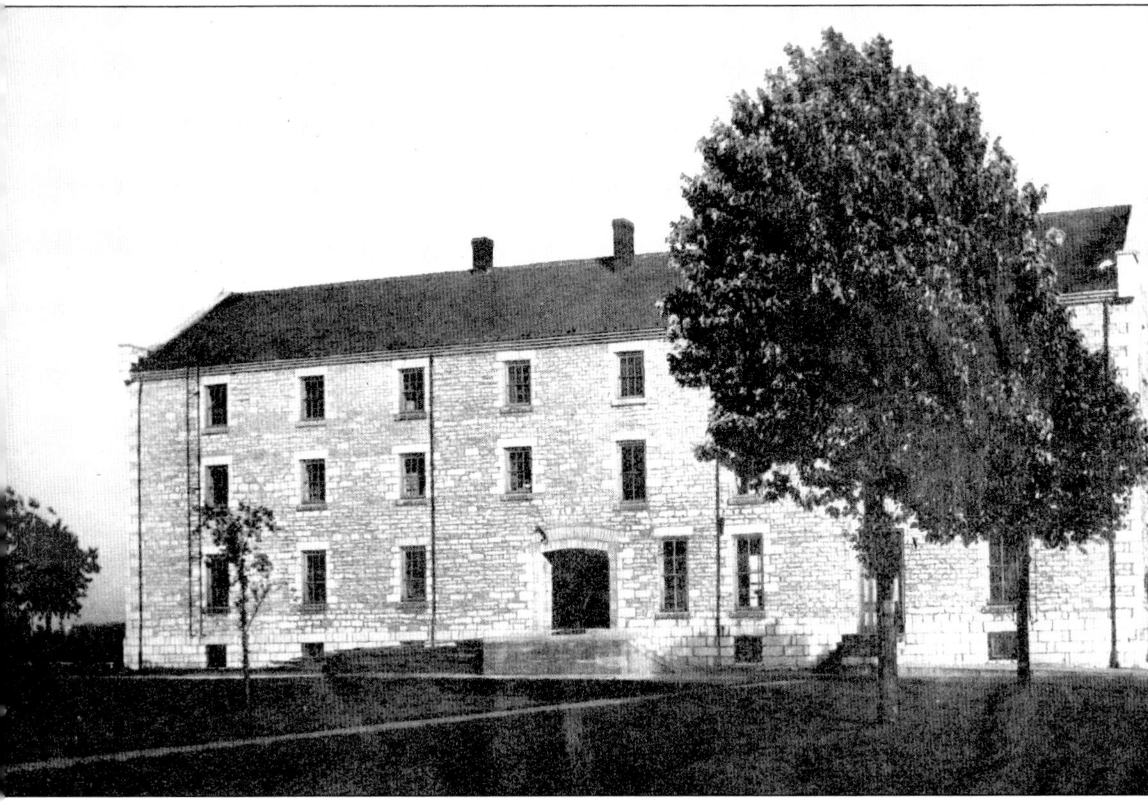

View of the Main Arsenal Building from the West. (Courtesy of NIMA) From 1828 through 1830, construction proceeded briskly at the arsenal. At least six new buildings were completed under the supervision of Lieutenant Thomas. The main arsenal building was finished early in November 1828, on schedule. Thomas wrote to headquarters reporting that he still held $2,000 in building funds, which, he suggested, should be used to purchase lumber for the next year's projects. The main arsenal building (later called the Small Arms Arsenal) overlooked the Mississippi near the center of the southeastern perimeter of the installation, was three stories high, and measured 40 by 120 feet. The walls were of locally quarried limestone, set on a stone foundation, the floors of thick timber, and the roof covered in Philadelphia slate. The first and second floors of this building had large main rooms, 89.5 by 35 feet in size, with small 35 by 16.5 foot rooms, perhaps offices, on the southwest end of the building. The third floor had a 35 by 57 foot large room, a 35 by 32 foot medium room, and two small rooms 16.5 feet square. The foundation of the northeast wall of this building was unearthed during the excavation of the site in 1983–84 by the archaeological crew from Southern Illinois University. Toward the end of the 19th century all of the buildings would be numbered and this would be designated #14.

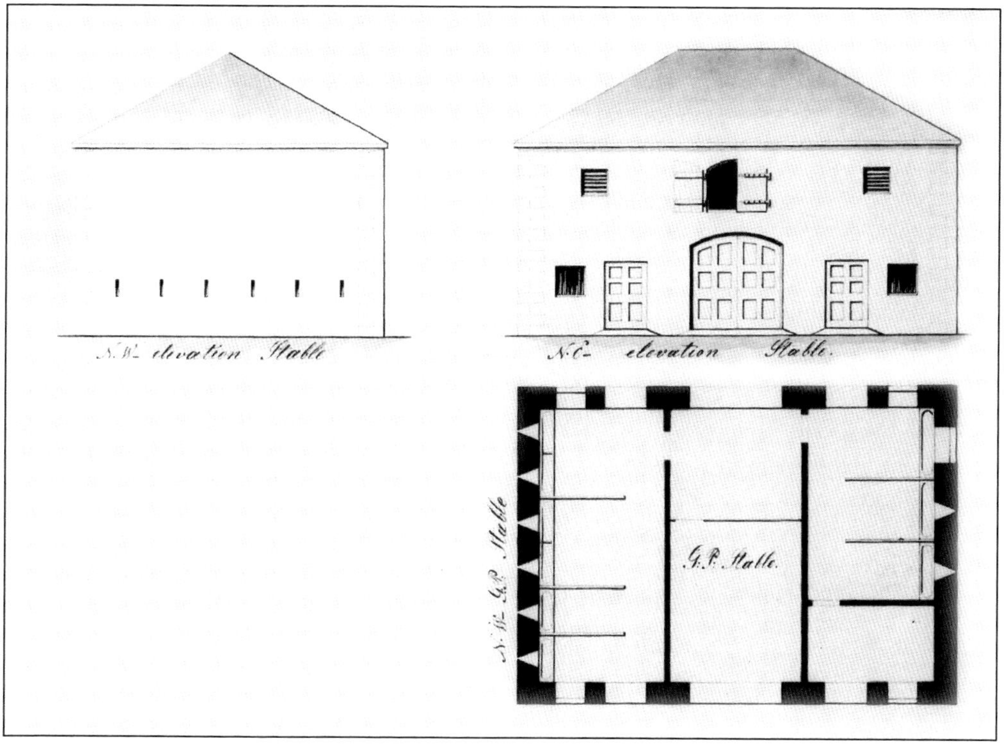

DRAWING OF THE FIRST STABLE BUILT AT THE ARSENAL, WINKELMAIER, 1840. (Courtesy of National Archives) North of the growing quadrangle of buildings, Lieutenant Thomas erected a simple stable of stone, roofed with wooden shingles and adjoined by outbuildings and a corral to house the installation's horses. The two-story building was approximately 43 feet wide by 30 feet deep. The floor plan shows that there were stalls for at least nine animals and additional rooms for livery equipment and supply storage. On the second floor there was room for storing sufficient quantities of hay and other feed for the horses. The stable was located just northwest of the carriage shop, near the roadway leading into the arsenal from the north gate. (See #5 on the site map, page 23)

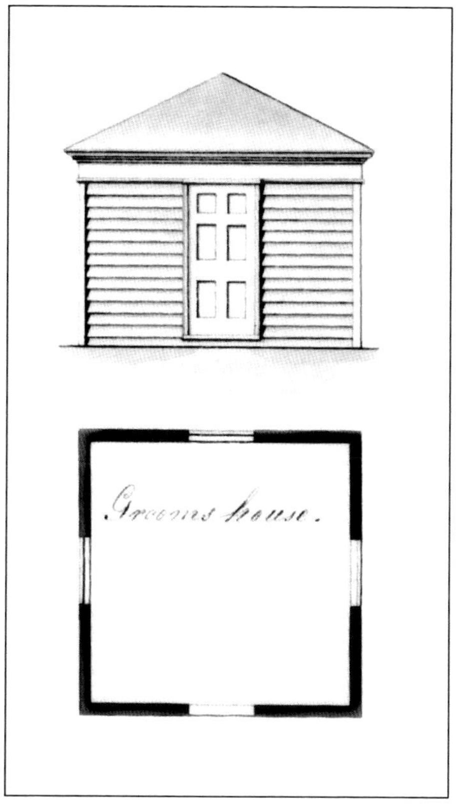

ILLUSTRATION OF THE GROOM'S HOUSE, WINKELMAIER, 1840. (Courtesy of National Archives) Close by the stable a small groom's house was built around 1830, from which the head of the stable oversaw its operation. This was a small, square, one-room building constructed of wood and roofed with wooden shingles. It had one access door and three windows. The interior floor plan measured 12 feet square.

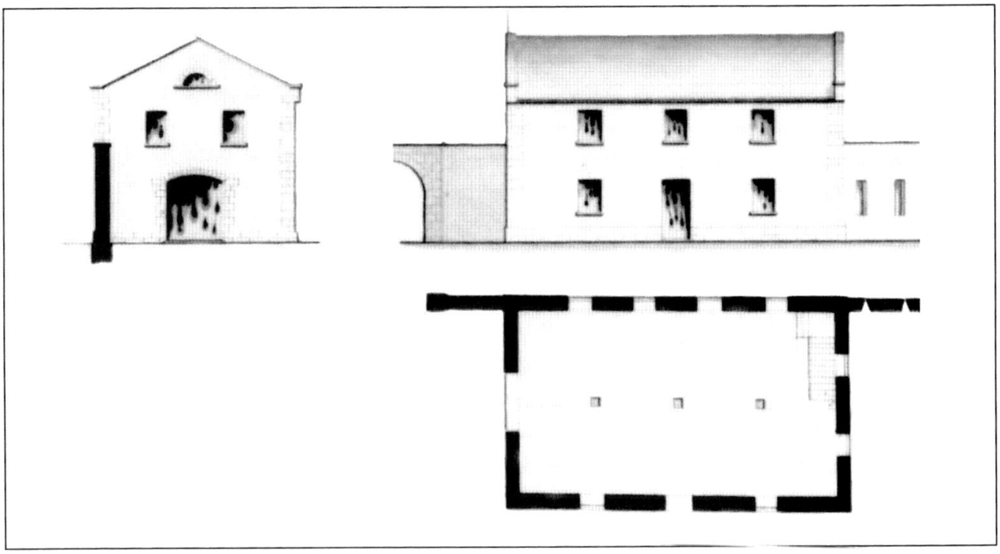

FIRST CARRIAGE-MAKER'S SHOP, WINKELMAIER, 1840. (Courtesy of National Archives) On the northeast side of the quadrangle, not far from the stable, a small rectangular building was erected in 1830, in line with the officers' kitchen. Constructed of native limestone and roofed with wooden shingles, the building stood two stories high. Each floor consisted of one large room and the exterior dimensions were 30 by 50 feet. Designed originally to be a carriage-maker's shop, it was soon found to be unsuitable and was converted to a storehouse. It was also at times referred to as a "small arsenal." Later in the century this would be designated Building #18.

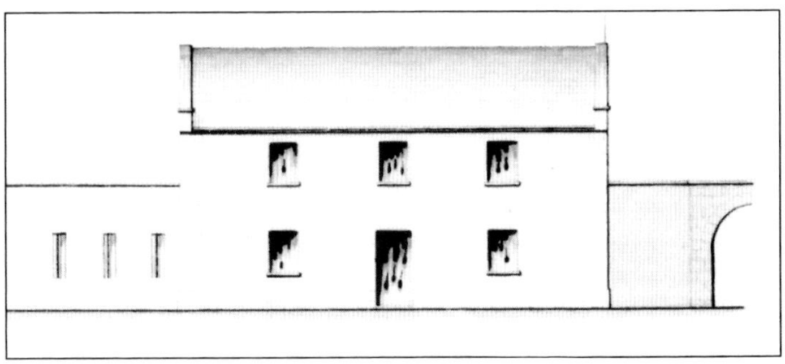

FIRST ARMORER'S SHOP, WINKELMAIER, 1840. (Courtesy of National Archives) Southwest of the carriage-maker's shop, straight across the parade ground, an armorer's shop was erected at about the same time. It ran along the southwest perimeter of the quadrangle, and would be in line with the eventual southwest wing of the commanding officer's quarters. A virtual mirror image of the carriage-maker's shop, this structure measured slightly smaller at 29 by 49 feet. It too was constructed of limestone and roofed with wooden shingles and had one large room on each floor. The building did not work well as an armorer's shop, however, because it did not have a chimney, nor was there room for a forge. So it was later recommended for conversion to a carpentry shop, and still later became another storehouse. Like the carriage-maker's shop, this was also sometimes called a small arsenal. This would be designated Building #12 later in the century.

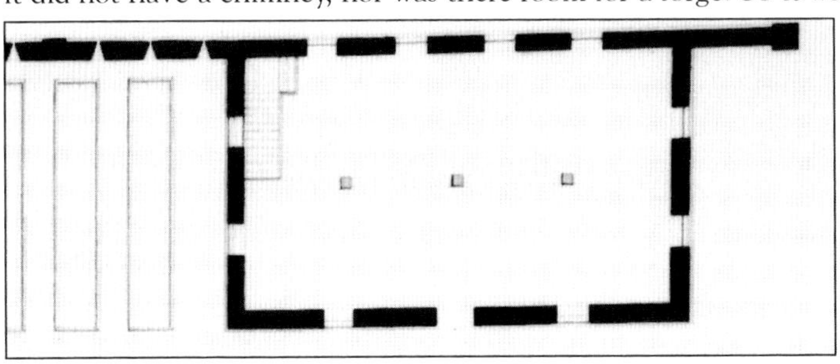

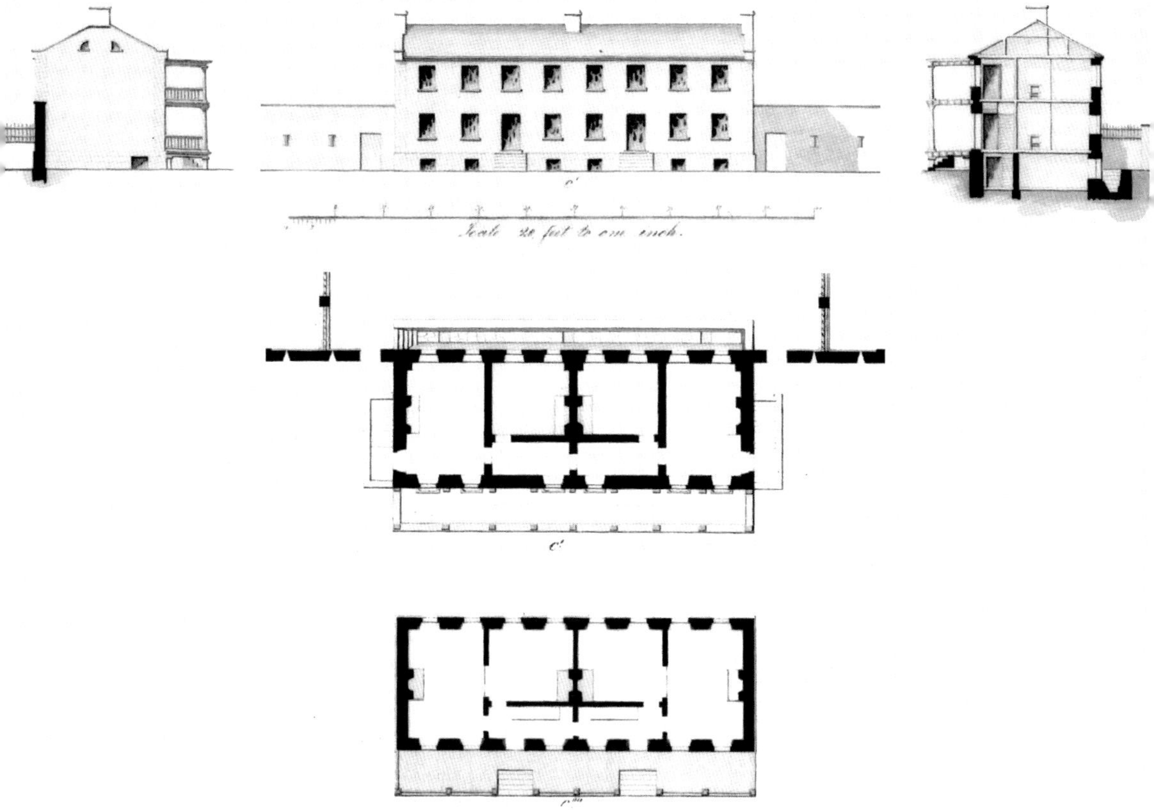

SOLDIERS' BARRACKS, WINKELMAIER, 1840. (Courtesy of National Archives) Finally, in 1830, with the prospect of a small garrison being stationed at the arsenal, a soldiers' barracks was constructed near the center of the quadrangle. This expansive edifice lay directly across the parade ground, about 230 feet northwest of the main arsenal building. It was two stories high, standing 22 feet at the eaves, with exterior walls of limestone, and it was roofed in slate. The edifice stood 75 feet long and 28 feet wide, with four commodious rooms on each of the two upper floors and in the basement. Large fireplaces heated the rooms.

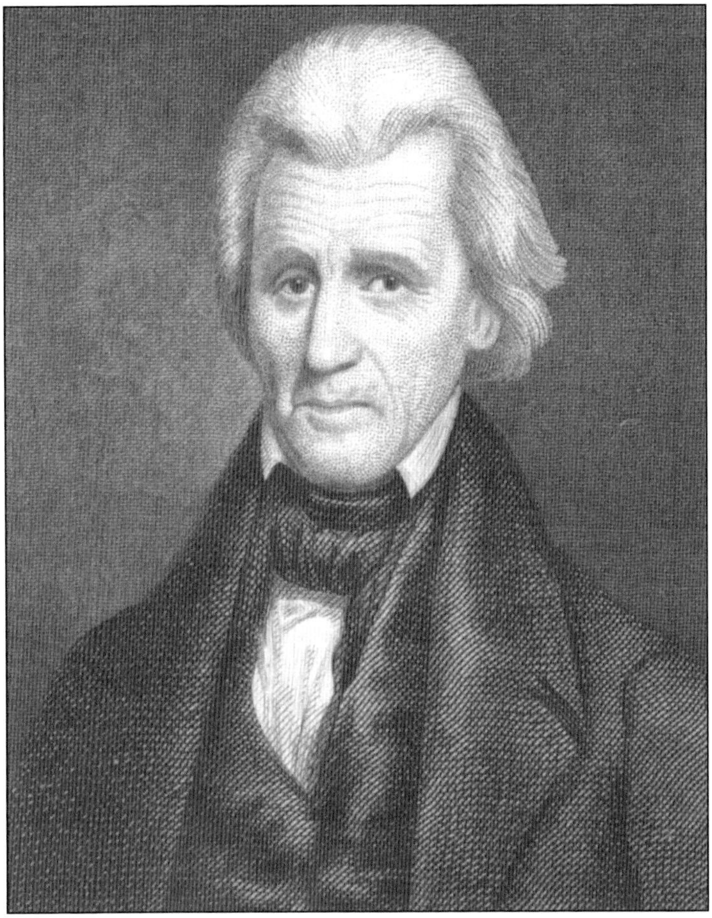

Lieutenant Thomas at Odds with Jackson Administration. (Dusenbery, SLU Archives) By 1830 the population of St. Louis was 5,852 and the city was prosperous and growing. Perhaps the business climate was too tempting, for during 1830 Lieutenant Thomas turned his attention more to local business prospects than to his military duties. Federal records reveal that Lieutenant Wheelwright took over most of the purchasing and contracting duties that normally would have been handled by the commander of the arsenal. Thomas, meanwhile, invested in a lumber mill operation with other local businessmen, became involved in private real estate transactions, and began participating in local politics. He was, in fact, an outspoken critic of the Andrew Jackson administration, which could not have endeared him to his commander-in-chief. He also neglected to submit the required quarterly reports to the Ordnance Office for at least three quarters of 1830, as stipulated in military regulations. So it may not be surprising that, in January 1831, Thomas was summarily dismissed from military service. The record is strangely silent about the specific reasons for his dismissal, but it probably related to some of the aforementioned activities. The dismissal did nothing to tarnish his reputation in St. Louis, however, for Thomas went on to become a wealthy businessman and politician, living and raising a family in the city for many years. He was, in fact, considered a sterling example of one who had come to the city during its infancy with little more than a will to succeed, and who, with hard work and calculated risk, became fabulously successful by the standards of the day.

After Lieutenant Thomas left, two officers shared intermittent command of the arsenal for the next two years. Lieutenant Wheelwright assumed command in January 1831. Then, late that summer, Brevet Captain Richard Bland Lee reported for duty. Captain Lee, an artillery officer, had served at many posts including the Artillery School for Practice at Fort Monroe. Command of the arsenal alternated between Wheelwright and Lee until January 1, 1833 when Lee was transferred to New York. He served with distinction at a variety of duty stations, was twice wounded in the Seminole Wars, and brevetted a major for gallantry in combat. During the 1840s, Major Lee returned to St. Louis as commissary of subsistence and became popular in the social and cultural circles of the city. He remained in federal service for 44 years until forced to make the painful choice of his beloved Virginia over further service to the Union.

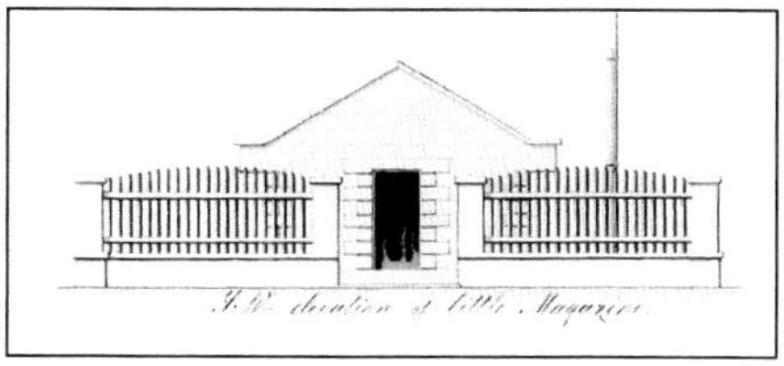

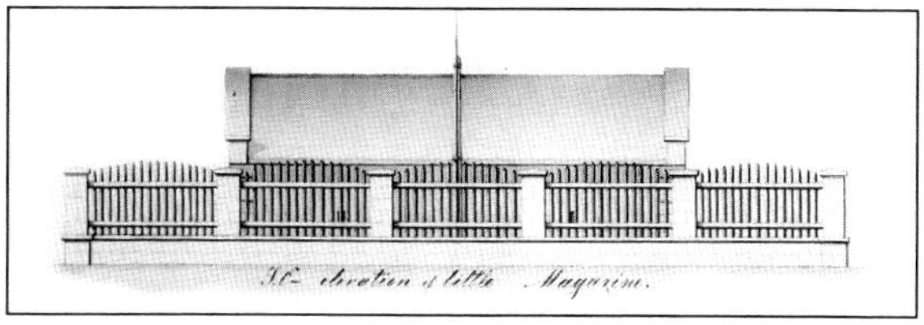

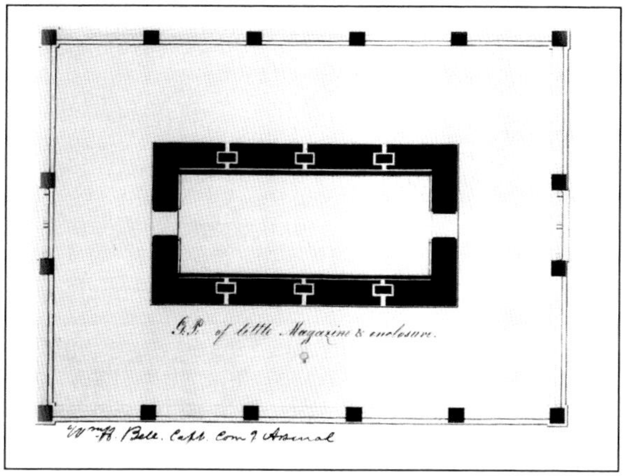

SMALL AMMUNITION MAGAZINE, WINKELMAIER, 1840. (Courtesy of National Archives) Somehow, during the tumultuous period of changes in command, building projects proceeded. The small ammunition magazine, proposed by Lieutenant Thomas in 1828, was finally constructed in 1831 in the extreme northwestern corner of the installation (approximately where the statue of General Lyon stands today). The so-called "little magazine" at the main installation was built of limestone in an attractive style, roofed with slate, and was separated from the primary buildings by some 800 feet. The magazine itself measured 20 by 38 feet and had a door at each end. Built low to the ground, it stood only 10-feet-high at the eaves and 16 feet at the peak of the roof. It was surrounded by a decorative 6-foot-high wooden picket fence set into a 2-foot-high stone base. The 48 by 67 foot fence provided minimal protection against vandalism and theft and seems to have been more for decoration than for defense. Inside the fence was a flagpole, clearly within sight of travelers on Carondelet Road.

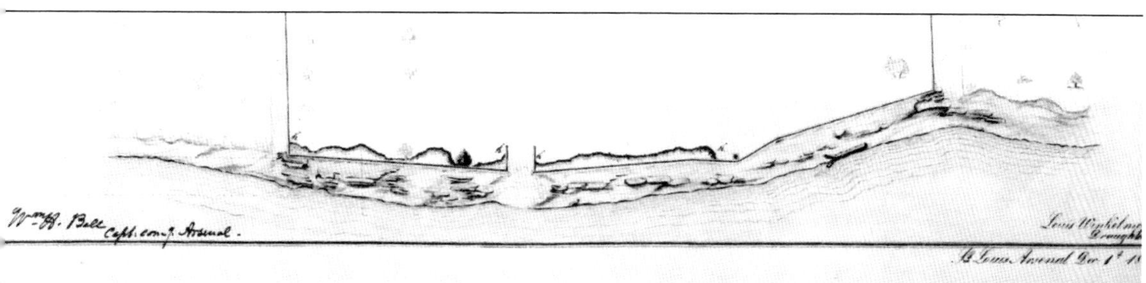

CONSTRUCTION OF THE RIVERSIDE WALL, WINKELMAIER, 1840. (Courtesy of National Archives) One of the most important arsenal building projects of 1832 was the riverside wall. Begun late in 1831, the wall was to be 8 feet thick at the base, tapering to 2 feet thick at the top. It averaged 14 feet in height. A stone coping ran the entire length of the wall, extending 2 inches beyond the sides and inclining from the top. A gate was built in the wall directly in line with the center of the main arsenal, giving access to the riverboat landing for ease of supply. The open areas inside the wall would be filled with rubble and graded evenly a few years later.

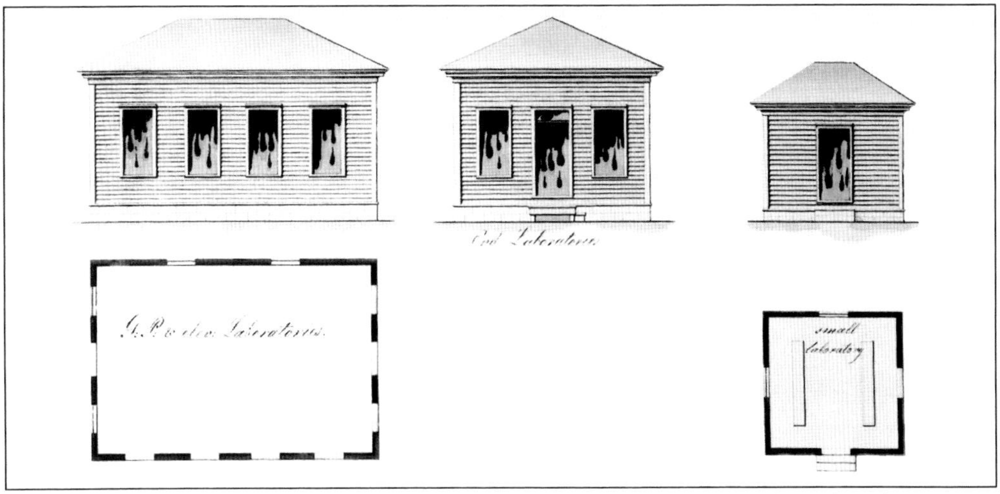

LABORATORY BUILDINGS, WINKELMAIER, 1840. (Courtesy of National Archives) Running about 100 feet east of the magazine was a line of three medium-sized laboratory buildings and one smaller one. The medium buildings measured 20 by 30 feet and stood 14 feet tall at the eaves. The small one measured about 14 feet square and stood 11 feet high. The laboratories were used to manufacture cartridges, pyrotechnics, and other explosives. Special safety measures were observed in the laboratories and in other buildings where gunpowder was in use. Laborers worked only during daylight hours since they could not afford to have open flames or even gas lamps anywhere near the explosive gunpowder.

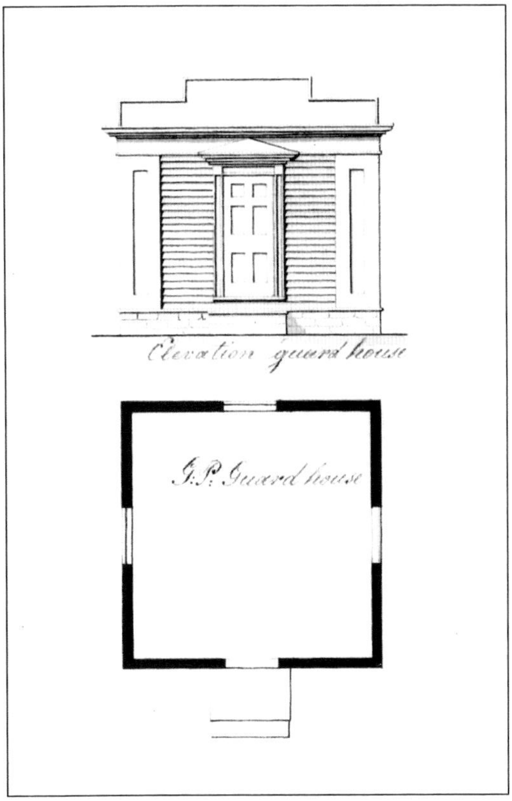

FIRST GUARDHOUSE ON THE INSTALLATION, WINKELMAIER, 1840. (Courtesy of National Archives) Between 1831 and 1833, with the construction of the north wall of the post, a small wooden guardhouse was erected near the entrance from Arsenal Street. During the 1830s the primary access to the arsenal was by a driveway leading from Arsenal Street, north of the officers' quarters, to a point near the stable. This might have been the original driveway created by the former owner of the property, Arend Rutgers. Once the exterior wall around the arsenal grounds was completed, an ornate gateway would be constructed at this northern entrance to the compound, and later, an elaborate brick guardhouse would replace the humble wooden structure.

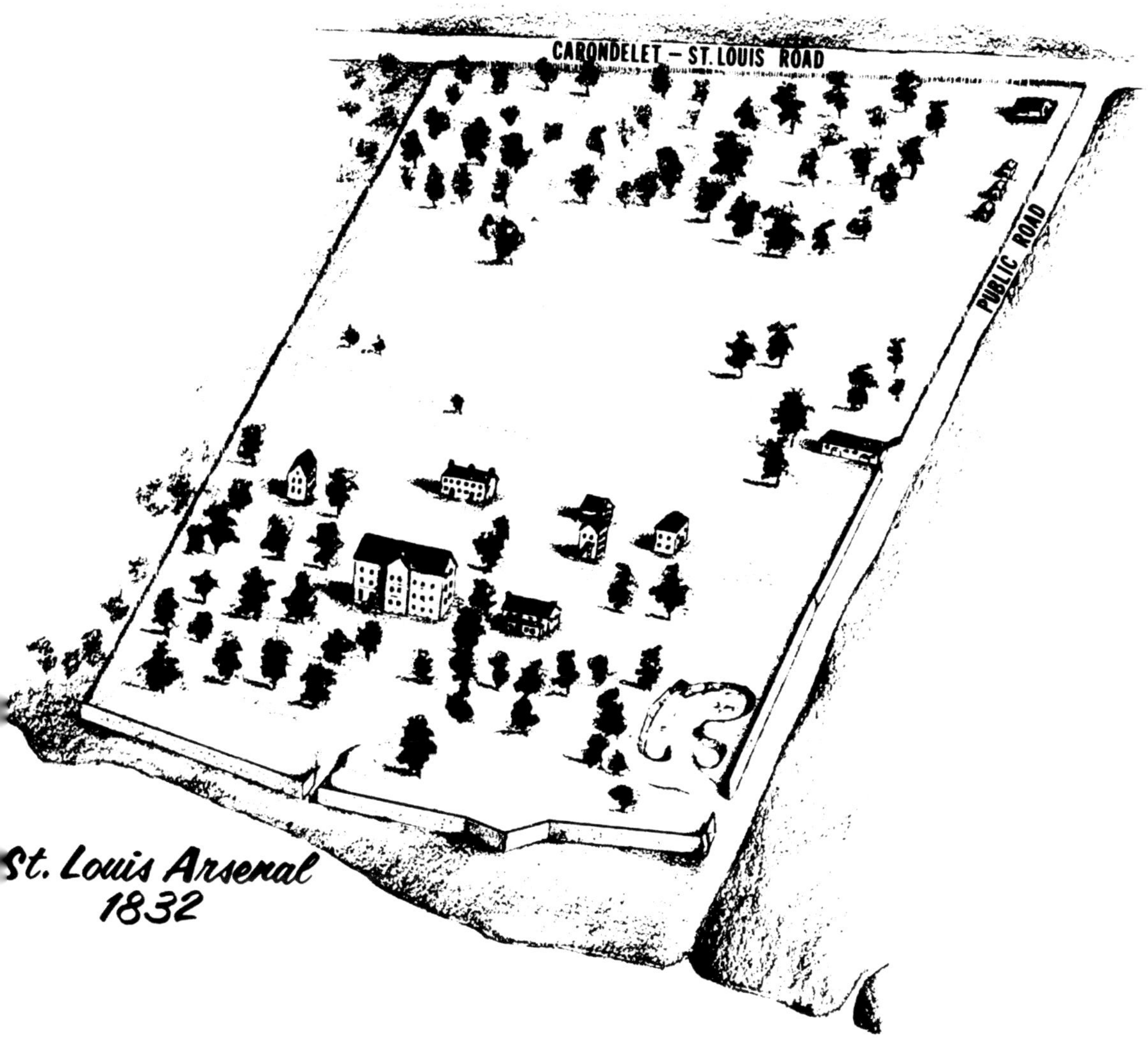

A BIRD'S-EYE VIEW OF THE ARSENAL IN 1832. (Courtesy of NIMA) This modern rendering by an artist at the Defense Mapping Agency illustrates how the arsenal may have appeared in 1832.

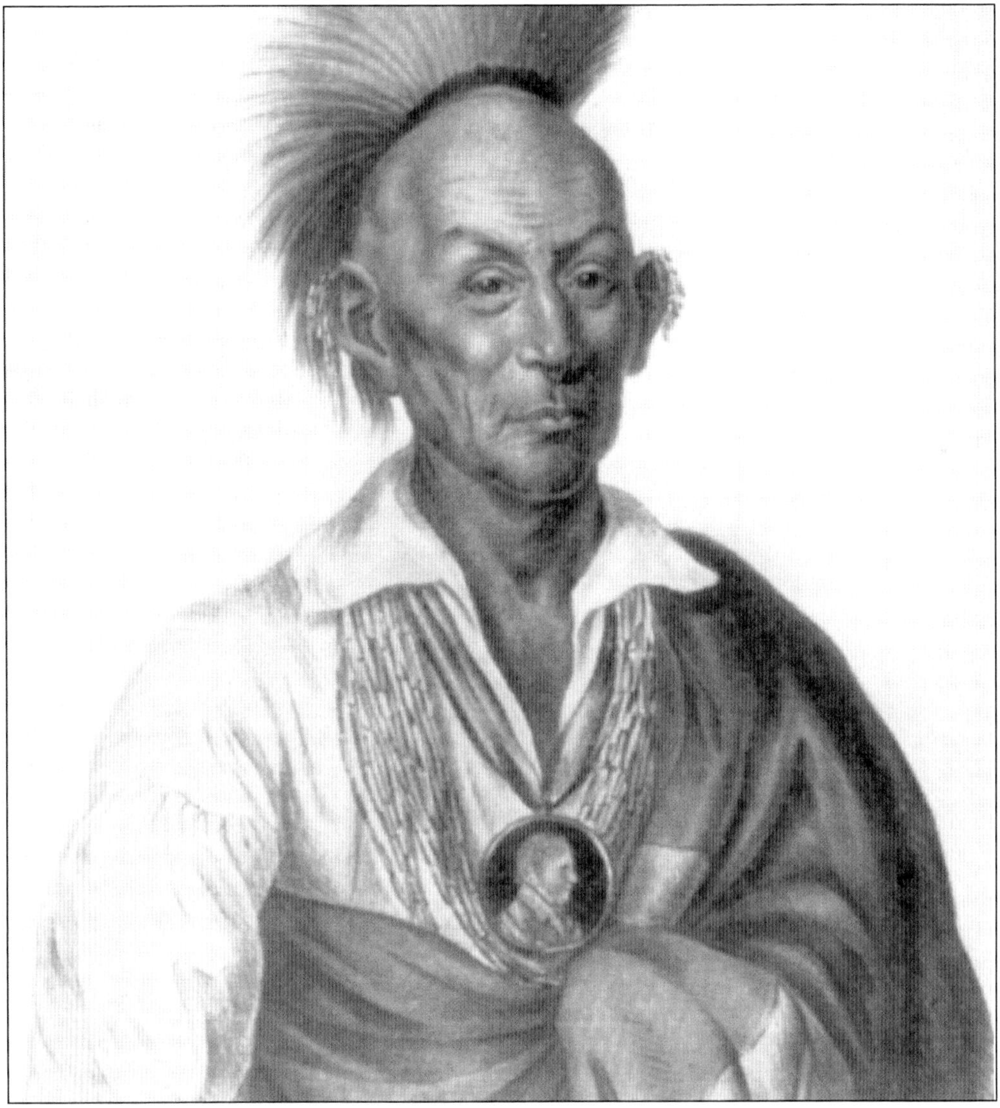

Black Hawk Rebellion Involves St. Louis. (Black Hawk, SLU Archives) In 1832, the Black Hawk War broke out in northwestern Illinois and the St. Louis Arsenal became a primary point for equipping U.S. troops and Illinois militia to subdue the uprising. On April 8, 1832, Lieutenant Wheelwright left the arsenal to serve as chief of ordnance under General Henry Atkinson with the 6th Infantry from Jefferson Barracks. The unit set out for Illinois immediately to subdue the rebellious Black Hawk, chief of the Sac and Fox tribes. Four months later Black Hawk was captured at the Battle of Bad Axe and was taken to Jefferson Barracks where he was confined in chains, to his great humiliation. A few weeks later he was sent to Washington D.C., to meet President Jackson. Thereafter he was confined under more humane circumstances at Fort Monroe, Virginia, and released in 1833 to return to his people in Iowa, where he died five years later. As for Lieutenant Wheelwright, he had accepted an assignment as colonel staff, chief of ordnance, with the Illinois Volunteers from May through the end of the war in October. Thereafter, he remained in upper Illinois as the superintendent of lead mines until the end of December when he returned to St. Louis. He resigned from the army in 1833 to engage in business in New York City.

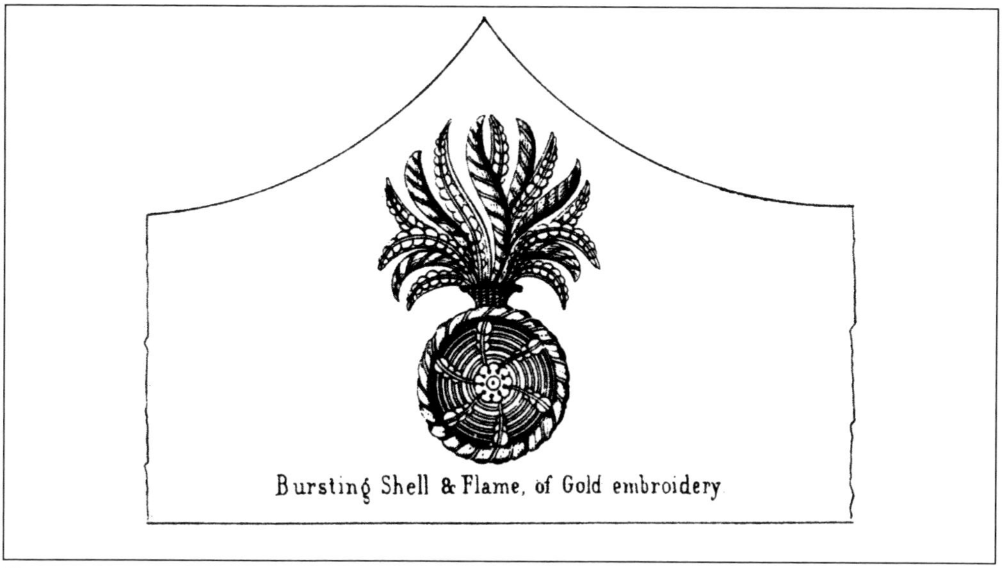

OFFICER'S EMBLEM OF THE ARMY'S NEW ORDNANCE DEPARTMENT. (Courtesy of SLU Archives) On May 30, 1832, an event of significance to the arsenal took place when the army reactivated the Ordnance Department as a distinct branch. Colonel George Bomford became its first reconstituted chief of ordnance and served in that position until March 25, 1848, from his headquarters in Washington D.C. Although Bomford had struggled for many years to see the Ordnance Department restored to an independent status, he was disappointed to learn that the new organization authorized only 14 officers to staff the corps' 18 arsenals, 2 armories, and 1 lead mine. During peacetime, there was need for at least 30 officers to staff these installations; half the contingent of officers on ordnance duty would still have to be detailed from other branches of the army. This would continue to undermine the continuity of the Ordnance Corps until the outbreak of the Civil War. The ordnance emblems reproduced above and below are excerpted from the 1851 Army Uniform Regulations and would be similar to those worn in the 1830s.

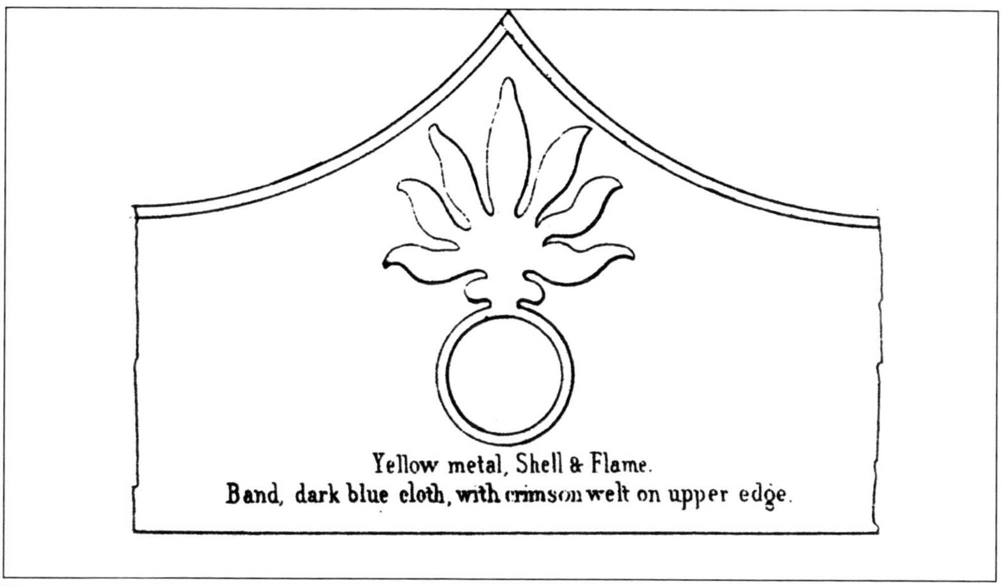

ENLISTED EMBLEM OF THE ORDNANCE DEPARTMENT. (Courtesy of SLU Archives)

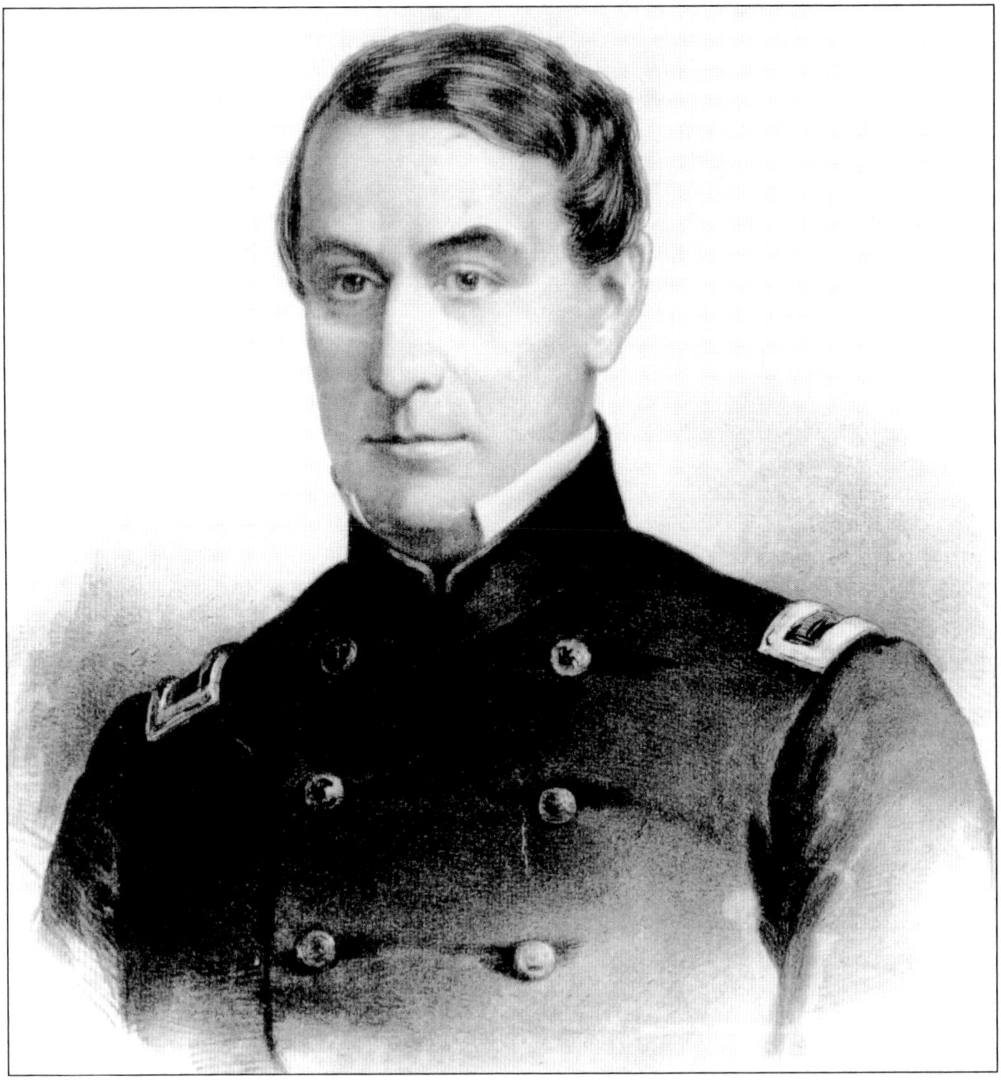

ROBERT ANDERSON, FUTURE HERO OF FORT SUMTER, GAINED VALUABLE EXPERIENCE AT THE ARSENAL. (Courtesy of Military History Institute) In February of 1833, a young army officer detailed from the artillery corps reported for duty at the arsenal. He was Second Lieutenant Robert Anderson, who had just completed a tour of duty at the Allegheny Arsenal in Pittsburgh. Anderson assumed temporary command of the St. Louis Arsenal from Lieutenant Lee, who left for New York. Anderson also performed duties as commissary of subsistence since he was the only officer on post for several weeks. When the new permanent commander, Captain John Symington, arrived in April, Anderson remained at the post as assistant ordnance officer and commissary of subsistence. During short periods of Symington's absence over the next few months, Anderson filled in as temporary commander. Then, in July of 1834, he left for garrison duty at Fort Constitution, New Hampshire. He would go on to serve in a variety of artillery posts and translate a French artillery manual into English. He would also be decorated for gallantry in the Florida Indian wars and in the Mexican War, and serve as writer and instructor in artillery in several distinguished positions. Still, Anderson's ultimate fame would be achieved as the determined commander of Fort Sumter in the opening days of the Civil War. He would finish out the war as a brevet major general, one of the most highly respected officers in the Union Army.

Three

Up and Running (1833–1840)

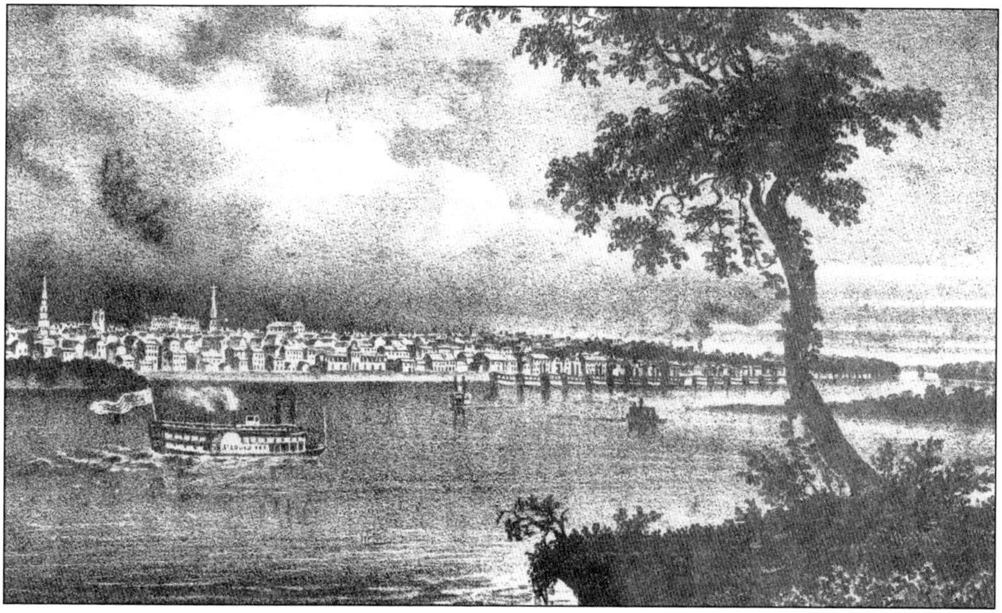

St. Louis, Gateway to the West. (Wild, SLU Archives) By 1833, St. Louis had reached the 7,000 mark in population. Since the depression of the early 1820s, the population had grown at a moderate but steady pace. The city's trade with Santa Fe and the Southwest had rapidly established St. Louis as a commercial capital of the West. A hundred steamboats made nearly 600 landings at the Mound City in 1833. Wagon trains and small boat traffic transported settlers and merchandise to all points west. To police this massive movement, the U.S. Army established its western operations at St. Louis. Jefferson Barracks became the training post and staging area for service in the West, while the arsenal provided most of the ordnance for the army and state militias.

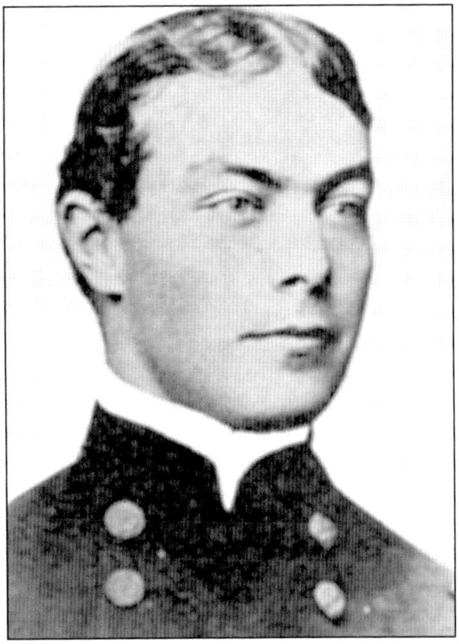

CAPTAIN JOHN SYMINGTON, ARSENAL COMMANDER, 1833–1840. (Courtesy of Watervliet Museum) After getting off to a rough start between 1827 and 1833, the arsenal contingent settled into a productive routine. In April 1833, Captain John Symington, the eighth ranking ordnance officer in the army, assumed command of the arsenal. It was a routine assignment for the army, but the choice of Symington proved to be fortunate, for the arsenal entered upon an era of uninterrupted growth, stability, and productivity. During his seven-year tenure as commander (1833–1840), Captain Symington expanded and standardized many ordinance activities and carried forward a multitude of construction projects. He came to the arsenal with over 18 years of service, one of only four soldiers to have spent his entire career as an ordnance officer.

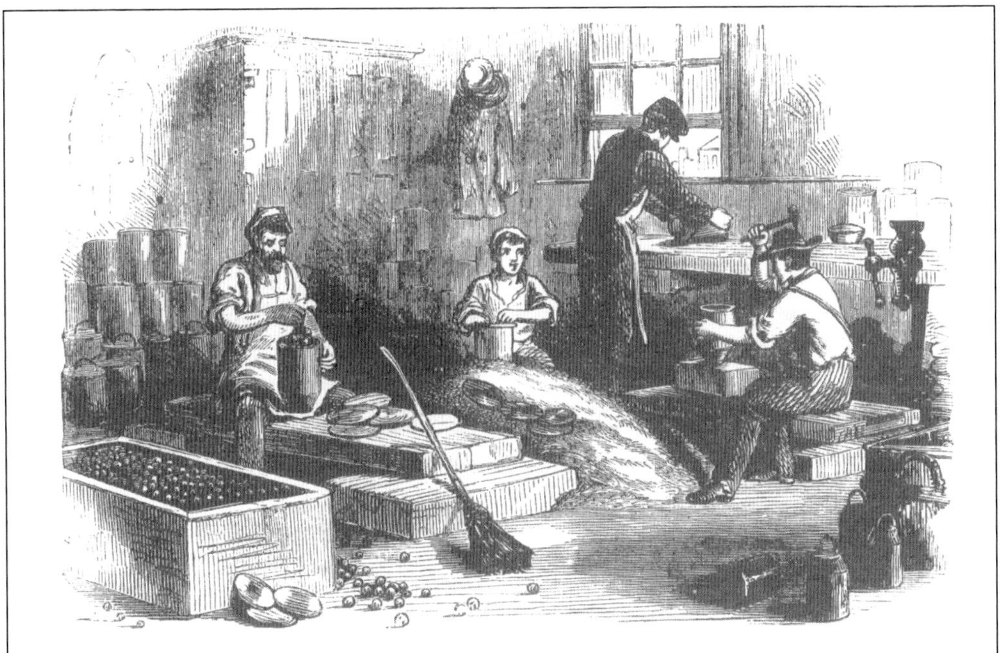

LABORERS FILL CANISTER IN ARSENAL WORKSHOP. (Courtesy of Watervliet Museum) The above image of workers at the Watervliet Arsenal is reminiscent of the way things were done in St. Louis. In the early 1830s, the primary activities of the St. Louis Arsenal involved repairing small arms, fabricating ammunition, building and repairing gun carriages, storing and preserving military materiel, and supplying local militias. During the first six years of arsenal activities, the army had spent an average of $17,000 per year on its operations. By contrast, during the first three years of Symington's command, an average of $26,000 per year was spent. The post was developing beyond its planners' fondest dreams.

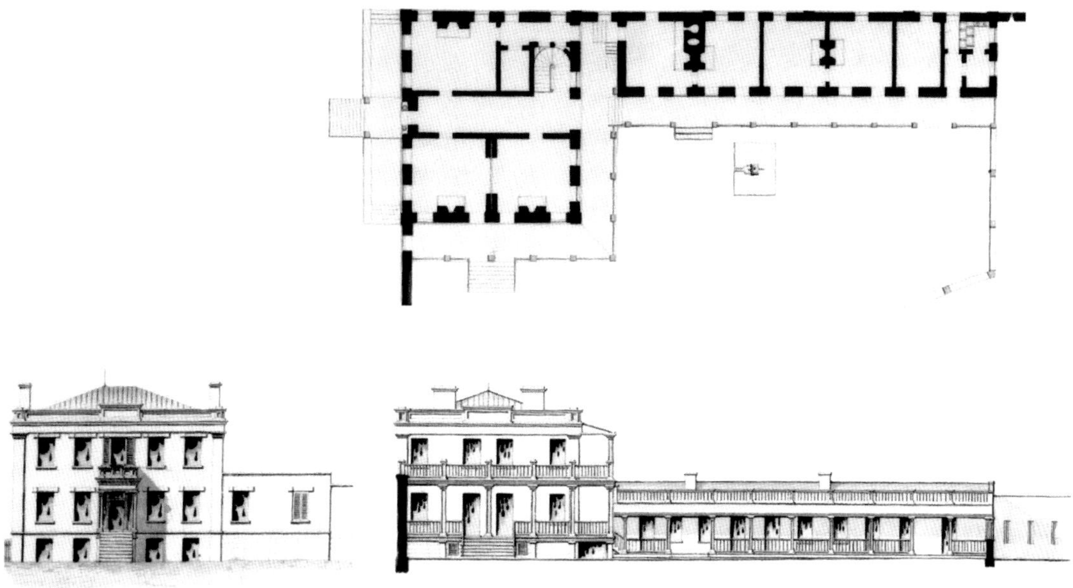

COMMANDING OFFICER'S QUARTERS, WINKELMAIER, 1840. (Courtesy of National Archives) During 1833, Lieutenant Anderson let three contracts for continuing construction at the arsenal. On July 20, he contracted with "Coutts and Witherell" to construct the walls of a two-story building and to provide the necessary brick and stone for the project. On July 26, he engaged Jonathan Biglow for carpentry work on "several buildings at the St. Louis Arsenal," and on September 1, he hired David Laurence to "erect a wall around a magazine." This probably refers to the "Great Magazine" located a half mile south of the arsenal on land purchased by Lieutenant Thomas for that purpose in 1829. The two-story dwelling erected by Coutts and Witherell was probably the commanding officer's quarters. This stately dwelling was located at the southeast corner of the post overlooking the river, a complimentary balance to the officers' quarters (the former Rutgers home) on the opposite corner. It consisted of two floors and a basement, which measured 41 by 48 feet, and an east-west wing of two stories, measuring 20 by 98 feet. Eight-foot-wide verandas encircled the house on all but the southwest side and continued along the northeast length of the west wing. Immaculately manicured lawns and gardens accented the landscape on the northeast side of the home. The dwelling, eventually designated #13, would serve as the home of each commanding officer and his family until the turn of the century.

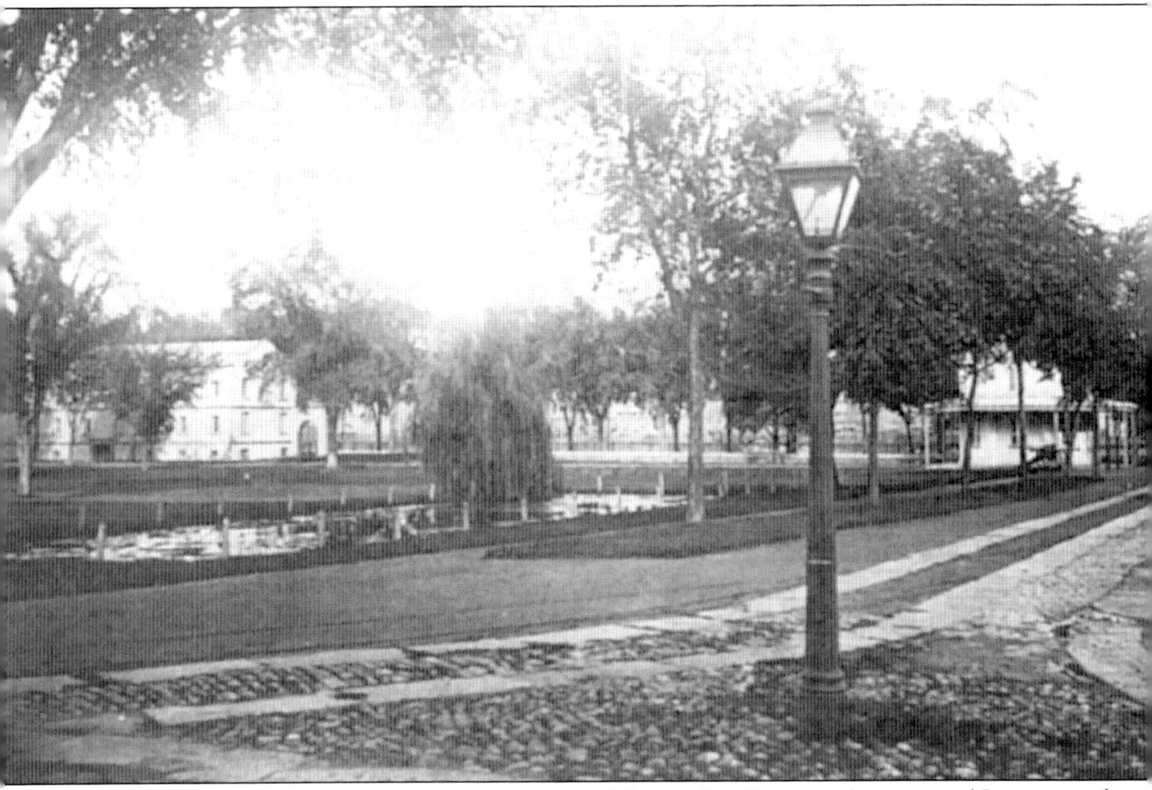

WATERVLIET ARSENAL, NEW YORK, THE NATION'S OLDEST ARSENAL. (Courtesy of Watervliet Museum) By 1834 there were 18 arsenals distributed across the U.S., with St. Louis located the farthest west. The Ordnance Department considered its three "principle arsenals" to be Watervliet, New York; Washington D.C.; and Pittsburgh, Pennsylvania. These were considered most important because they were "arsenals of construction," meaning that they built field carriages, fabricated all types of ammunition, and repaired and preserved a variety of small arms and militia stores. Watervliet became one of the most important cannon manufacturers and research facilities in the country. From these primary locations, materiel was shipped to the second level installations, which were classed "important arsenals." They were responsible for repairing gun carriages and small arms, fabricating all but the largest types of ammunition, and distributing ordnance and supplies to the militia in accordance with the Act of 1808. By 1834, St. Louis was considered the most prominent of this class of arsenal, ranking third for the year in expenditures, reflecting its growing importance on the western frontier and in the Mississippi River Valley. Colonel Bomford reported that progress on building the St. Louis Arsenal had gone so well, and it had functioned so efficiently as a medium ordnance installation, that it should be upgraded to an arsenal of construction. Such action was never taken, however.

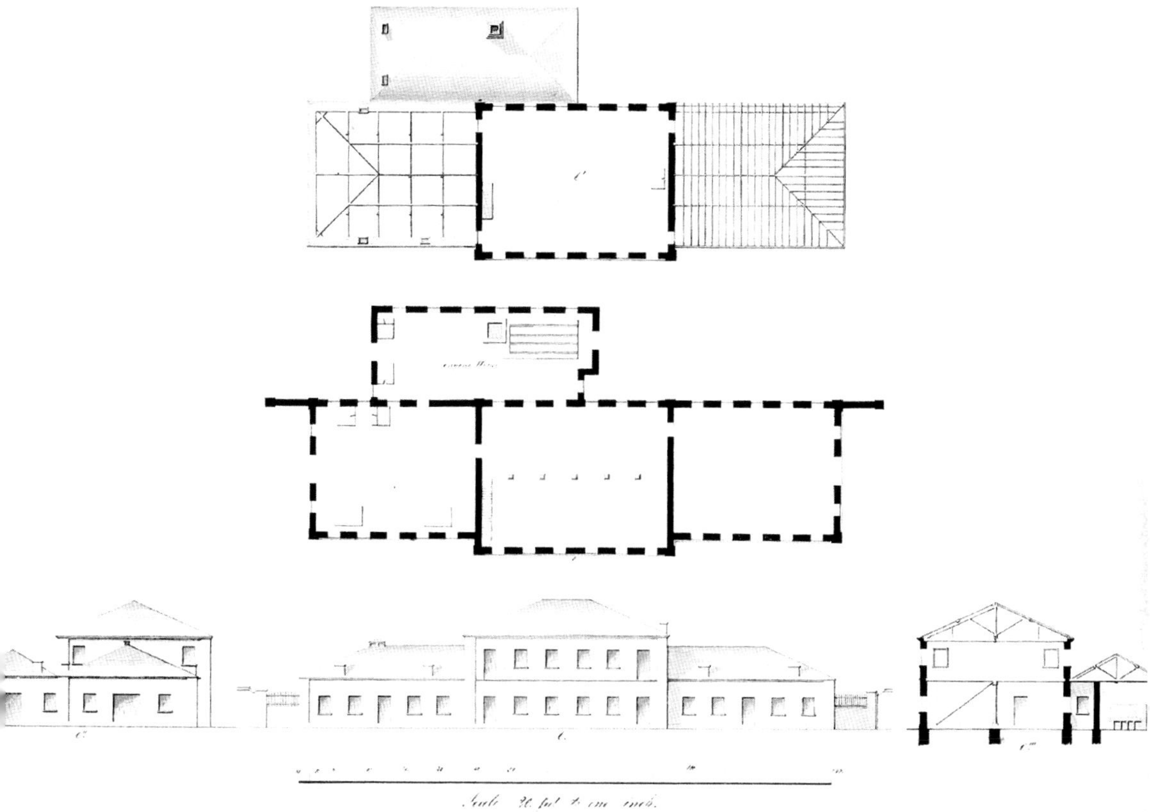

ARMORY AND WORKSHOPS, WINKELMAIER, 1840. (Courtesy of National Archives) A rather complex building constructed during 1834 and 1835 was the armory. Built of limestone and roofed in slate, this structure consisted of a central section, two stories high, measuring 44 by 58 feet, which was flanked on the northeast and southwest by one-story workshops of 40 by 48 feet. On the northwest side of the building, positioned slightly off-center toward the south part of the structure, was an attached one-story steam engine room. The steam engine supplied power for the machinery housed in the center section and the two workshops, which consisted of carpentry and blacksmith facilities. The length of the entire complex was 154 feet. It was located some 200 feet northwest of the enlisted barracks, centered on a line running from the main Arsenal building, through the enlisted barracks, to the armory. It formed the central portion of the northwest side of the quadrangle.

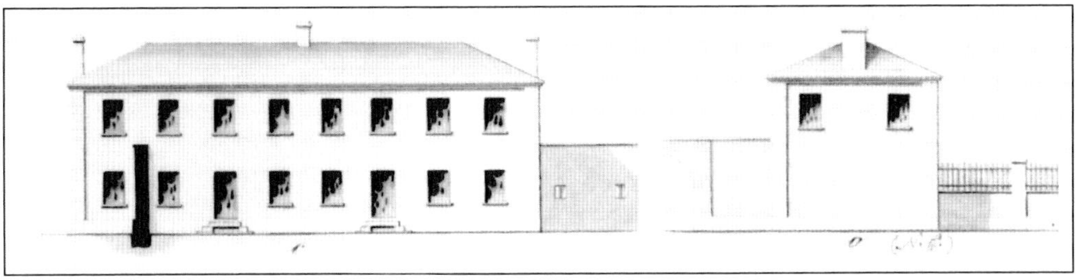

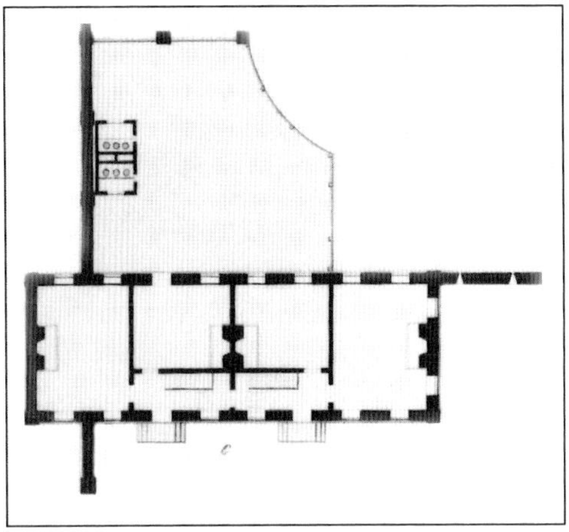

POST HOSPITAL BUILDING, WINKELMAIER, 1840. (Courtesy of National Archives) Three new buildings were erected during 1834 and 1835. The exterior walls were of limestone, the inner walls and chimneystacks of brick, and the roofs of slate. By late summer the walls were lathed, plastered, and painted. One of these structures was the post hospital (later designated #10). It was two stories high, with four rooms and a closet on each floor. The external dimensions were 22 by 61 feet, and the building was situated on a northeast-southwest axis, in line with the enlisted men's barracks and the office and storekeeper's quarters across the center of the original quadrangle. It lay perpendicular to the small storehouse building (#12), which was located on the southwest side of the quadrangle. The photograph below depicts the building in the early 20th century when it served as a dwelling for two civilian employees.

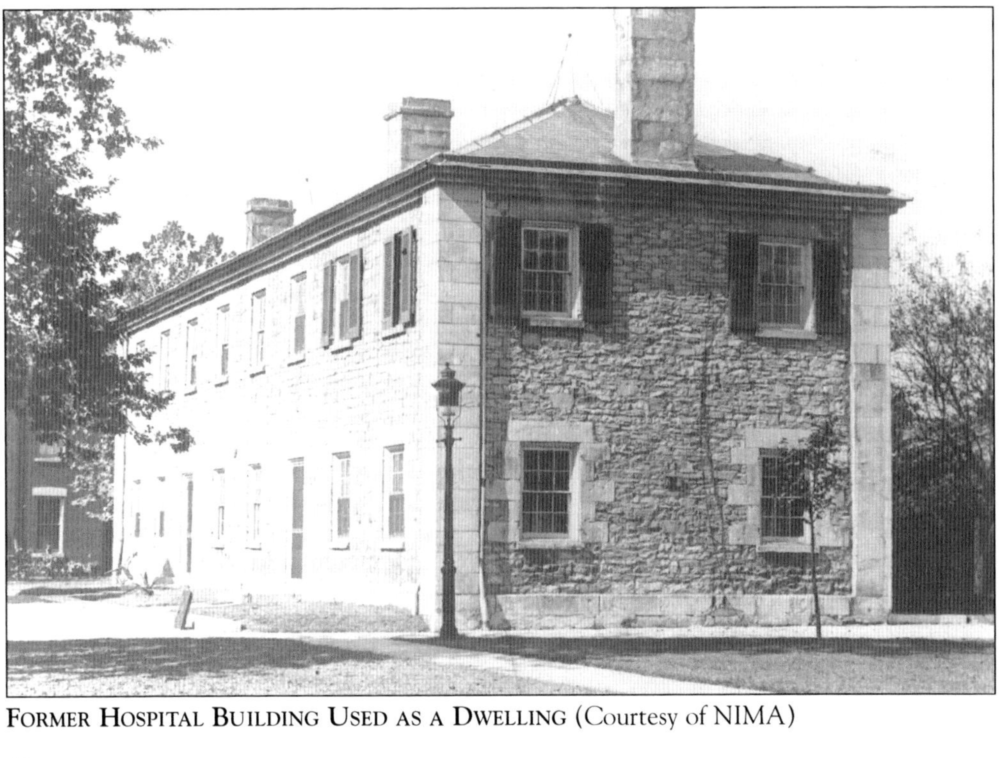

FORMER HOSPITAL BUILDING USED AS A DWELLING (Courtesy of NIMA)

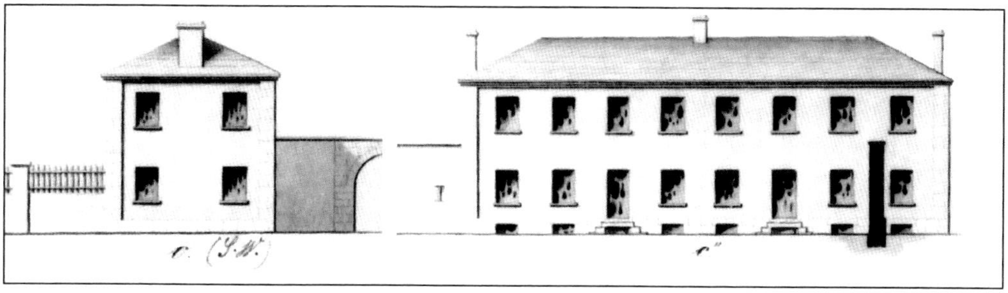

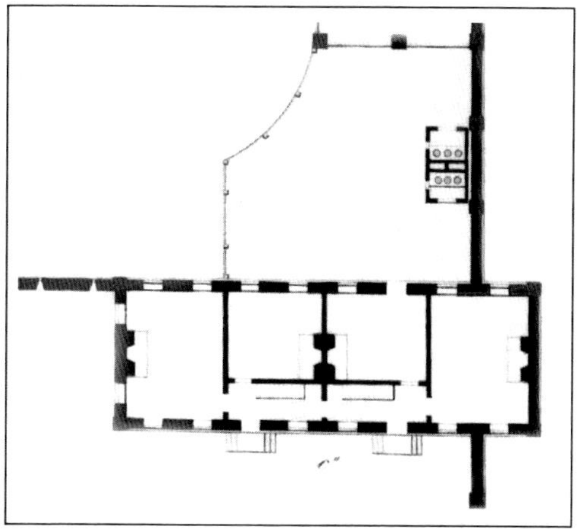

OFFICE AND STOREKEEPER'S QUARTERS, WINKELMAIER, 1840. (Courtesy of National Archives) Straight across the quadrangle, in line with the post hospital and the enlisted barracks, the office and storekeeper's quarters (#19) were built for the arsenal storekeeper. The structure was a mirror reflection of the hospital building and lay perpendicular to the small storehouse (#18), which ran along the northeast side of the quadrangle. Like the hospital, the storekeeper's building was constructed of limestone, with a stone foundation and a slate roof. It consisted of two stories of four rooms each, with a closet only on the second floor. The external dimensions, similar to the hospital, were 22 by 61 feet. This building was also converted to use as a dwelling for a civilian employee near the turn of the century.

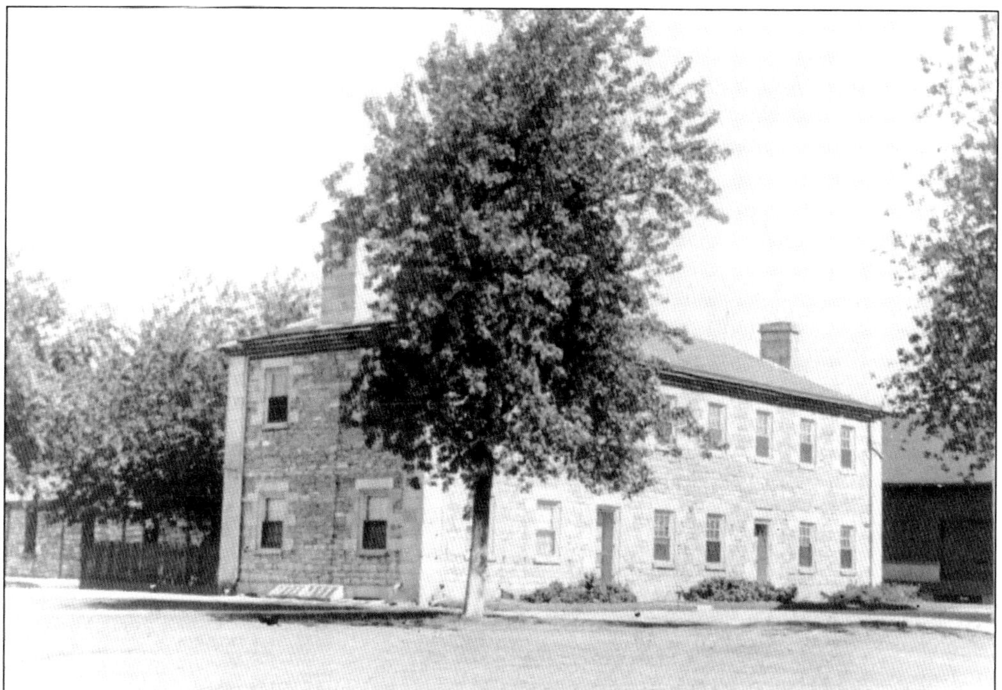

FORMER OFFICE BUILDING USED AS A DWELLING (Courtesy of NIMA)

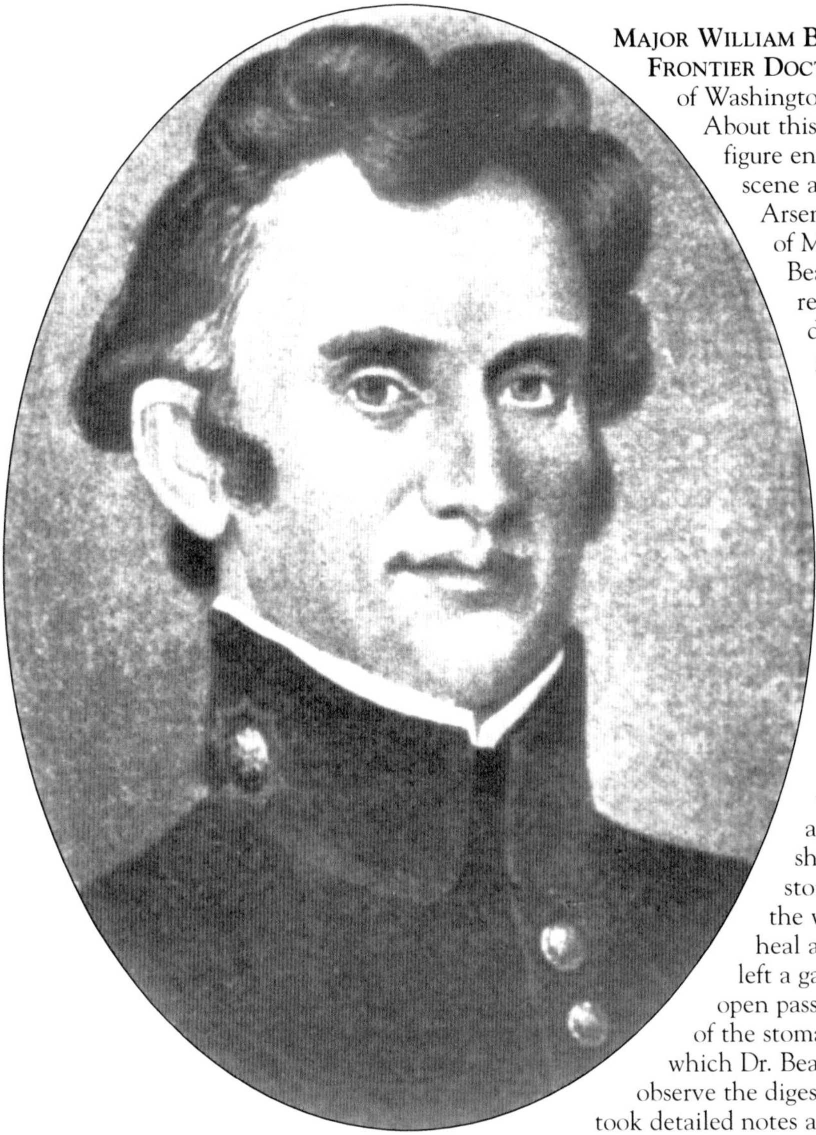

MAJOR WILLIAM BEAUMONT, FRONTIER DOCTOR. (Courtesy of Washington University) About this time a new figure entered the scene at the St. Louis Arsenal in the person of Major William Beaumont. This renowned army doctor had gained recent fame in the publication of the most advanced book of its time on the human digestive system. He had treated a young French-Canadian trapper, Alexis St. Martin, who had been accidentally shot in the stomach. When the wound did not heal as expected, it left a gastric fistula or open passage in the wall of the stomach through which Dr. Beaumont could observe the digestive process. He took detailed notes and conducted extensive experiments over several years on the digestion of different types of foods, publishing his findings in 1833. He quickly gained a worldwide reputation in the medical community. Major Beaumont and his family arrived at the arsenal in July of 1835 where he served as post surgeon, working out of an office at the new hospital. He also received permission from the surgeon general to treat civilian patients, and he quickly carved out a lucrative clientele among the leading families of the city. Biographer Alma Myer points out that such names as Cabanne, Carr, Mullanphy, Vandeventer, and Benton were commonly found in his accounts. In fact, his civilian patient load soon outweighed his military responsibilities. Sometime later Beaumont moved to the city to be closer to his civilian practice and left his hospital steward, George Johnson, in charge of affairs at the arsenal. Beaumont had himself trained Johnson and rationalized that he could deal with all but the most severe military cases. Johnson had a brilliant mind for medicine. Beaumont would eventually sponsor him at medical school and the two would become partners in a St. Louis practice.

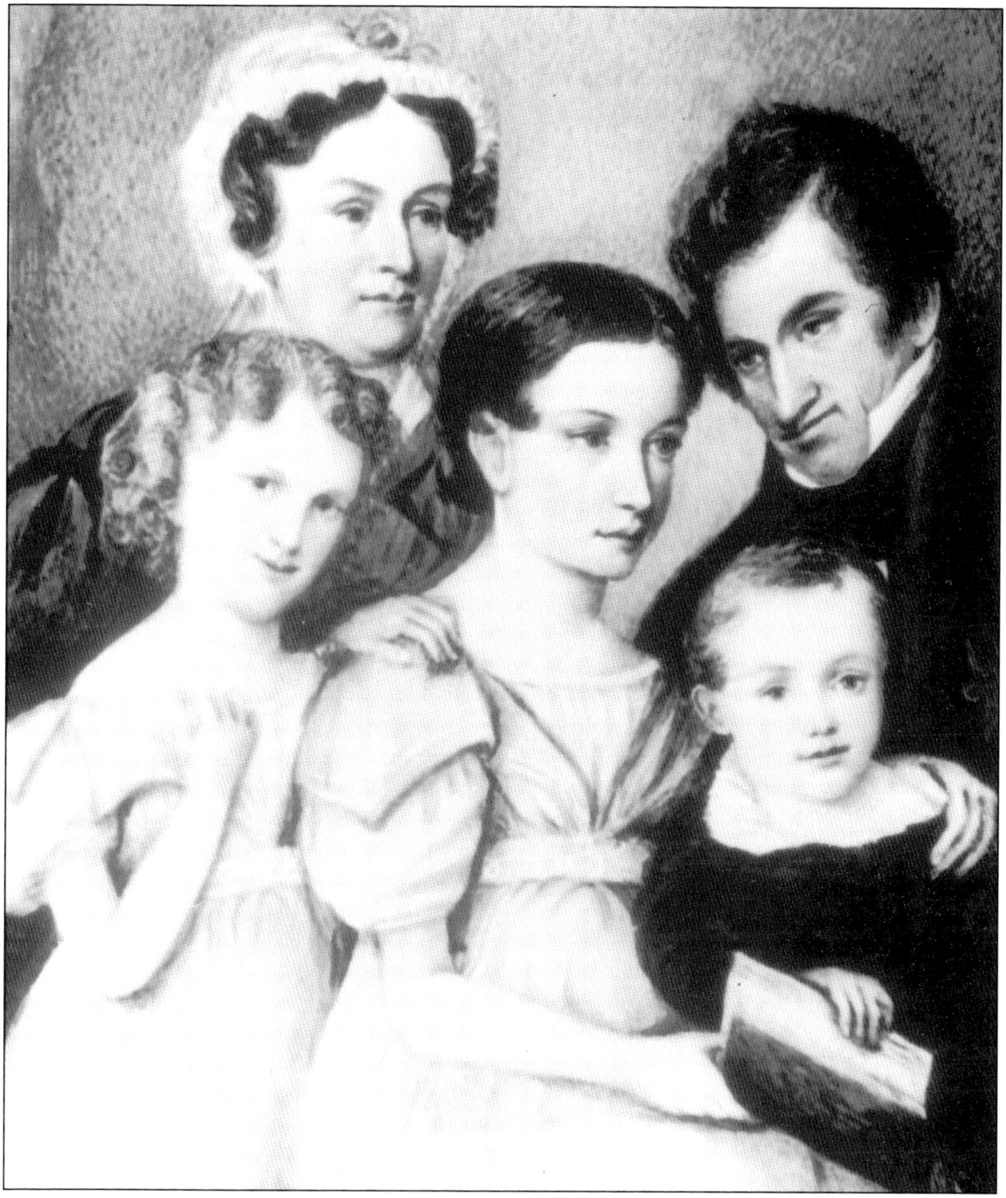

THE WILLIAM BEAUMONT FAMILY. (Courtesy of Washington University) With wife Debby and their three children, the Beaumonts settled into their temporary home in the officers' quarters at the arsenal until they could find "suitable housing" in the city. Alma Myer described the picturesque scene which first greeted the Beaumonts: "The gray limestone walls of the officers' quarters were warmed by the bright gardens and fruit trees which surrounded them. The arsenal's 40 acres were not so filled with sheds, laboratories, and shops but that many spots were available where children could play. Down by the river, two pet deer were kept; along the stonewalls that shut off the upper roads were rows of cannon and pyramids of cannonballs which afforded excellent hiding places. Sometimes the children were allowed to look in at the smiths' forges or at the steam-engine house. Two ropewalks, in long low stone houses on the north side of the arsenal, where 600 slaves twisted the fibers, held them fascinated for hours on end." This privately owned rope factory north of the arsenal shows how close the city had already grown by 1835.

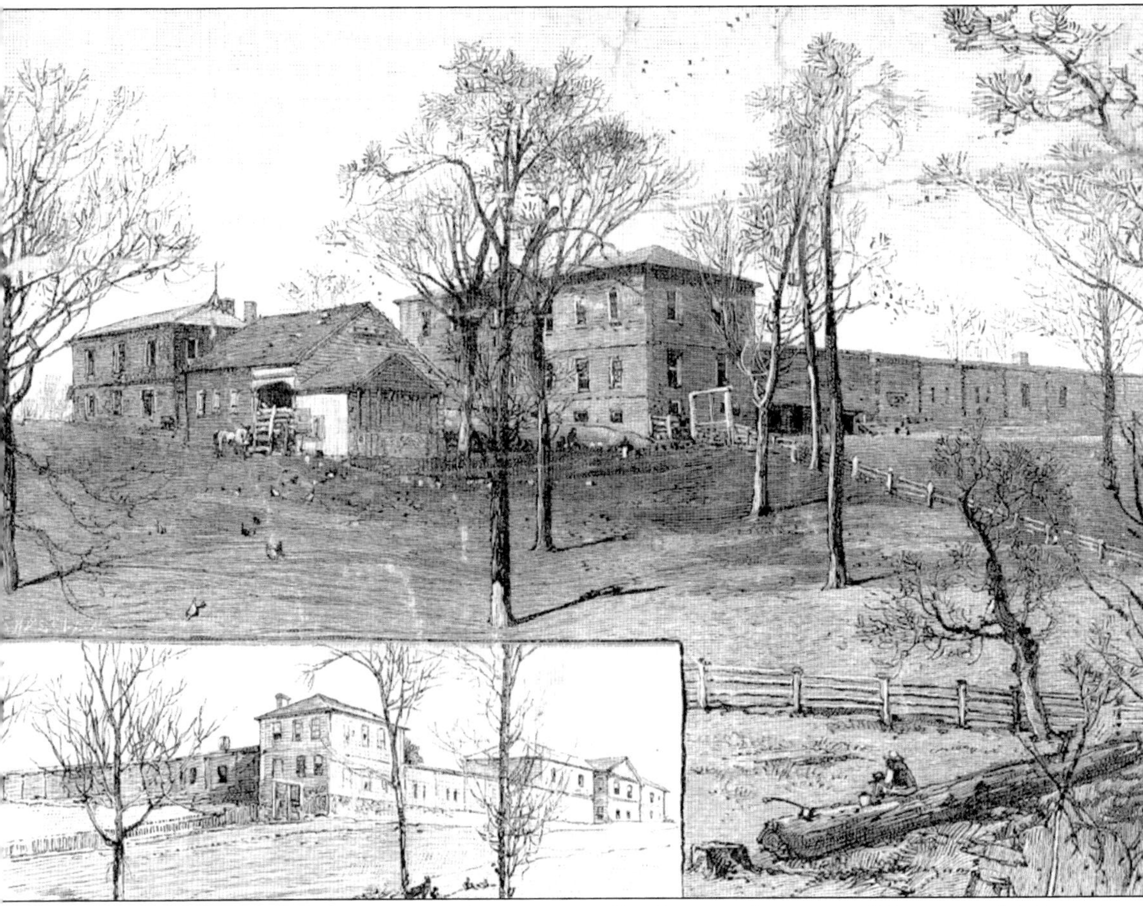

LIBERTY MISSOURI ARSENAL, OUTPOST OF ST. LOUIS ARSENAL. (Courtesy of Missouri Historical Society) After the U.S. government forcibly removed Native Americans to the western banks of the Mississippi to keep them from clashing with the relentless waves of white settlers, a series of "Indian Wars" broke out across the western and northern frontiers. The state legislatures of Missouri, Tennessee, and Arkansas urged the U.S. Congress to provide ordnance depots and munitions to arm local militias for their defense. So, in 1836, as the St. Louis Arsenal approached the completion of its first phase of construction, Colonel Bomford announced that two small "arsenals of distribution" would be erected at Liberty, Missouri and Memphis, Tennessee, and that a larger facility already planned for Little Rock, Arkansas, would commence construction. Since there were not enough officers in the ordnance branch to assign to these new projects, Captain Symington was ordered to oversee all arrangements for the building of these installations. Though burdened with maintaining the pace of construction at the St. Louis Arsenal, Symington proceeded to his duty. Federal funds appropriated for these projects exceeded $34,000 during 1836. This amount included some $7,800 for "current expenses of the ordnance service," over $18,000 for "arsenals," $350 for "arming and equipping the militia," $1,800 for "the suppression of Indian hostilities," and $5,000 specifically for the purchase of sites and construction of the arsenals at Liberty, Memphis and Little Rock. The appropriations included about $3,000 for the St. Louis Arsenal. Symington managed to spend nearly $25,000 of this whopping budget in one year and carried the remainder over into 1837.

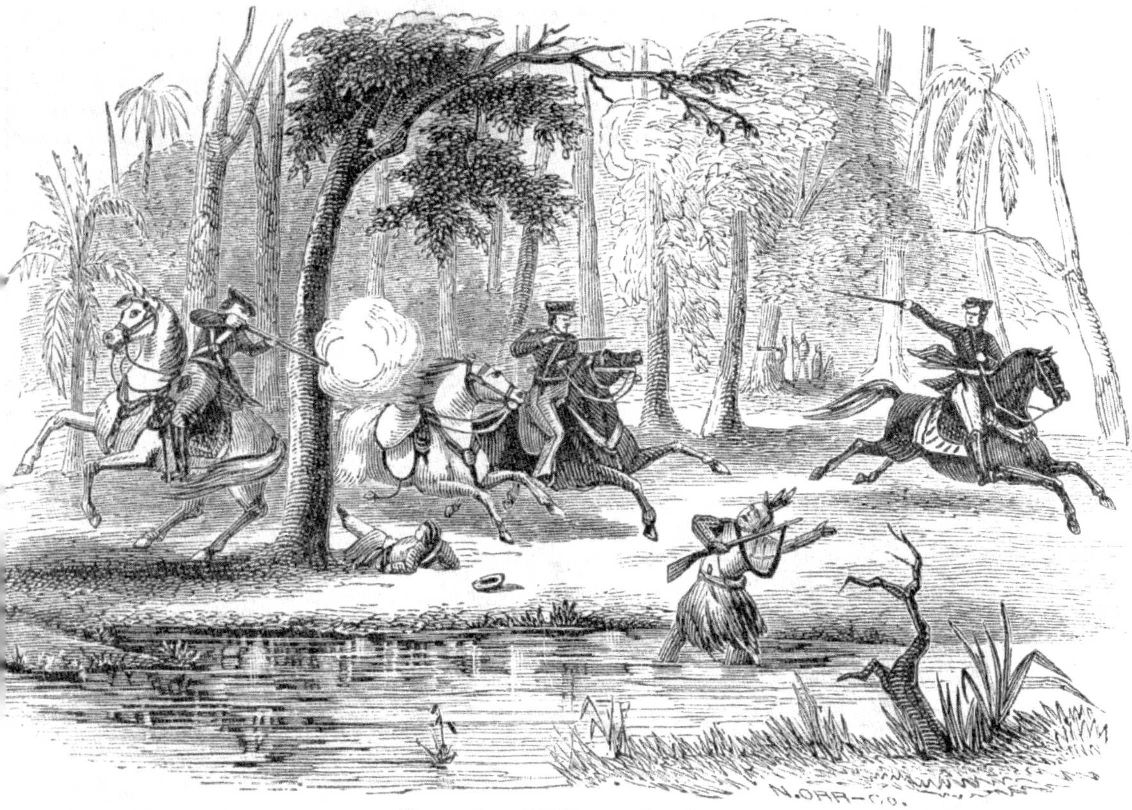

Death of Waxe-hadjo.

SEMINOLE WAR RAGES IN FLORIDA. (Giddings, SLU Archives) Another "Indian hostility" broke out in Florida when the Seminoles resisted the attempts of the U.S. government to oust them from their reservations and send them west to less favorable lands in the Indian Territory (Oklahoma). White settlers coveted the Florida land and President Andrew Jackson, veteran of an earlier Seminole War, promoted the Indian Removal Act of 1830 to clear the land east of the Mississippi of all Indian tribes. Tens of thousands of Native Americans were forcibly removed from the southeastern states during the 1830s and a quarter of them died en route to new reservations, but the Seminoles did not go easily. From 1835 to 1842 they took refuge in the Florida Everglades and waged fierce guerrilla warfare against U.S. troops and militia, killing as many as 2,000 soldiers and wounding hundreds more. The U.S. government spent between $40 and $60 million to suppress the conflict. As the fighting escalated, the St. Louis Arsenal shipped ordnance and equipment to the front-line troops, even though its primary mission continued to be the supply of troops and militia on the western frontier. In some cases, officers and enlisted men who had served at the arsenal were dispatched to Florida.

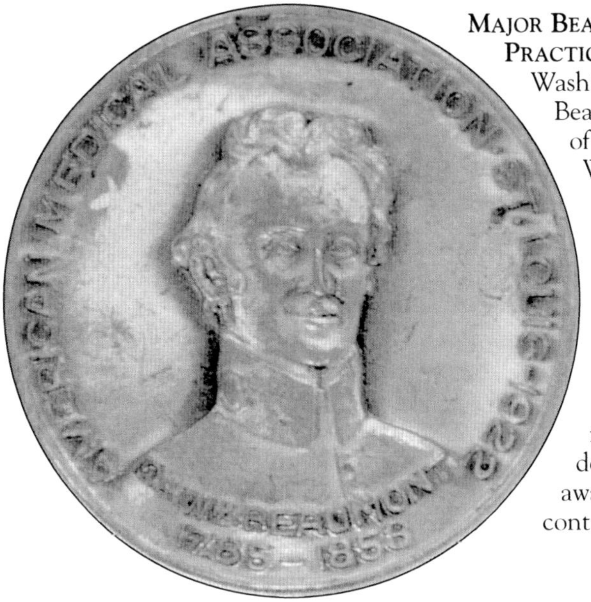

Major Beaumont Retires to a Busy Practice in St. Louis. (Courtesy of Washington University) Even Major Beaumont was not beyond the reach of orders to report for duty in Florida. When he refused on the grounds of his advancing age and busy medical practice, he tendered his resignation. Though discharged on December 31, 1839, he continued providing medical care for arsenal personnel, without compensation, until his replacement arrived many months later. Dr. Beaumont practiced medicine in St. Louis until his death in 1853. He received numerous awards and recognition for significant contributions to medicine.

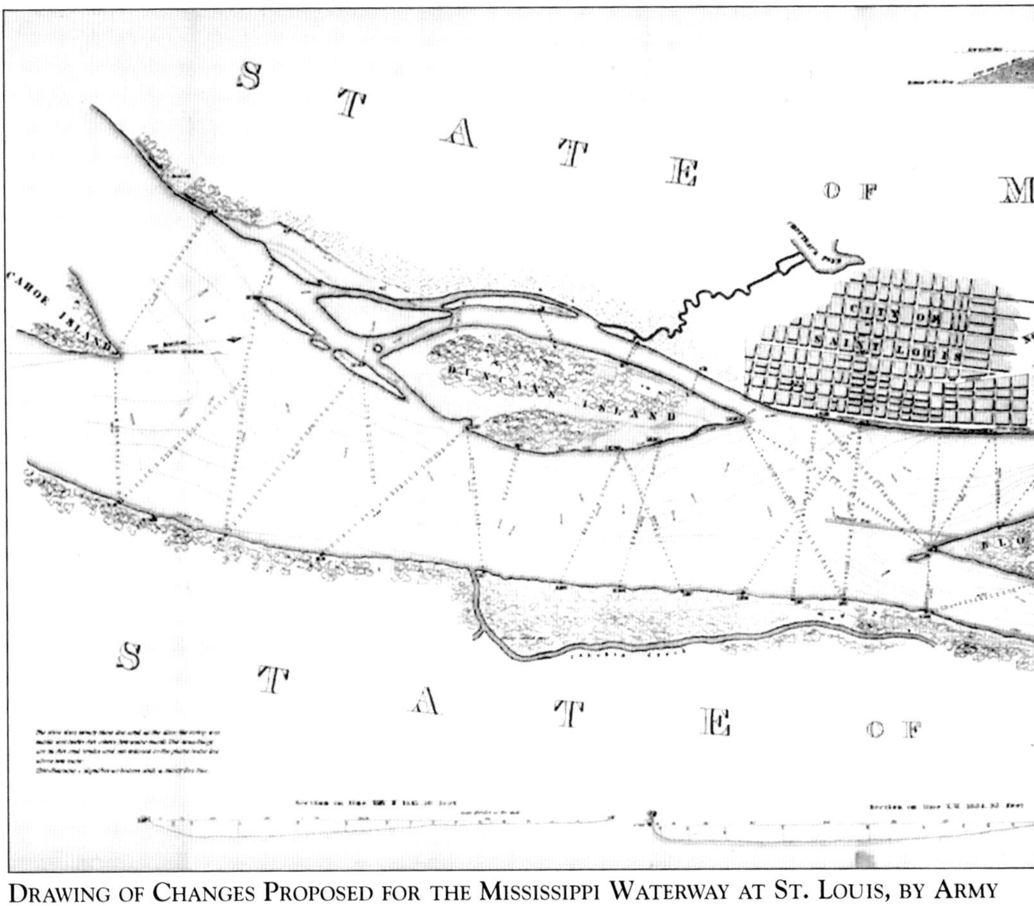

Drawing of Changes Proposed for the Mississippi Waterway at St. Louis, by Army

Robert E. Lee, Engineer on the Mississippi. (Courtesy of Missouri Historical Society) First Lieutenant (soon to be Captain) Robert E. Lee, a U.S. Army engineer, was assigned to St. Louis to attempt to remove the sand bars that were blocking access to the port of St. Louis. Since it was too late in the season to begin construction on the project, Lieutenant Lee returned to Virginia to escort his wife and three young children back to St. Louis before the next season's work. They arrived in St. Louis in May 1838. Lieutenant Lee had arranged to rent a small cottage in the city, but the house was not vacated until a month after their arrival. The Beaumonts took them in until they could move into the cottage, and the two families became lifelong friends.

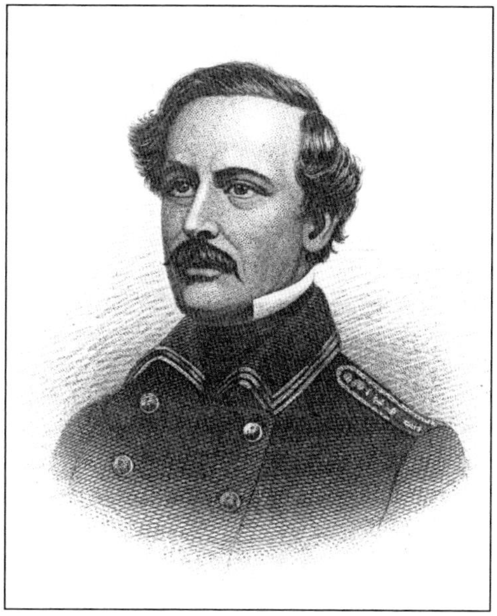

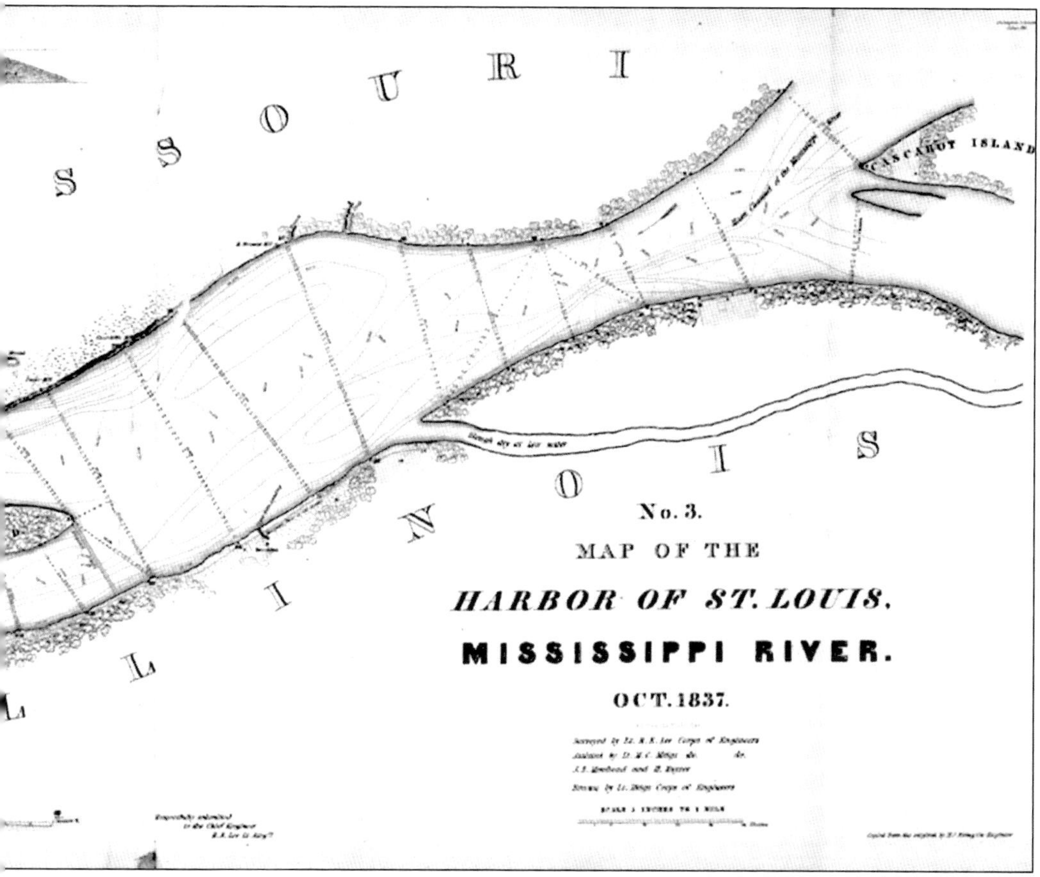

Engineer Robert E. Lee. (Courtesy of Missouri Historical Society)

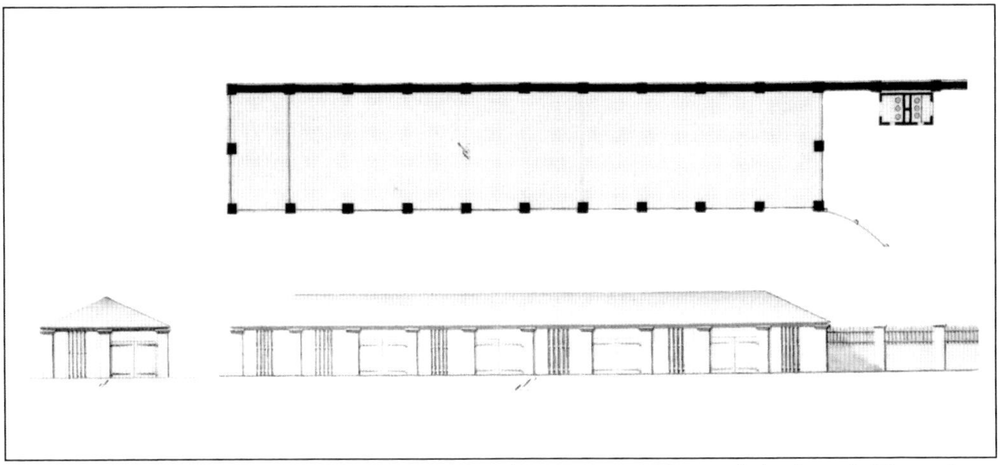

NORTH TIMBER SHED, WINKELMAIER, 1840. (Courtesy of National Archives) Throughout the Indian Wars, the press of construction activity at the arsenal continued unabated. The building projects required immense amounts of lumber and basic building materials. In 1836 and 1837, two large timber sheds were built to provide space for stacking and curing lumber and room for woodworking. These two long, slender, one-story buildings, measuring 30 by 151 feet, were located along the northeast (Building #21) and southwest (Building #9) perimeters of the original quadrangle. The buildings were supported by eleven pillars along each side of their length, the walls were of timber, the roofs of wooden shingles, and each building was served by four sets of double swinging doors on the inside of the compound.

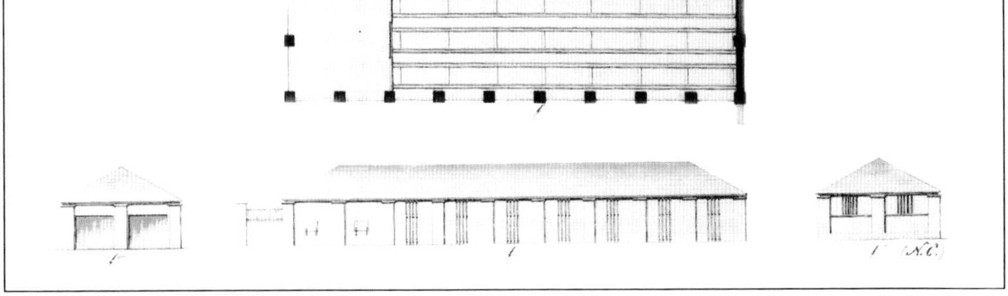

NORTH GUN SHED, WINKELMAIER, 1840. (Courtesy of National Archives)

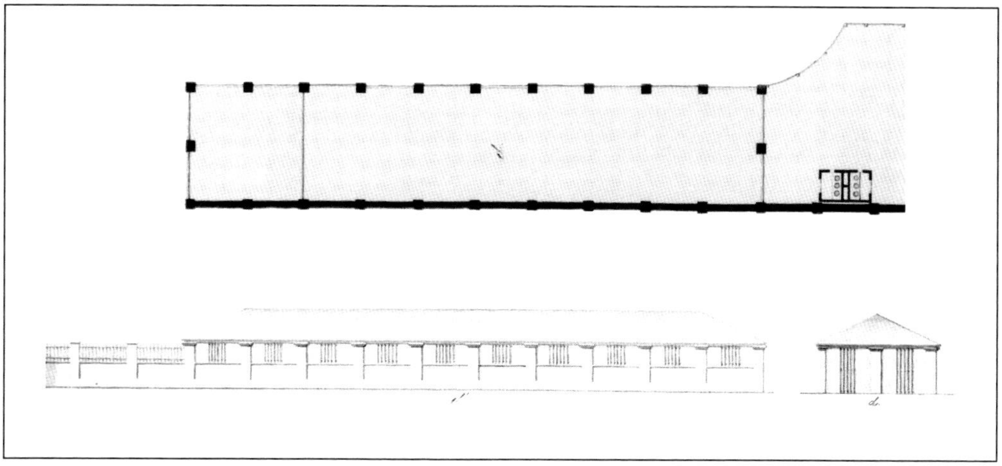

SOUTH TIMBER SHED, WINKELMAIER, 1840. (Courtesy of National Archives) During the same two years, two gun carriage sheds were also built, flanking the armory along the northwest wall of the quadrangle. These too were built of timber and roofed with wooden shingles. Each structure measured 30 by 106 feet, being supported by 2 parallel rows of 10 pillars, with vertical planks forming the walls. Access to the carriage sheds was provided by two sets of double doors on the sides closest to the armory, and by two more sets of doors on one end of each building. Three pairs of gun skids ran in parallel down three-quarters of the distance of the sheds. They provided supports for gun barrels which were not mounted on carriages and would thus maximize the use of the limited storage space. Carriage sheds provided storage for gun carriages and caissons apart from the gun sheds.

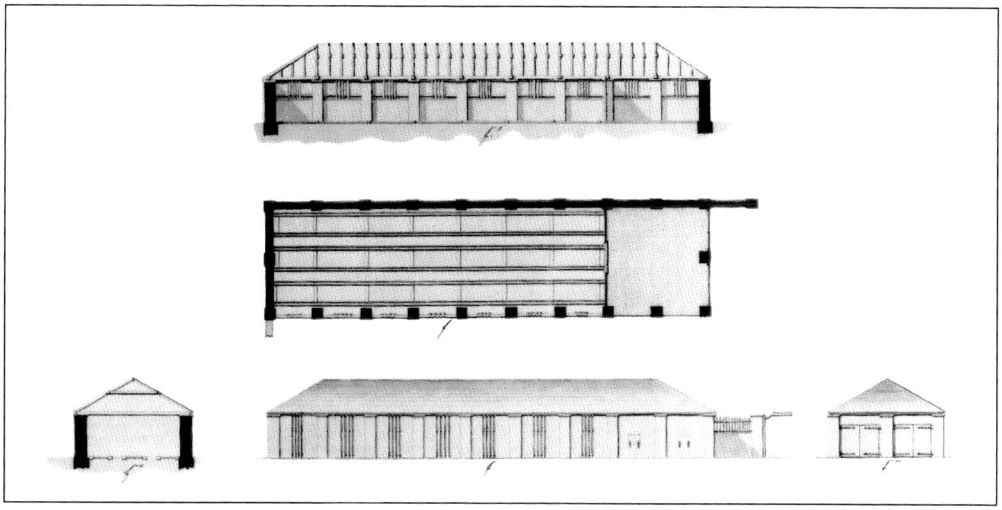

SOUTH GUN SHED, WINKELMAIER, 1840. (Courtesy of National Archives)

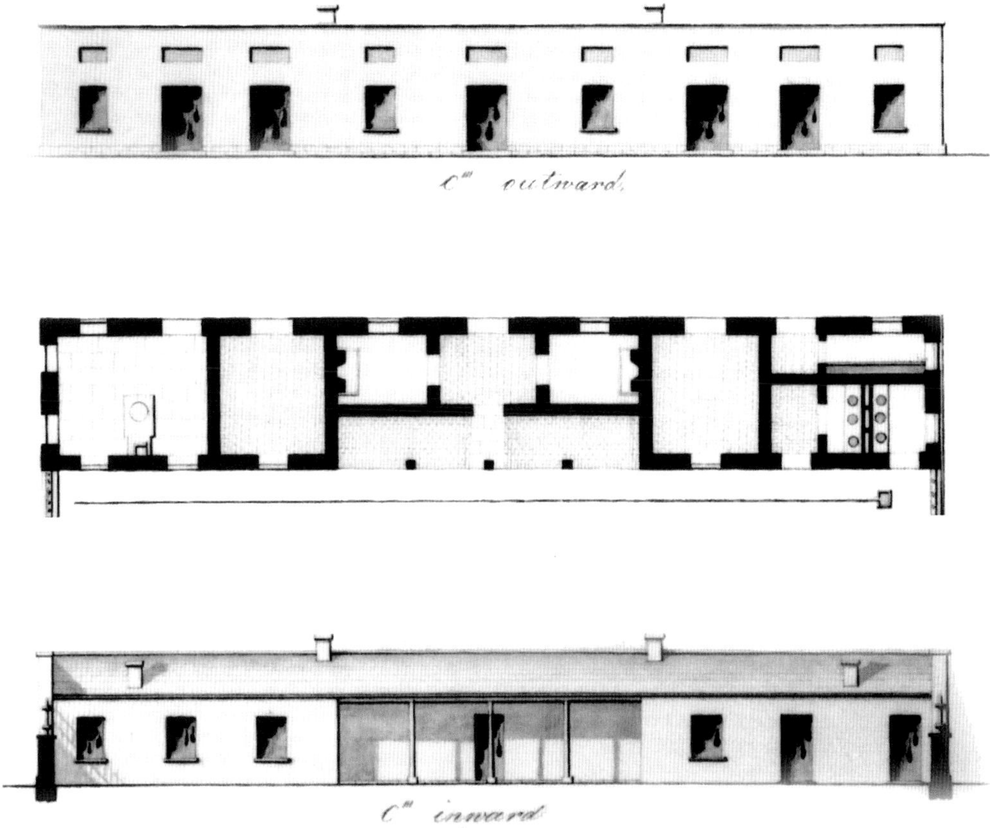

CASTING HOUSE, WINKELMAIER, 1840. (Courtesy of National Archives) In 1836 a "casting house" was built northwest of the soldiers' barracks. It measured 106 by 17 feet and, among other things, housed a melting furnace for casting lead. In addition to the casting function it held a guardroom, tool room, fire engine room, and what appears to be two three-holed latrines. The construction of this structure, in addition to the three laboratories and the small magazine, completed the complex of buildings or rooms required for the safe and proper manufacture of ammunition. In order to manufacture small arms ammunition, lead was melted in a furnace room and cast into musket balls. The finished lead balls were then moved to a cartridge room, one of the laboratory buildings where workers seated at a 2.5 by 12 foot table would fasten paper and flannel cartridges to the lead balls. Another lab would serve as a filling room where cartridges were packed in cases for later use or shipment. Finally, all finished products were moved immediately to the small magazine, which was purposely placed as far as possible from the casting room. From there it was shipped to other arsenals for distribution or was issued directly to militias and active army units.

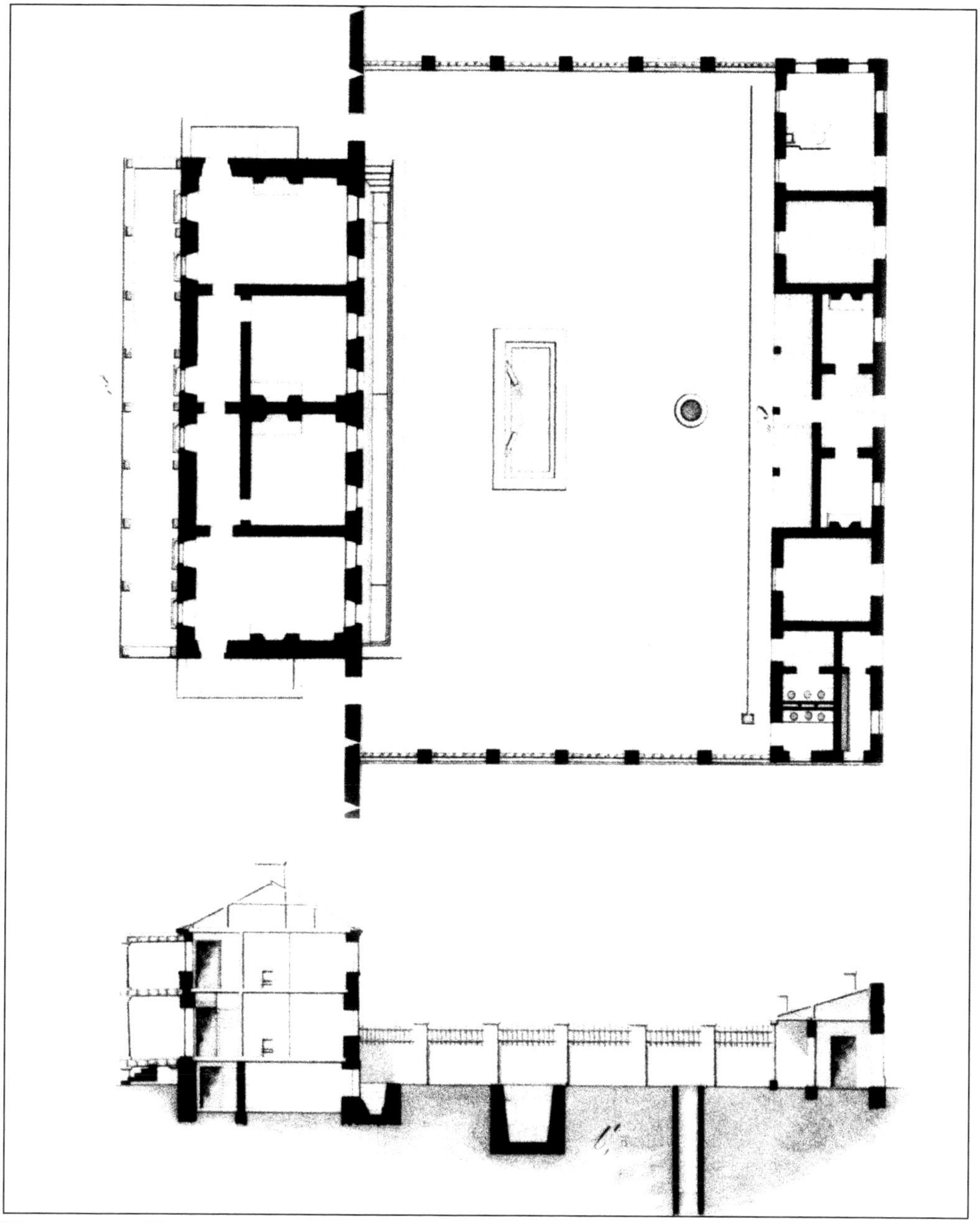

VIEW OF THE BARRACKS YARD, WINKELMAIER, 1840. (Courtesy of National Archives) With the completion of the casting house in 1836, interior connecting walls were built between it and the barracks, creating a private yard for the soldiers, measuring 63 by 102 feet. The walls of the enclosure were about 9 feet high, constructed of 6 feet of stone and topped off by 3 feet of "paling" (upright wooden or metal pickets). Inside the barracks yard was a 12 by 24 foot stone cistern to collect rainwater for fire protection and a deep well. Two other smaller stone cisterns were built elsewhere on the installation that same season. The upper image above shows the yard with the barracks on the left (southeast) side and the casting house on the northeast side of the quadrangle. The lower image depicts a cross section of the yard and the two buildings from the northeast side. Note the cistern on the left of the yard and the well on the right.

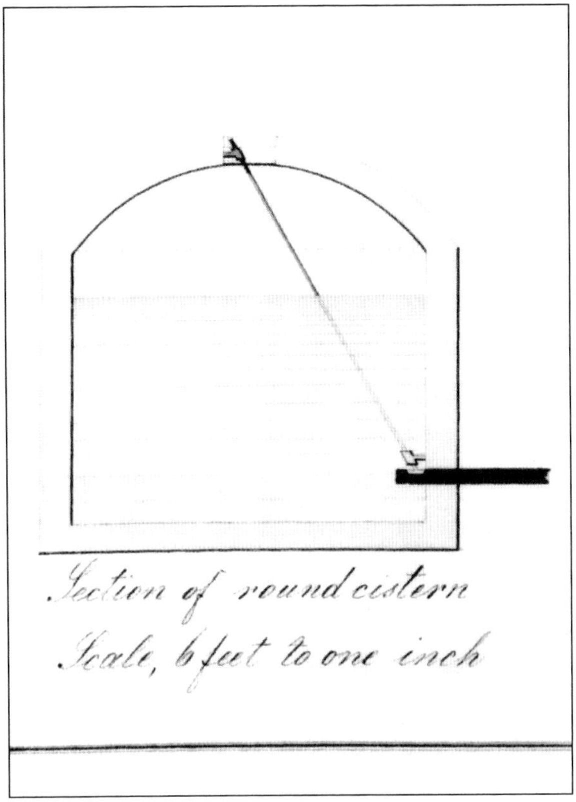

PATENTED BRICK CISTERN, WINKELMAIER, 1840. (Courtesy of National Archives) During the 1837 building season Captain Symington hired stonemasons Coutts and Withnell to complete the connecting walls between the sheds and their adjoining buildings, and to begin erecting the exterior enclosing wall around the arsenal complex. The original wall around the arsenal had been made of wood and the timbers were well-decayed by 1837. Specifications for the exterior wall called for it to be "about 7.5 feet high, and 18 inches thick, of dry stone, well-bedded, to the height of 5.5 feet." Symington also hired Thomas A. West to install three of his patented brick cisterns at underground locations around the arsenal. These were to measure 12 feet deep from the crown of their arch to the bottom of the reservoir, with a 15-foot diameter at the base of the cistern. This would also require the laying of 1,350 feet of iron pipe all over the arsenal to connect the cisterns with run-off spouts from various buildings. By 1840 the arsenal could boast 12 cisterns of different size and manufacture, scattered widely about the post. They were the primary source of water used in firefighting.

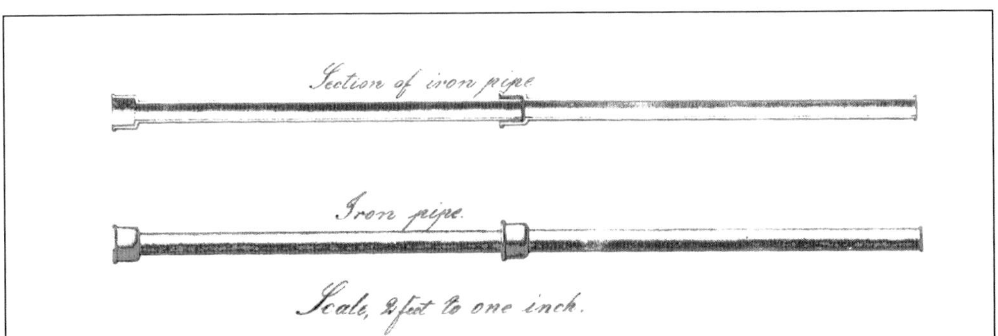

WATER PIPES SKETCHED BY LOUIS WINKELMAIER IN 1840. (Courtesy of National Archives)

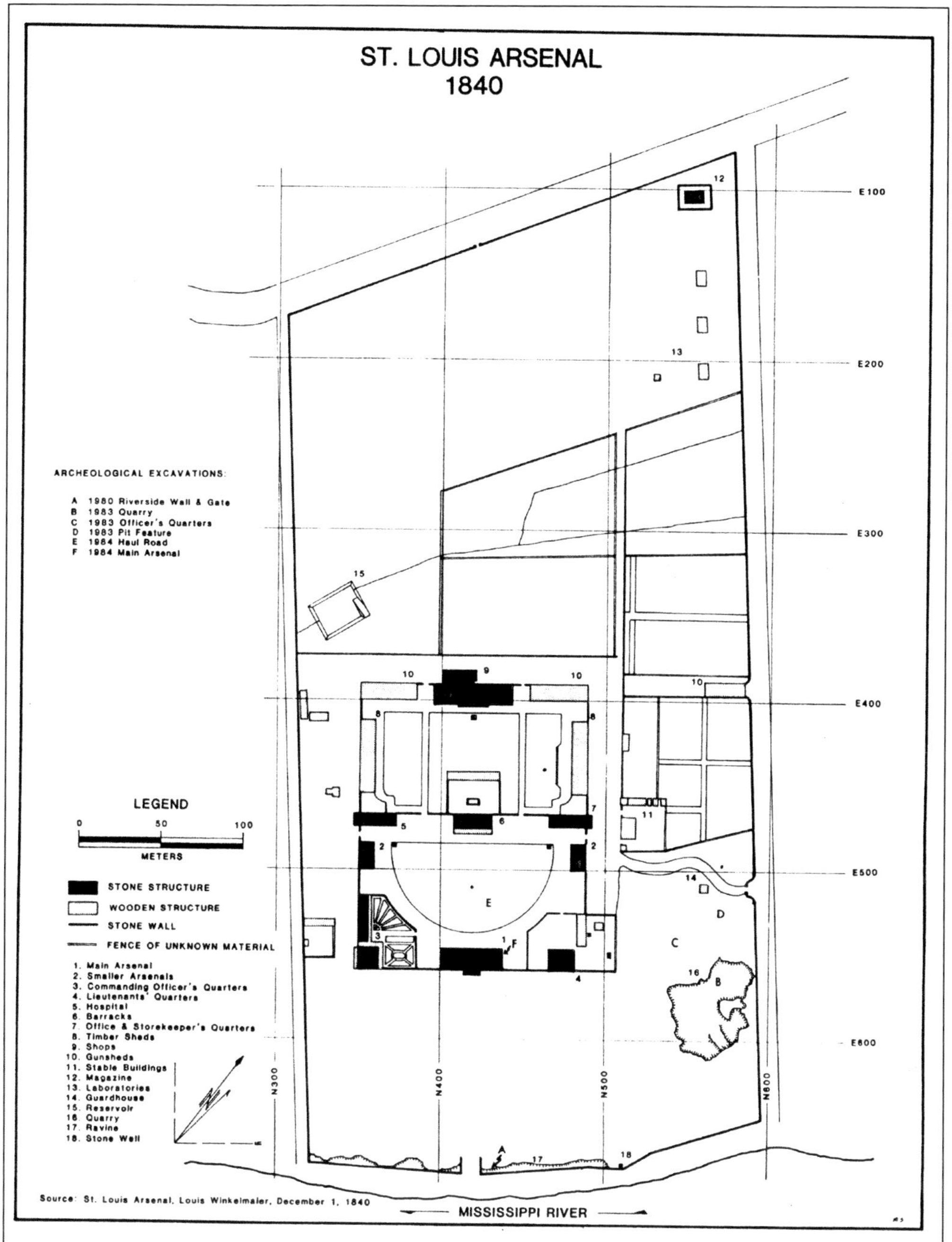

DRAWING OF THE INSTALLATION AS IT APPEARED IN 1840. (Courtesy of William Woods) This map was created from information provided in an 1840 drawing by Louis Winckelmaier and from work on the site in 1983 and 1984 by the archaeological team from Southern Illinois University. This map accompanied their final report.

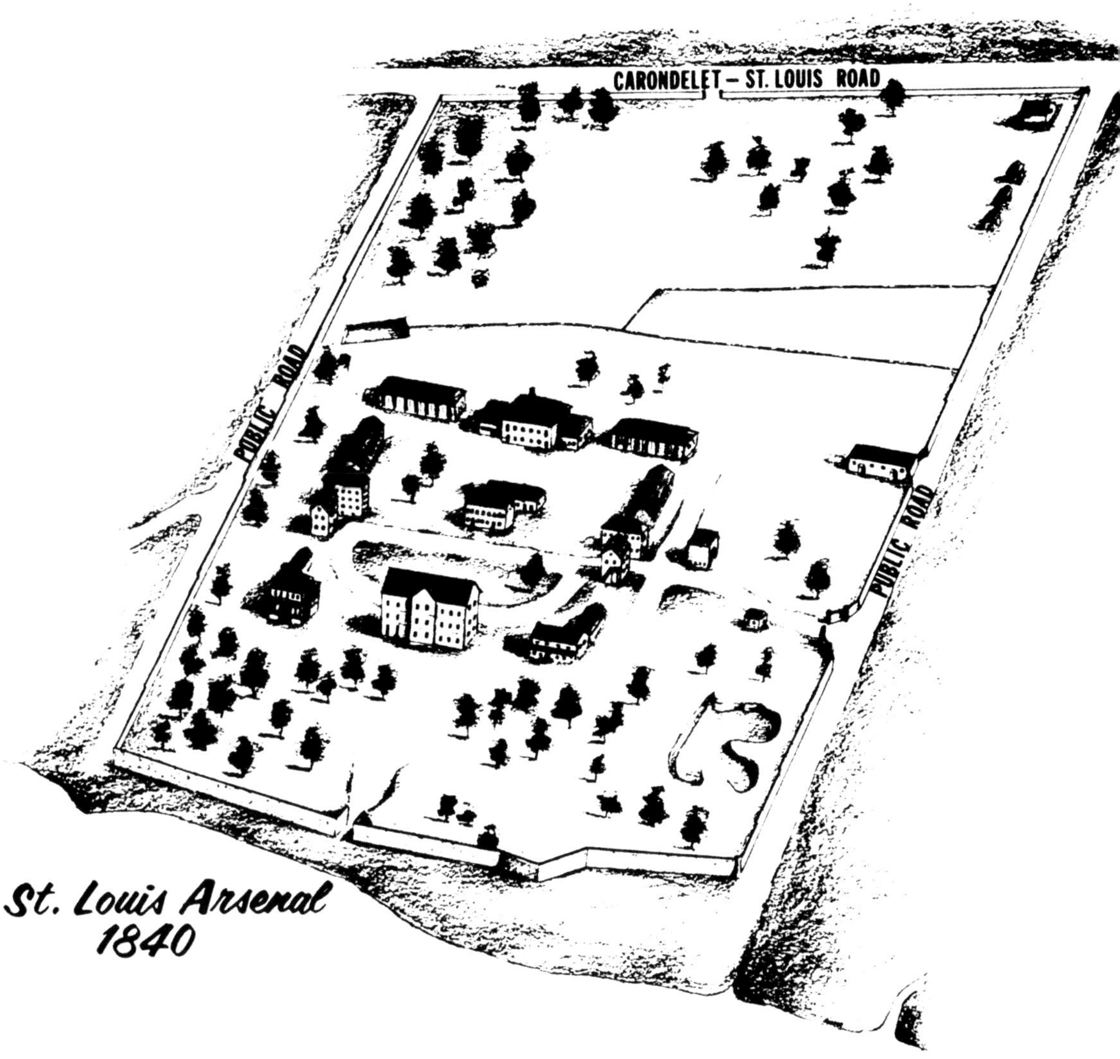

PRINCIPLE BUILDINGS OF THE ARSENAL IN 1840. (Courtesy of NIMA) By 1840 the arsenal had evolved into an impressive and beautiful installation in the countryside south of St. Louis. The initial construction of the complex spanned more than a decade, commencing in 1827 and culminating in the erection of 22 buildings and a stone enclosing wall by the end of 1839. Although three commanders and numerous architects and builders had a hand in fashioning this picturesque bastion of the western frontier, the primary credit should probably rest with Captain Symington for rescuing the arsenal from its unstable beginnings and engineering it into one of the finest examples of its kind in the United States. Furthermore, Symington was the chief architect of the arsenals at Liberty and Memphis during the same period, so his accomplishments were nothing less than spectacular. Soon, however, the St. Louis Arsenal would experience severe testing as the countryside surrounding it was transformed into a thriving urban landscape. By 1840, the city boasted a population of 16,439, and within a decade its borders would encompass the entire vicinity of the Arsenal, presenting new challenges to its existence.

Four

Armory of the West (1840–1849)

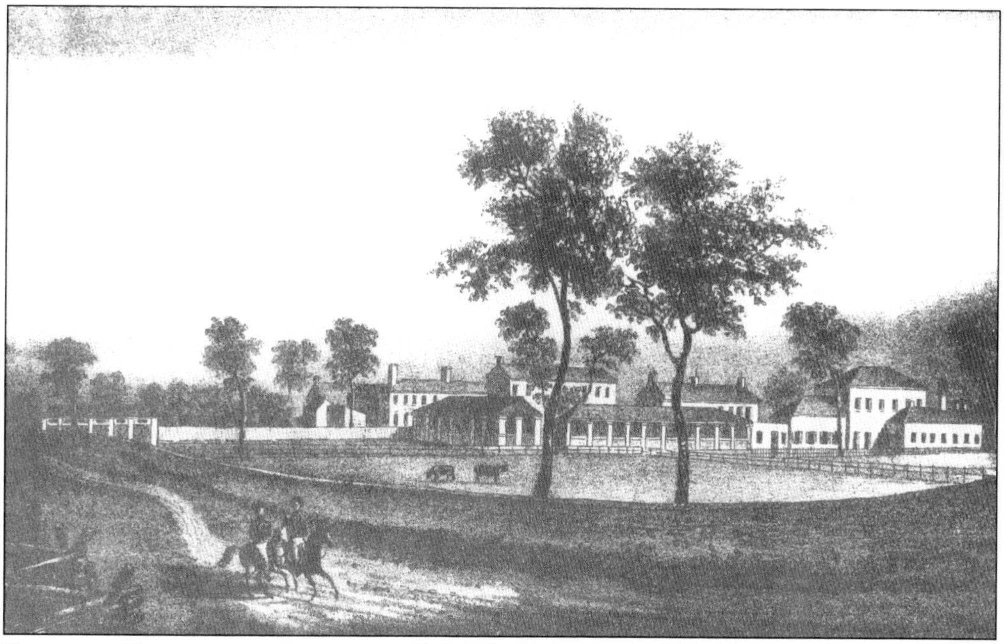

Pastoral View of the Arsenal by J.C. Wild, 1841. (Wild, SLU Archives) In his travels around the St. Louis area, artist J.C. Wild was most impressed with the beautiful setting of the U.S. Arsenal. Its martial function was subdued by the lush green meadows surrounding it and its tastefully structured architecture. Nevertheless, it was a powerful catalyst in the winning of the West, which the decade of the 1840s would prove beyond a doubt. The above rendering by Wild depicts the arsenal grounds as seen from the northwest. The soldiers seen in the left foreground are riding west on what is now Arsenal Street. Off the picture to the right would be the small magazine and the three laboratories. The building seen on the far right is the armory with its telltale steam engine room and tall chimney. The left wing of the building was one of the shops associated with the armory and is today designated Building #4. The tall structure in the center of the picture, at the far side of the installation, is the main arsenal building (later numbered 14). As the picture indicates, the primary layout of the arsenal installation was well established by 1841.

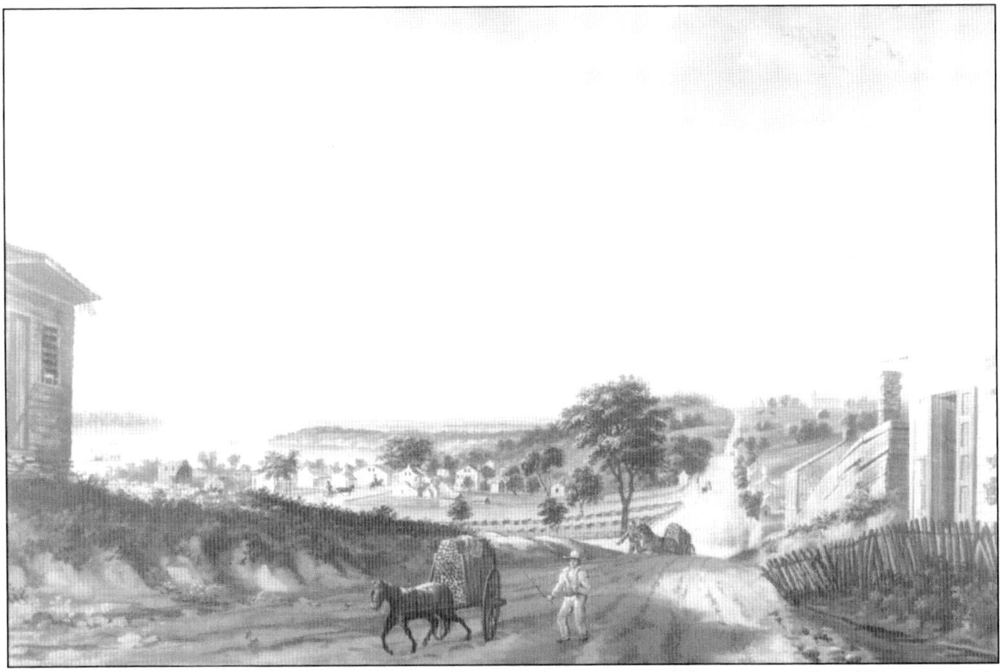

VIEW OF CARONDELET ROAD, RUNNING SOUTH ALONG THE MISSISSIPPI, J.C. WILD, 1841. (Courtesy of Carondelet Historical Society) The main thoroughfare running south of St. Louis and skirting the Mississippi for many miles was Carondelet Road. It led to Carondelet (the former Vide Pouch) and on to Jefferson Barracks. Today it is called Broadway and it still mostly follows the path laid out by its earliest creators. Carondelet Road ran along the east side of the St. Louis Commons and provided access to the common fields cultivated by many St. Louis residents. At various points along the way the road topped hills that provided breathtaking vistas of the river. This road formed the westernmost boundary of the original Rutgers and Chenie properties which became the arsenal tract, and it would provide direct egress for the arsenal in later years. It also would be the main access route to the south magazine once a connecting road was constructed to the site. It is interesting to note that the image above is from a painting by J.C. Wild, not from one of his usual lithographs. A lithograph of this same scene is found in his 1841 *The Valley of the Mississippi Illustrated*, but its detail is not as pronounced as that of the painting.

Itinerant traveler Henry B. Miller of Pennsylvania spent most of 1838 in and about St. Louis, recording scenes of his visit in a journal. In May he wrote: "Spent the time mostly walking about in which time I visited the United States Arsenal which is about 2 miles below the city and is a most beautiful place; the whole buildings are surrounded by a rough stone wall about 7 feet high; the plat is an oblong square about 600 yards by 325; the buildings are near the river and consist of a house for the commanding officer (now General [Edmund Pendleton] Gaines) who is commander in chief of the Western Army, with houses for the staff and inferior officers, with the hospital building where the arms are deposited, which form a square with a beautiful plot in the centre and carriage way round it. Where the buildings do not meet there is a wall with port holes about 12 or 15 feet high; the buildings are all built of limestone and roofed with slate; there are a number of stables and work shops round, the whole occupying not more than half the ground; the rest is planted with trees, on a beautiful green sward. About a half mile below is the magazine; it is in a beautiful and romantic country surrounded by trees of a sand growth. It is surrounded by a stonewall about 20 feet high, about 150 feet by 350 feet, with one gate way. The building is covered with slate and is altogether fire proof outside." Miller has captured here a compelling image of this beautiful and active installation in its earliest years.

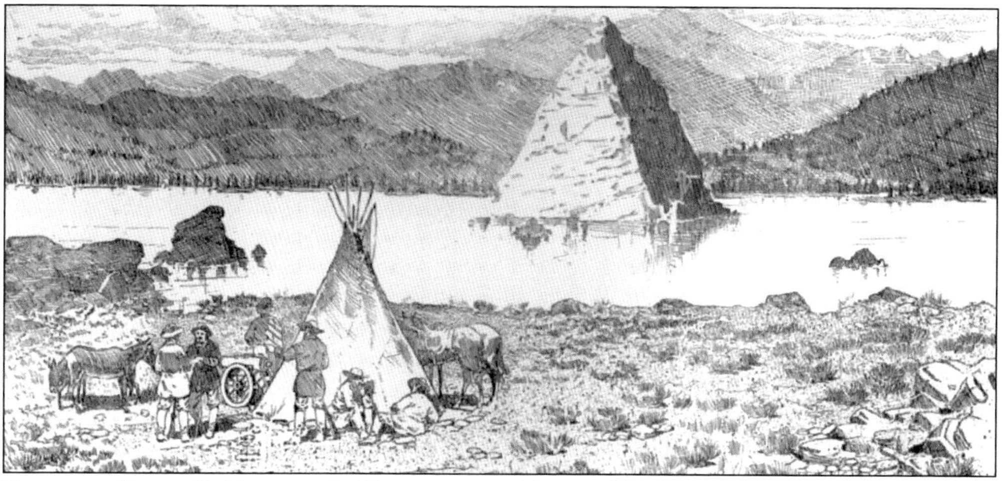

EXPLORER JOHN C. FREMONT'S CAMP IN THE ROCKY MOUNTAINS, 1843. (Fremont, SLU Archives) The St. Louis Arsenal served as an equipping point for many expeditions heading west. In 1843, soldier and explorer John C. Fremont, son-in-law of the influential Senator Thomas Hart Benton, reported to the arsenal to outfit his party with weapons, ammunition, and accouterments for the exploration of a trail to the Pacific Northwest and California. Among the weapons Fremont acquired at the arsenal was a small 12-pounder mountain howitzer, intended to impress the Indians with its superior firepower. After he had set out on the trek, Fremont's commander in Washington D.C. heard of this extravagant acquisition and sent a letter ordering Fremont to Washington to explain himself. But the letter was intercepted by Jessie Benton, Fremont's wife, who refused to forward it, in order to prevent further delay of the expedition. The howitzer proved to be both a blessing and a curse. Although it was used to great effect in repelling Indian attacks, it proved so burdensome to transport that it was eventually abandoned at the Sierra Nevadas. The image above shows Fremont's encampment at Pyramid Lake with the howitzer at the ready near a teepee. The image below depicts the army's official equipment for packing a mountain howitzer. It was normally transported on the backs of three pack animals or pulled behind one, on a carriage, with the remaining equipment and ammunition packed by two other mules or horses.

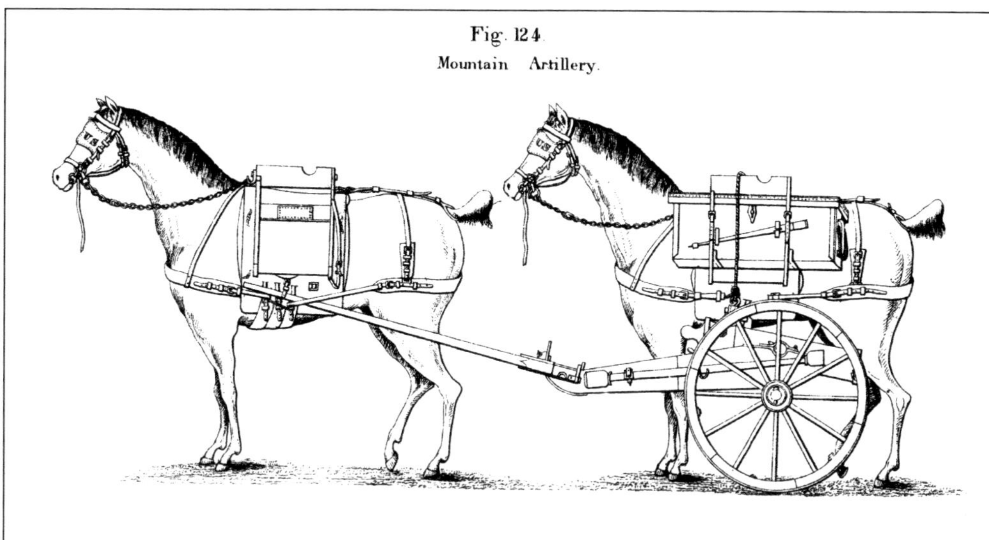

ARMY EQUIPMENT FOR MOUNTAIN ARTILLERY. (Gibbon, SLU Archives)

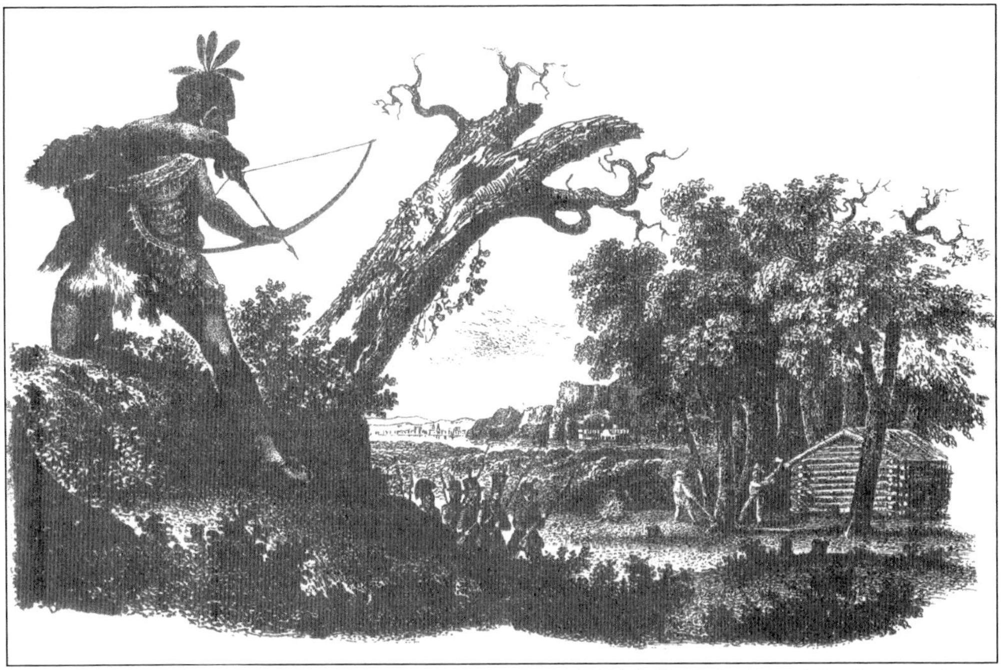

Taming the Western Frontier, J.C. Wild, 1841. (Wild, SLU Archives) In the significant "Act of 1808," Congress charged the U.S. Ordnance Department with responsibility for "arming and equipping" militia units of the United States. Annual budgets were established and distributed among the existing arsenals for this purpose. The arsenals were responsible for arming and equipping two categories of troops: those units activated for U.S. service, and those enlisted only for state and territorial service. Both categories were issued similar weapons and equipment, with the notable difference (and a nod to private business interests) that troops serving the states were first issued ordnance manufactured by private armories, whereas U.S. troops received equipment manufactured by one of the national armories (Springfield or Harper's Ferry). The image above depicts J.C. Wild's impression of militia troops coming to the rescue of settlers threatened by the Indians whose lands they were taking over.

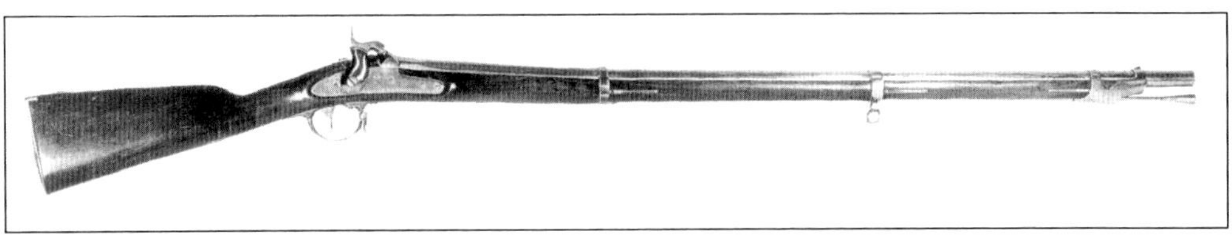

U.S. Model 1842 Musket. (Courtesy of NIMA) One of the early workhorses of U.S. firearms was the U.S. Model 1842 musket. This was the first smoothbore, percussion musket in U.S. service and was actually an adaptation of the 1840 flintlock musket, which had recently been adopted for standard use. There were very few copies of the Model 1842 made under private contract. The national armories produced nearly 273,000 of these muskets between 1844 and '55. Ironically, they were not extensively used by regular infantry until after the Mexican War because of supply problems with the early percussion caps. Production of this weapon essentially ceased with the introduction of "Minie ball" rifling in 1855, but most were eventually rifled and many saw service on both sides in the Civil War. The St. Louis Arsenal issued large numbers of these muskets between 1844 and the Civil War.

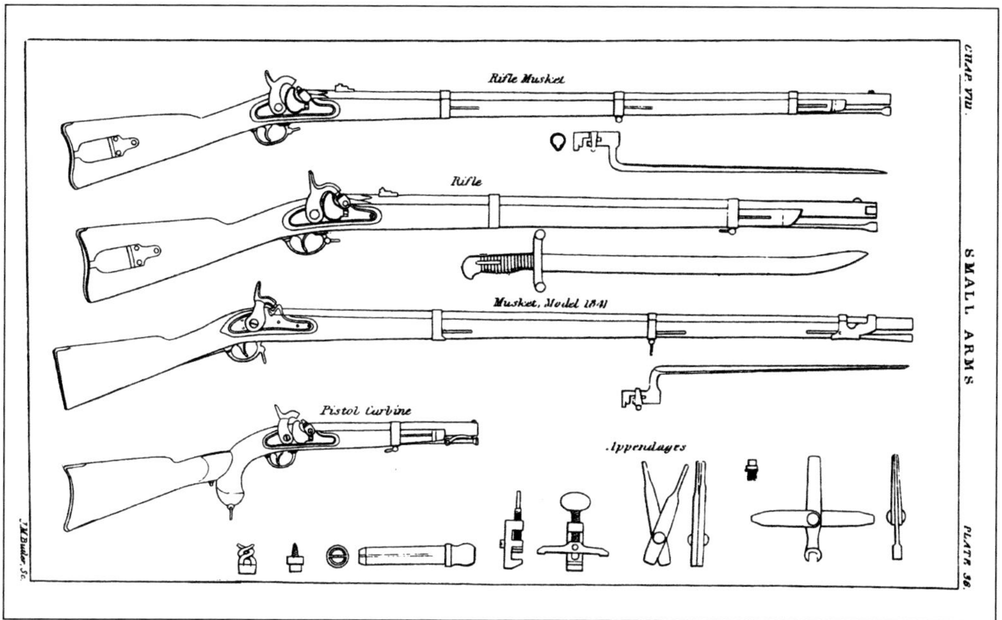

SMALL ARMS OF THE 1840S AND '50S. (U.S. Army Ordnance Manual, SLU Archives) U.S. ordnance manuals defined, in minute detail, the care, packing, storage, and use of arms and equipment. The head of ordnance in Washington D.C. was ultimately responsible for the maintenance of all arms and accoutrements awaiting issue to regular troops and militia. This responsibility devolved upon the commanders of arsenals and upon their subordinate ordnance officers. Once the items were issued, however, responsibility lay with the commanders of the receiving units and each soldier was thereafter held accountable for the care and upkeep of his individual equipment.

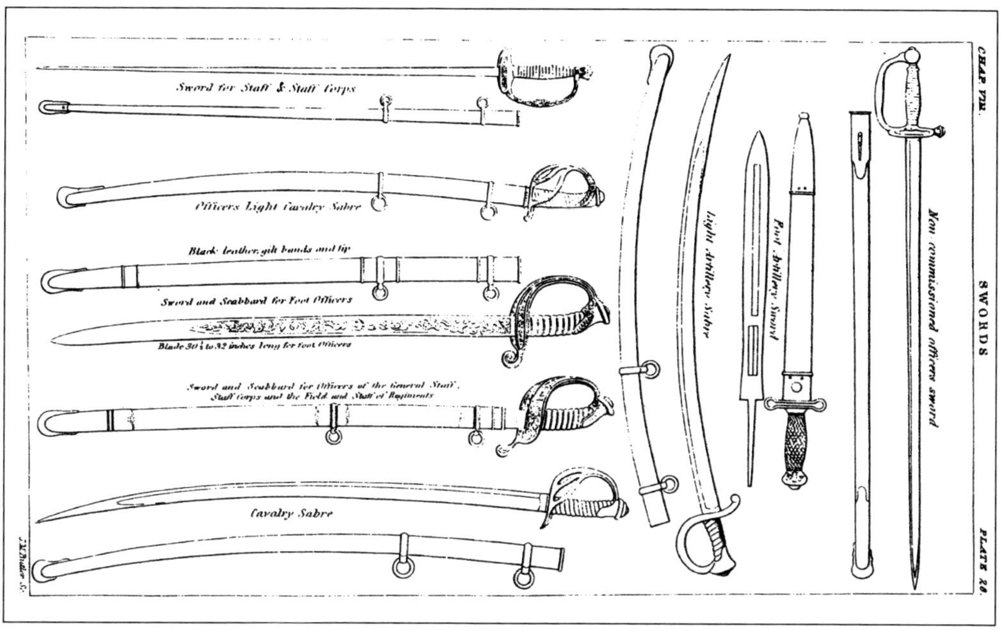

EDGED WEAPONS OF THE 1840S AND '50S. (U.S. Army Ordnance Manual, SLU Archives)

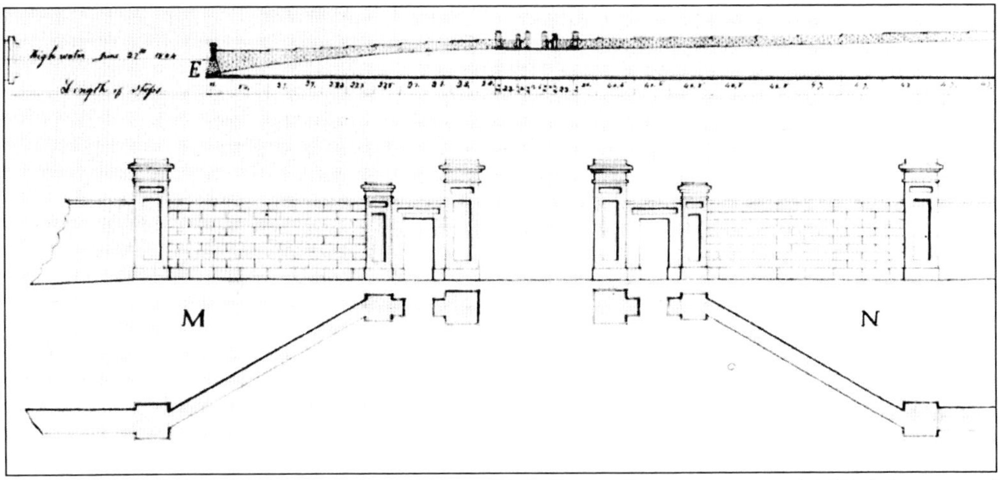

North Gateway from St. Louis Arsenal Site Plan, Shoemaker, c. 1847. (Courtesy of National Archives) The earliest enclosing wall of the St. Louis Arsenal had been constructed in the mid-1830s. It proved to be of inferior quality, so a new stonewall was built around the arsenal in 1844 and '45. In those days, the main entrance to the post was on the north side, directly from Arsenal Street, not far from the river. When the wall was rebuilt, a new, 12-foot-wide, ornate gateway was constructed. The image above shows both top and front views of the gateway, which was built back from the wall by several feet and connected by diagonal sidewalls. The very top portion of the image shows a reduced sketch of the north wall as it runs toward the river and indicates the placement of the gateway.

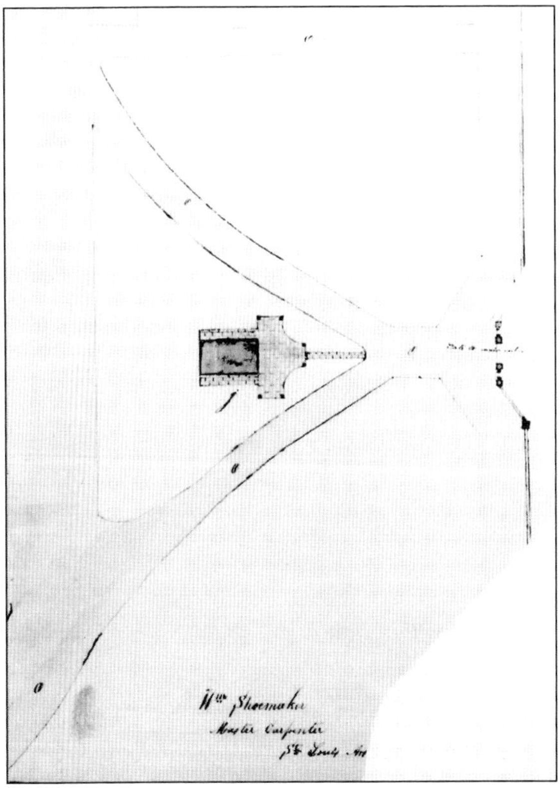

Brick Guardhouse from St. Louis Arsenal Site Plan, Shoemaker, c. 1847. (Courtesy of National Archives) Just inside the new gateway a large brick guardhouse was built to replace the smaller wooden structure. An 1847 map indicates it was constructed "of brick painted and sanded imitation of stone, and cov'd with slate." This was, therefore, the first brick structure built at the arsenal. Its dimensions measured 34 feet long by 19 feet wide. A cobbled brick walkway surrounded the building on three sides, probably to accommodate inspections and guard mount. In later years, when it was no longer used as a guardhouse, it would serve as the post adjutant's office. Then, in about 1872, a 62 by 14 foot wing would be built off the west side, converting it to an officers' quarters.

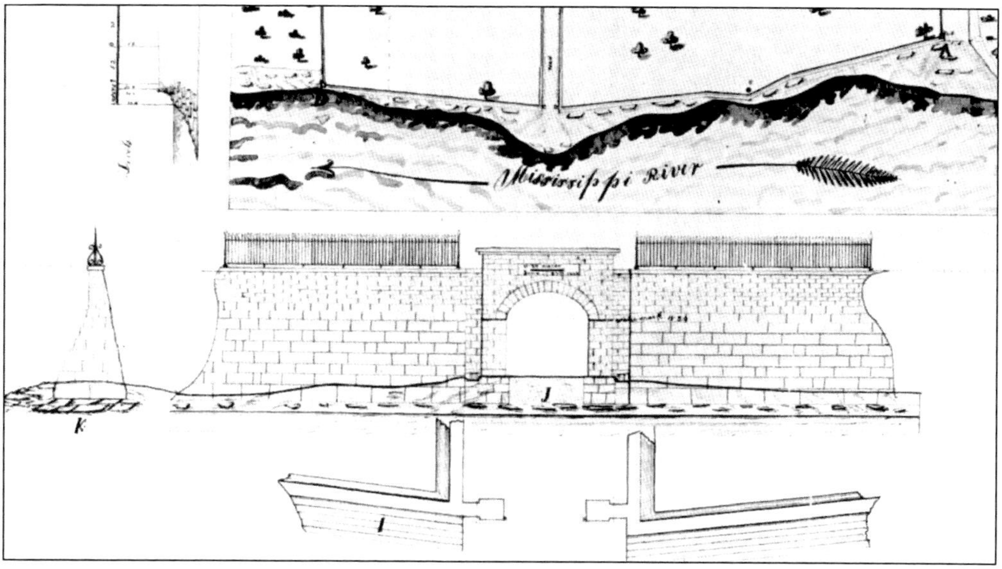

Riverside Gate from St. Louis Arsenal Site Plan, Shoemaker, c. 1847. (Courtesy of National Archives) The inhabitants of the arsenal learned at a very early date that the Mississippi River could pose a dangerous threat to the eastern wall. When the original riverside wall was constructed in 1831–32, it was built 1 foot higher than the previous high-water mark of 1826. Severe flooding in 1844 brought river levels to the top of the wall, so an 1845 building project extended the height of the wall to 3 feet above the 1844 high water mark. An extensive new riverside gate and a sally port leading to the interior of the post were built in conjunction with this improvement.

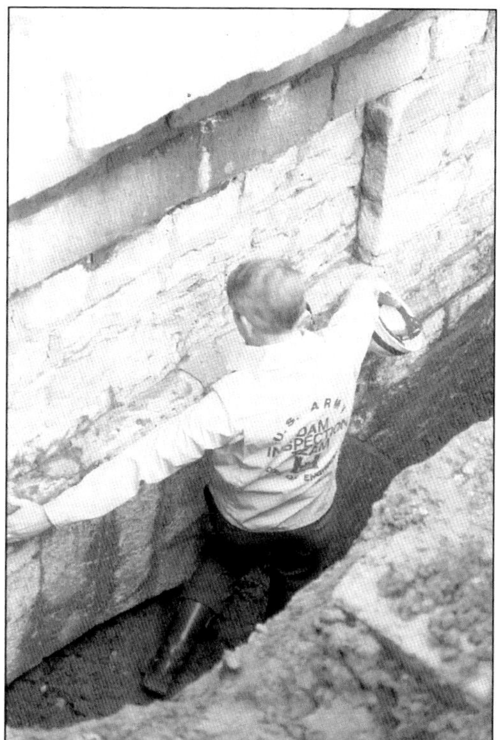

USACE Officer Measures Riverside Gate During Archaeological Excavation, 1981. (Courtesy of William Woods) The U.S. Army Corps of Engineers (USACE) built a service base on the land between the wall and the river late in the 19th century. All evidence of the lower wall and the gate were buried and forgotten with subsequent building activities. In 1981, during excavation for the construction of a new maintenance building, USACE personnel uncovered a portion of the old riverside wall and gate. Dr. William Woods and a team from Southern Illinois University at Edwardsville were called in to conduct archaeological testing of the site to establish its cultural significance. The image to the right shows the upper arch of the gate being measured by a USACE officer prior to being reburied.

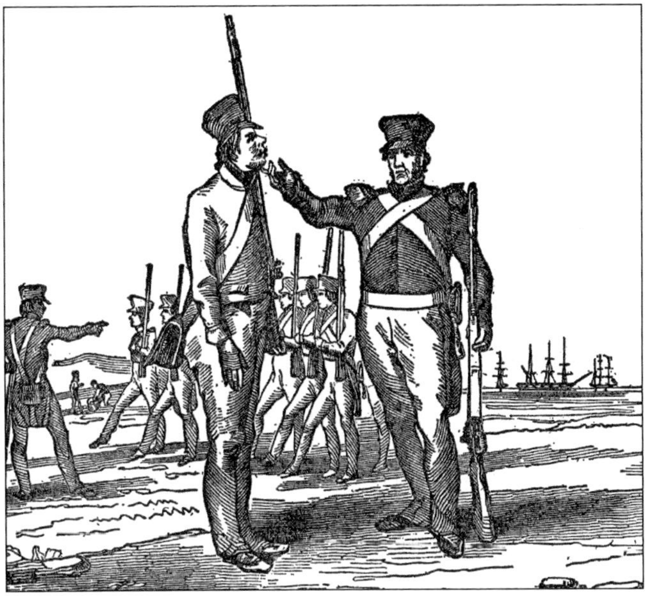

Raw Recruits are Drilled in the Field at Outset of Mexican War, 1846. (Henry, SLU Archives) The war with Mexico brought abrupt changes to the quiet routine of arsenal operations. The civilian workforce grew from 47 to 517 at the height of hostilities. As the westernmost outpost of ordnance operations, the St. Louis Arsenal bore responsibility for equipping several western units and supporting the ongoing war effort. Some of the militia units outfitted at the arsenal were the 64th Missouri Infantry Regiment, Battery A of the Missouri Light Artillery, and the "Flying Artillery" Battalion of St. Louis. Regular army units equipped were Captain Braxton Bragg's Company C of the 3rd U.S. Artillery and the 1st and 2nd Dragoons. The outbreak of hostilities caught U.S. forces so unprepared that many fresh recruits, as in the scene above, had time for only the most rudimentary training before being engaged in combat.

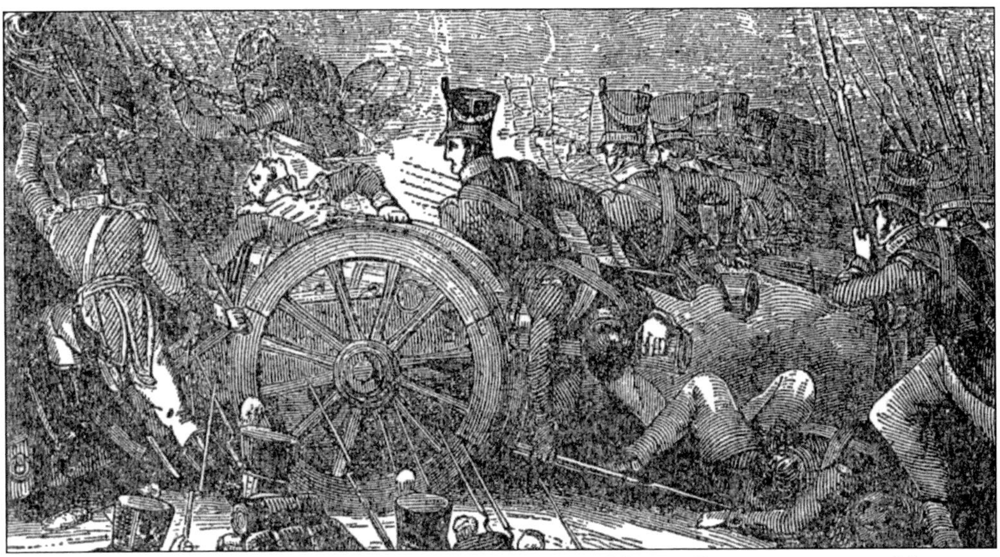

American Ordnance Faces the Ultimate Test in Heavy Fighting in the Mexican War, 1846–48. (Henry, SLU Archives) A wide range of weapons and ammunition were pressed into service during the Mexican War. Captain William Bell, arsenal commander for 16 years, reported to the St. Louis Board of Aldermen the contribution of the St. Louis Arsenal to the war effort. The numbers were impressive for those days: 19,500 artillery rounds; 8.4 million small arms cartridges; 13.7 million musket balls; 4.7 million rifle balls; 17 field cannon with equipment; 15,700 complete sets of small arms; 4,600 edged weapons and much more. Then, once the fighting was over, the arsenal regrouped to receive the large influx of returned arms and equipment as militia units demobilized.

Five

Civilization Overtakes the Arsenal (1850–1860)

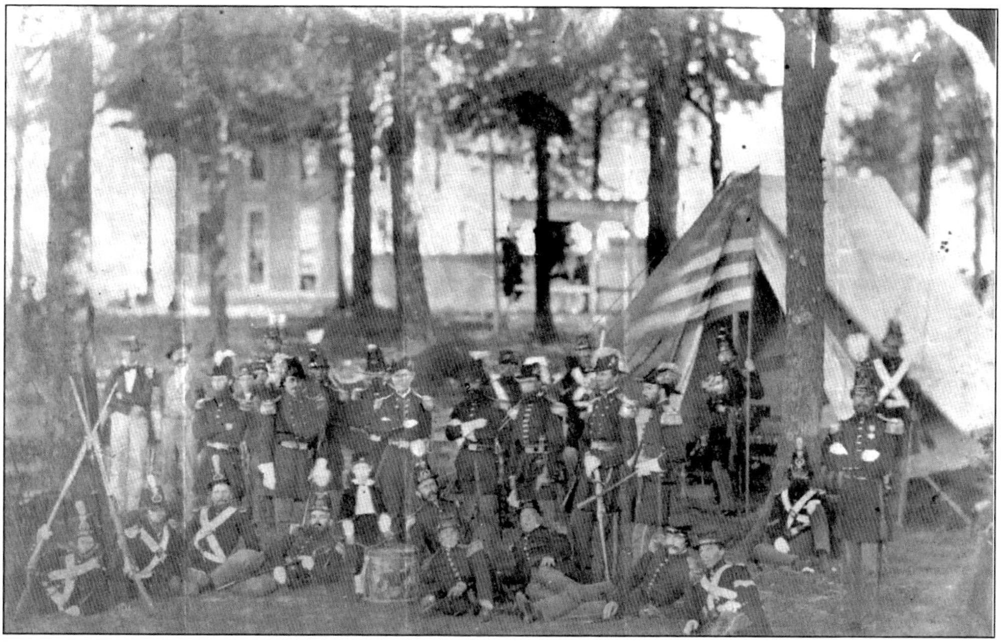

MISSOURI VOLUNTEER MILITIA, 1860. (Courtesy of Missouri Historical Society) The 1850s were a critical time for the St. Louis Arsenal. The city grew steadily until all of the property in the vicinity of the arsenal had been sold to private parties. There was no longer room for the arsenal to grow. Sentiments soon arose proposing that the arsenal be sold and its property subdivided into lots. The common wisdom declared that this dangerous facility was now too close to civilization and its threat should be removed. The U.S. government was in the initial stages of agreeing with this proposal when the threat of Civil War scuttled their plans. Soon the arsenal proved to be a key to the salvation of Missouri for the Union. Border troubles with Kansas had kept the arsenal active in the mid-1850s, outfitting militia units such as the Missouri Volunteer Militia pictured above. Organizations like this would form the basis of Union and Confederate units mustered into service during the coming conflagration.

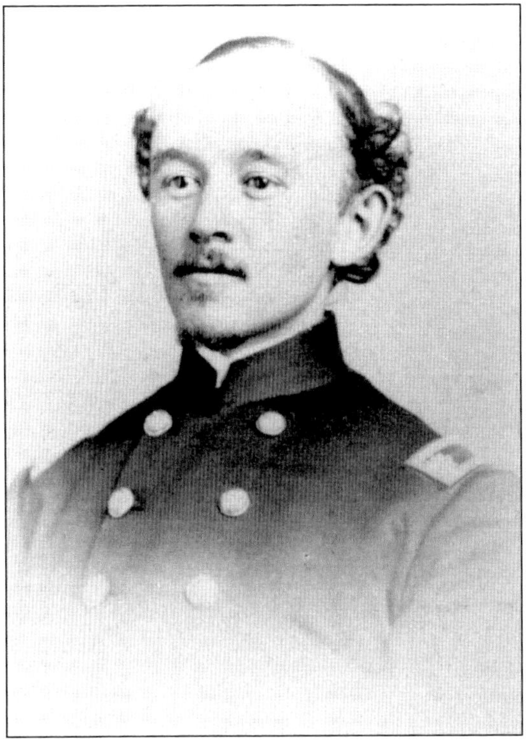

Charles P. Kingsbury, Inspector of Armories and Arsenals, 1851. (Courtesy of Military History Institute, Barrett Collection) In 1851, First Lieutenant Charles P. Kingsbury was attached to the arsenal to serve as inspector of armories and arsenals. Kingsbury was an 1840 graduate of West Point. He had served as assistant ordnance officer or commander at eight different arsenals in the decade before reporting to St. Louis, bringing a wealth of experience to his post. He had distinguished himself in the Mexican War, serving as chief of ordnance under Major General Wool and aide-de-camp to Zachary Taylor. Shortly before coming to St. Louis he wrote an *Elementary Treatise on Artillery and Infantry.* After a year in this station he moved on to command the Little Rock Arsenal and eventually served the Union during the Civil War, achieving the rank of brevet brigadier general. He retired in 1870.

Robert H.K. Whitely, Commander of St. Louis Arsenal, 1851–54. (Courtesy of Military History Institute, Barrett Collection) Robert Whitely arrived at the St. Louis Arsenal in September 1851 to succeed Major William Bell in command. Whitely, an 1830 graduate of West Point, had begun his career as an artillery officer but was transferred to ordnance as a result of the act of 1838, which authorized an increase in the size of the Ordnance Department. He was a veteran of the Seminole War and had commanded the significant Washington and Baton Rouge arsenals before reporting to St. Louis. Whitely was a family man, living with his wife, a son, and two daughters in the elegant commander's residence. Both daughters were married at the arsenal. The Commander had a succession of assistants, many of whom recently graduated from West Point. He presided over accelerated ordnance activities and the construction of several more buildings at the arsenal and the magazine site near Jefferson Barracks. Captain Whitely transferred to New York in 1854. During the Civil War, he remained with the Union and was promoted to brevet brigadier general in 1865.

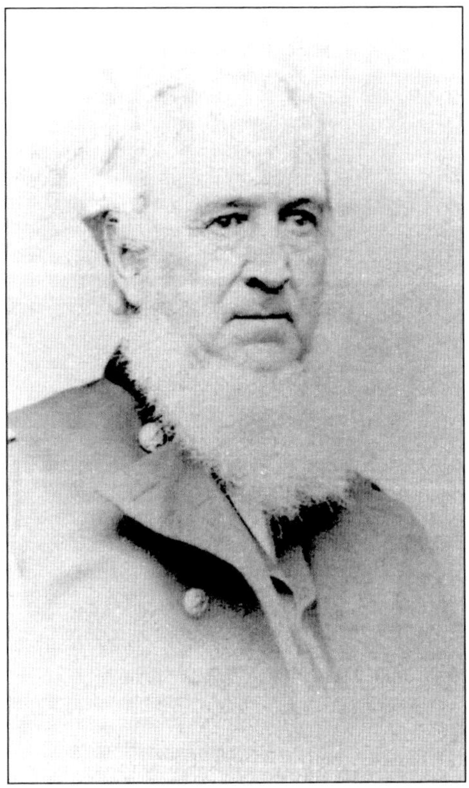

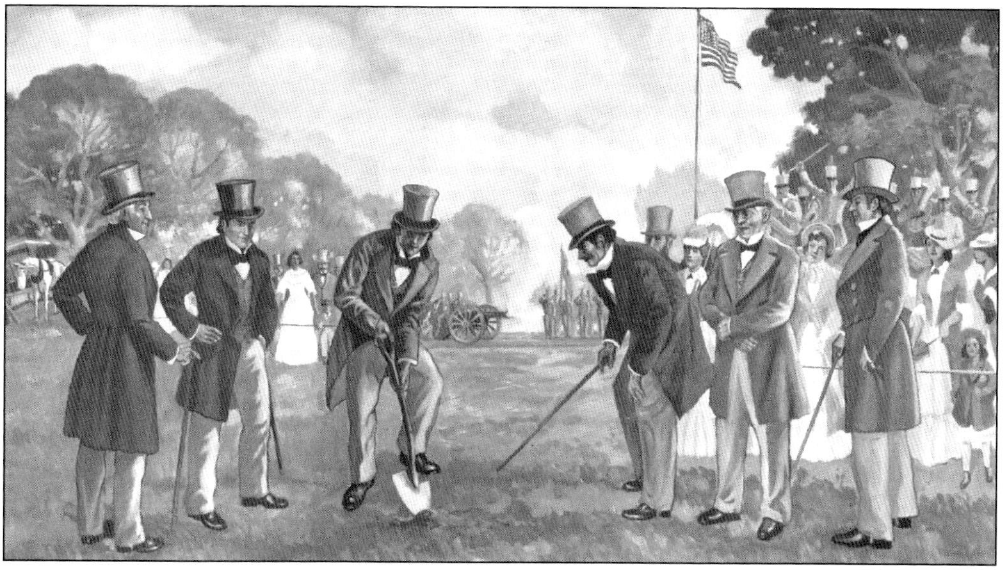

THE ARSENAL CONTRIBUTES LIBERALLY TO LOCAL CELEBRATIONS. (Courtesy of SLU Archives) The arsenal played a very important role in the community by supporting its many local celebrations with a military flare. Events such as the ground-breaking pictured above were often attended with martial displays by local militia units, marching bands, fireworks, and parades. It was very common for arsenal personnel to participate in or support these activities to the great delight of the local populace.

Fig. 258.

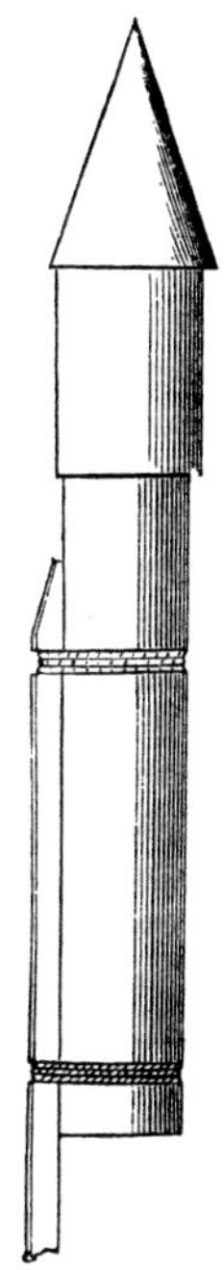

ARSENAL FIREWORKS ARE POPULAR WITH THE COMMUNITY. (Gibbon, SLU Archives) In addition to its production of all types of ammunition, the St. Louis Arsenal produced a wide array of pyrotechnics. Although rockets such as the one pictured here served particular military purposes, they were soon adapted to uses of a celebratory nature. Many of the German artisans employed at the arsenal brought their old-world techniques with them and manufactured fireworks that were second to none. Captain Bell was the first arsenal commander to use this commodity as a popular tool of public relations and the commanders succeeding him followed suit. Harold Iverson describes the community's response to the arsenal's fireworks displays on national holidays: "The Fourth of July fireworks held by the city were too late, at the wrong place, and mishandled, as opposed to the fireworks inside the arsenal. 'There, the rockets and other works were magnificent, and managed systematically, with safety and with fine effect, doing credit to the day, and to the officers in charge of the works.'"

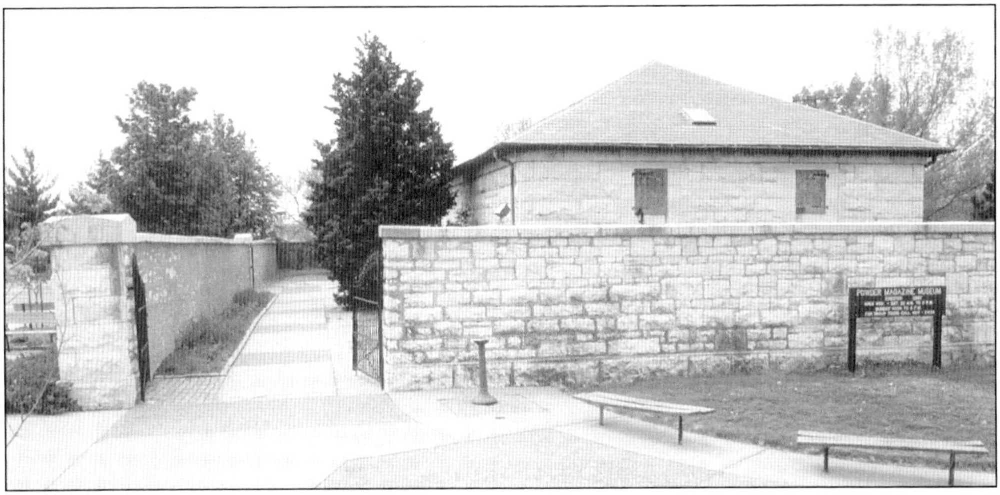

Powder Magazines at Jefferson Barracks. (Courtesy of NIMA) In 1850 Major Bell began the search for a location for the construction of two new powder magazines. A marine hospital was being built on the site of the south magazine and civilization was rapidly encroaching upon the area, so Bell concentrated his search on the northern reaches of the Jefferson Barracks reservation. In January 1850, 110 acres were set aside for the purpose. In May 1851, Bell contracted with Francis A. Quinette to build the first magazine (without an enclosing wall at this time), along with a keeper's house, a small laborer's house, a stable, and a road leading to the river wharf. Bell was transferred in September 1851, but oversight of the construction continued under Captain George Ramsay. The first magazine cost $17,626, while the second, which was a little larger than the first and was beset with delays, cost about $25,000. The second magazine was completed in early 1858 by Charles H. Peck. In 1859 "879 boxes and 247 barrels of powder munitions" were moved from the old magazine at the marine hospital site to the new ones near Jefferson Barracks. Still, structural problems with the new magazines would plague the arsenal command for several more years.

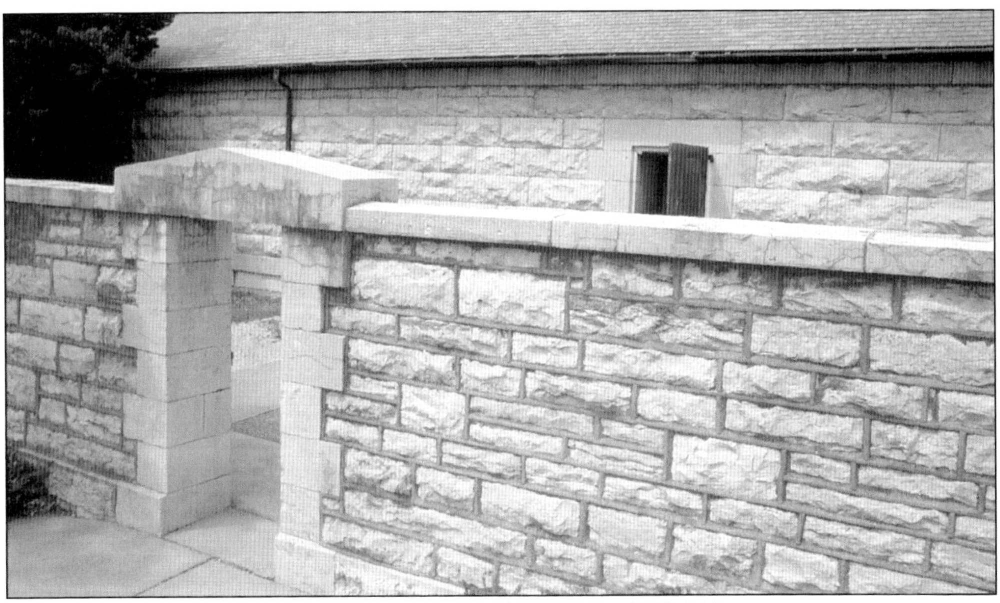

Side Entrance to the Powder Magazine. (Courtesy of NIMA)

JEFFERSON DAVIS, U.S. SECRETARY OF WAR, 1853–57. (Courtesy of Missouri Historical Society) Post-Civil War generations frequently forget that Jefferson Davis had a life and a very active career in public service before his fated term as President of the Confederate States of America. As a young U.S. Army officer, Davis served at Jefferson Barracks and came to know St. Louis well. During the Mexican War he saw distinguished service and was severely wounded at the Battle of Buena Vista. In 1853, President Franklin Pierce appointed Davis secretary of war, at which he was considered "outstandingly successful." During this time, the St. Louis and Iron Mountain Railroad petitioned Congress for permission to build their line along the west bank of the Mississippi, cutting through the arsenal and Jefferson Barracks, and very near the new powder magazines being built north of the barracks. The military strongly opposed this plan, but the political ramifications of the project were immense and Congress was inclined to grant permission for right-of-way through the government installations. Secretary Davis fought the proposal with every tool at hand, but ultimately lost the political fight. The railroad was built in 1856.

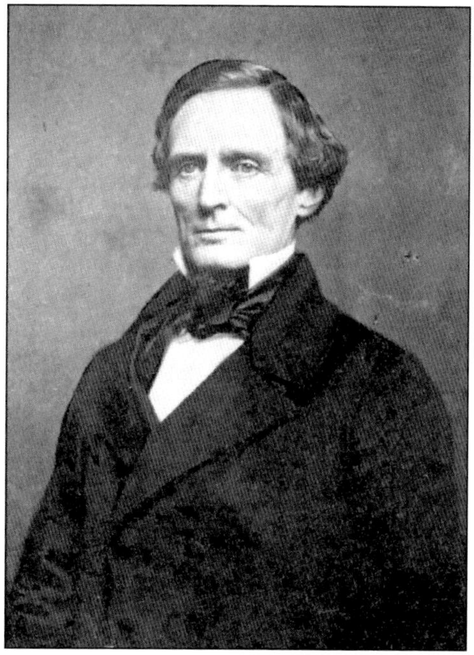

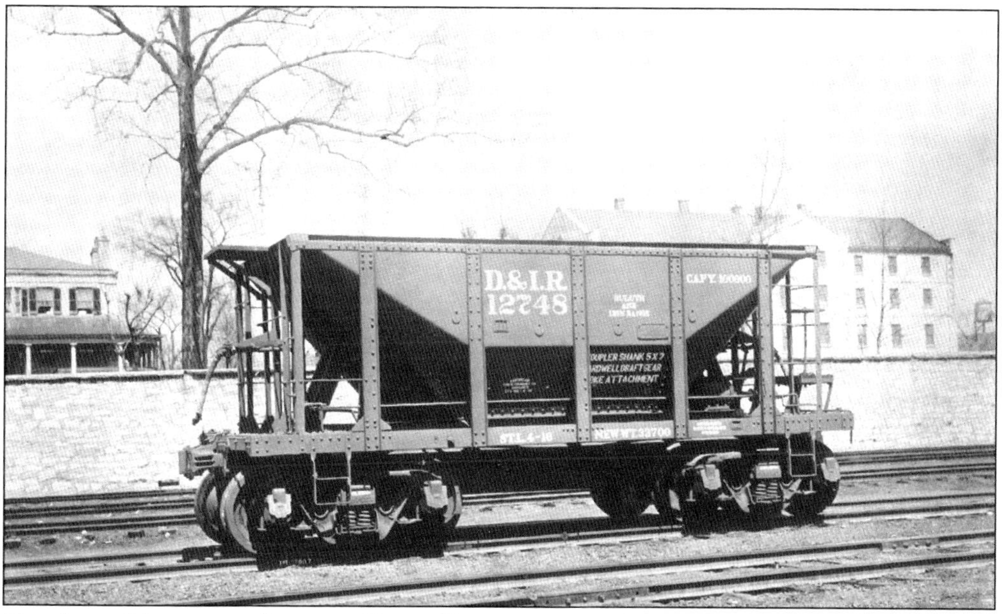

THE IRON MOUNTAIN RAILWAY RUNS THROUGH THE ARSENAL (Courtesy of Carondelet Historical Society) The image above shows a railroad car built by the American Car Company about 1916, photographed against the backdrop of the arsenal. This is next to the tracks built by the Iron Mountain Railway in 1856. In the end, the safety of neither the arsenal nor Jefferson Barracks was compromised and the railroad served well the commercial interests of eastern Missouri.

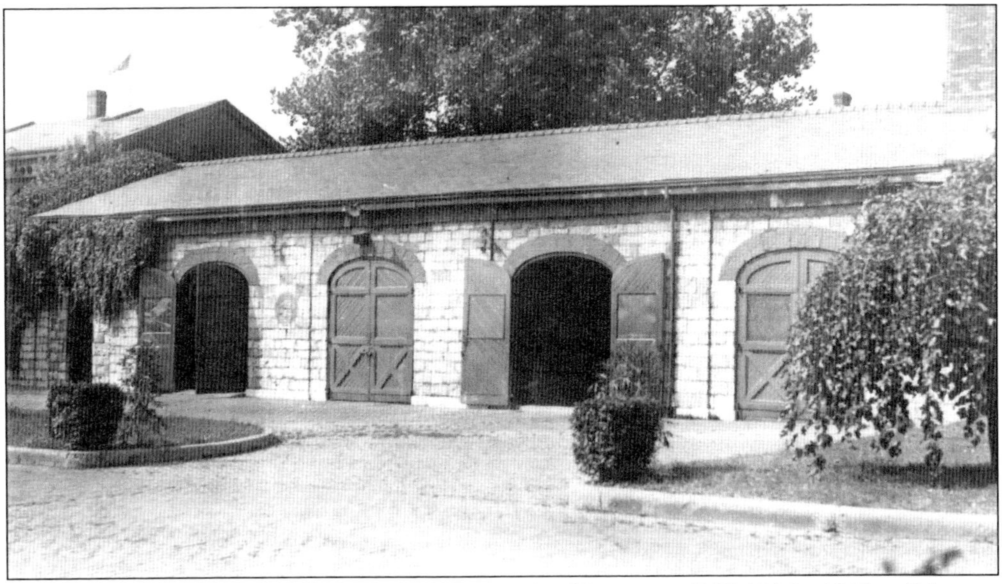

QUARTERMASTER COAL HOUSE, BUILT IN 1849–50. (Courtesy of NIMA) In 1849 well-known St. Louis architect Charles Peck, was hired to design two coal-storage buildings. Arsenal labor was used to quarry the stone and construct the buildings. Exterior dimensions of the Quartermaster Coal House were approximately 30 by 85 feet. This was a multi-purpose structure, with coal stored in the two western bays for heating quarters and non-ordnance buildings, a fire engine housed in the central bay, and a paint shop occupying the east bay. During the Civil War the structure was altered to store small arms ammunition. This was later designated Building 2.

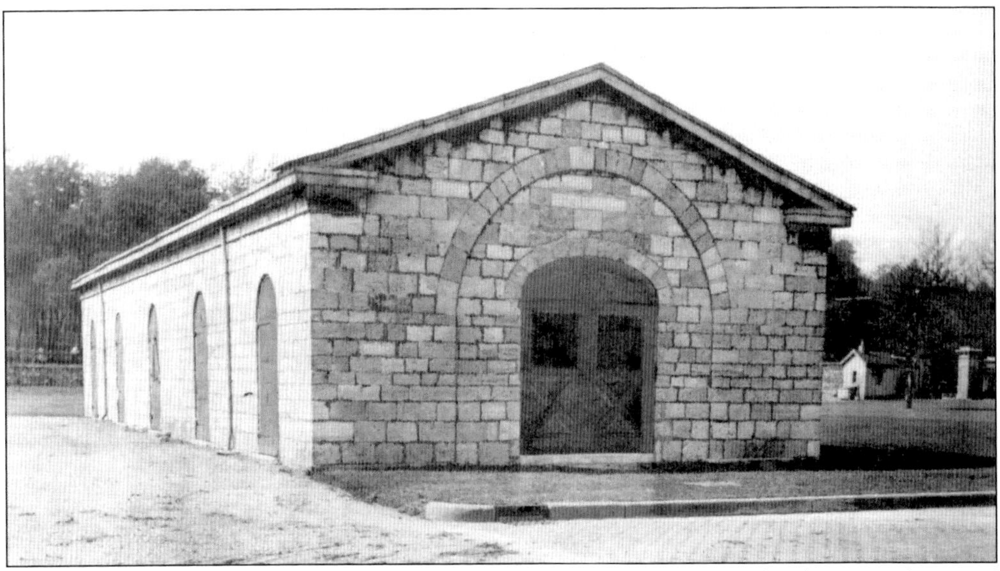

ORDNANCE COAL HOUSE, BUILT IN 1849–50. (Courtesy of NIMA) The second arsenal structure designed by Peck was the Ordnance Coal House. It was designed to hold enough coal to feed the voracious appetite of the steam-driven machinery in the armory building. The Ordnance Coal House was similar to Building 2, built of limestone and roofed in slate, but was slightly smaller, measuring approximately 27 by 83 feet. During the Civil War, it too was used to store small arms ammunition. This was designated Building 7.

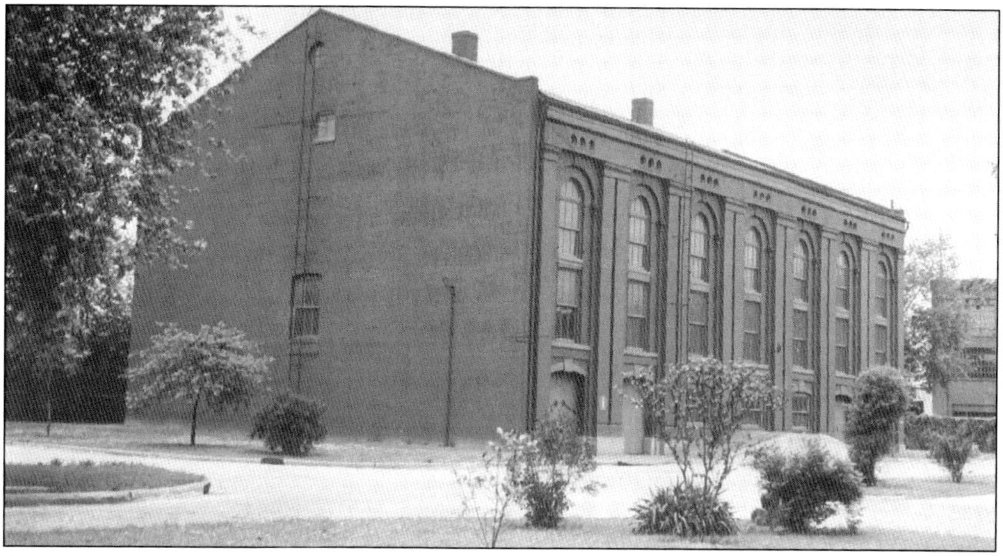

ARTILLERY STOREHOUSE, BUILT IN 1850. (Courtesy of NIMA) The 71 by 106 foot artillery storehouse was also planned by Peck. This was the first major building at the arsenal to be built of brick. It stood three stories high and was roofed with slate. The first floor was cement and the upper ones of wood. The purpose of this building was to store artillery carriages. At full capacity, it was designed to hold 192 of them. The building served this purpose until the post was converted to a cavalry recruit depot in 1871. This was designated Building 1.

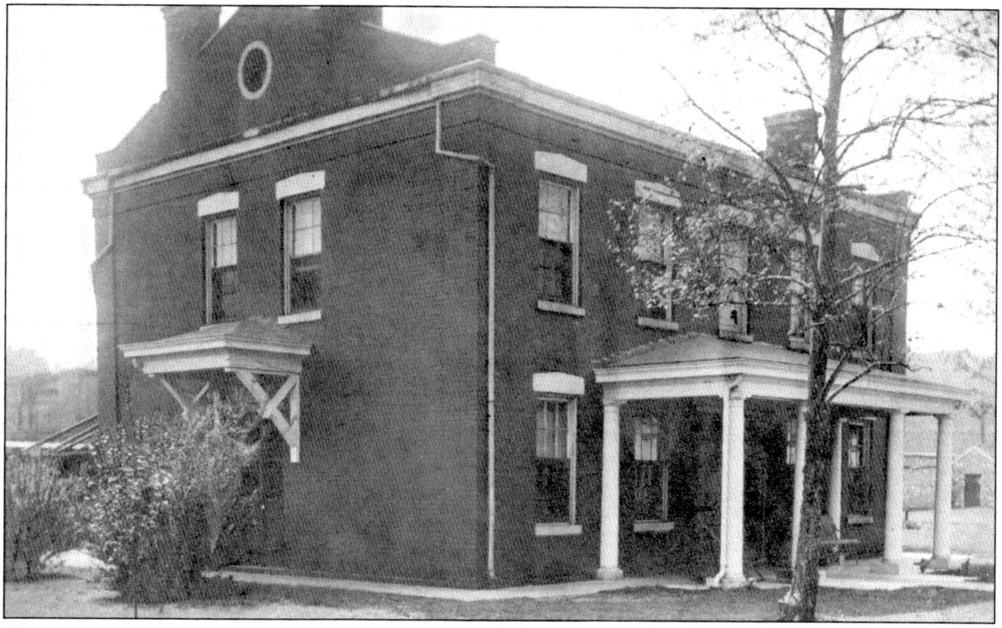

ENLISTED FAMILY QUARTERS, BUILT IN 1852. (Courtesy of NIMA) Charles Peck designed this building (#8) and its "twin" (#11) in 1852. Each structure was a two-family dwelling, intended to be occupied by enlisted personnel and their families. The buildings were constructed of brick, roofed in slate, and measured 30 by 40 feet. Each family had two rooms on the first floor and two rooms and a large closet on the second floor. After the military population declined at the arsenal, civilian employees lived in these quarters.

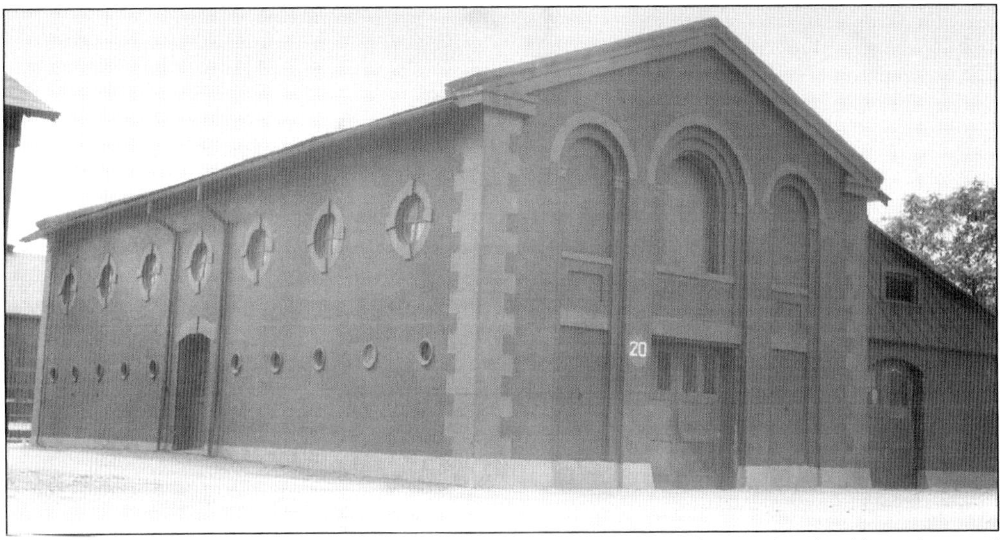

STABLE BUILDING, CONSTRUCTED IN 1852. (Courtesy of NIMA) Another building designed by Charles Peck was the stable. Measuring 34 by 68 feet, it stood two stories high, was built of brick and roofed in slate. Seven distinctive circular windows lined the two long sides of the building. The stable provided housing for nine animals and storage space for harnesses, feed, and other necessities. The stable replaced an earlier one and was located just west of the "ball yard" where mounds of cannon balls and cannon barrels were stored. The photo on page 77 shows the stable in the background, as seen from the ball yard. This was designated Building 20.

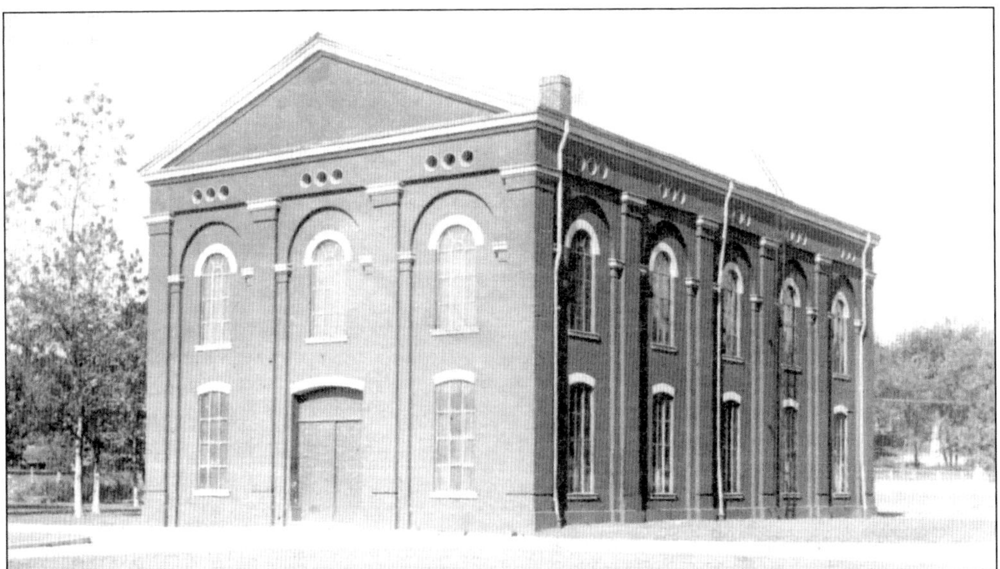

CARRIAGE-MAKER'S SHOP, BUILT IN 1852. (Courtesy of NIMA) This building appears to have been designed by Peck as well, though no record has been found to verify it. The design, however, is almost identical to Building 3, which is known to have been done by Peck. The carriage-maker's shop measured approximately 42 by 70 feet, was constructed of brick and roofed in slate. The floors were of wood. It stood two stories high and had an attic. The exterior displayed high, arching windows. During the Civil War this building was used as a saddler's shop. This was designated Building 6.

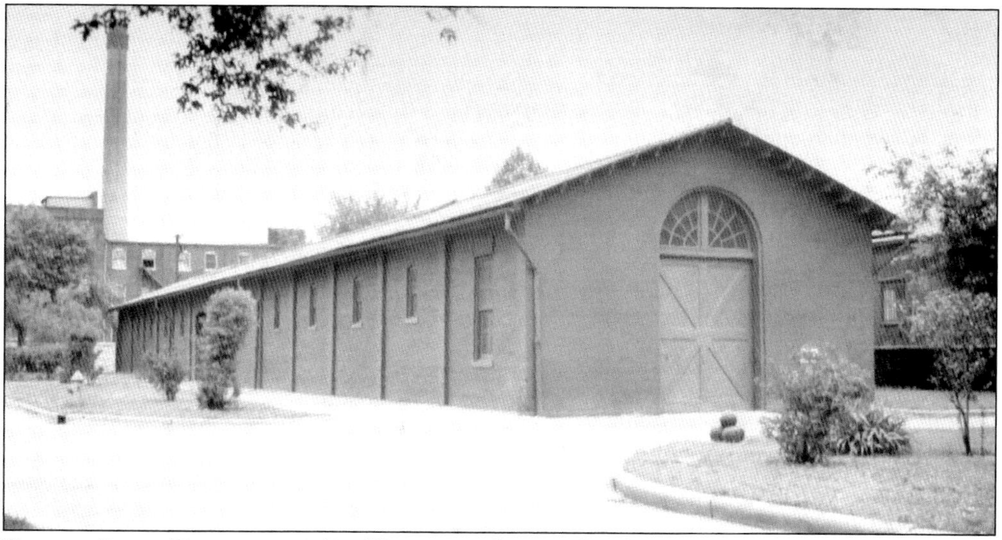

TIMBER SHED, BUILT C. 1853. (Courtesy of NIMA) About 1853 a new timber shed was built just east of the artillery storehouse. It measured approximately 30 by 193 feet and was constructed with open bays covered by wooden slats. The roof was supported by 14 pairs of 15 inch brick columns and was covered with slate. The building was used to store and cure timber until 1871 when the installation's functions changed. Thereafter it served as a warehouse and occasionally as an extra stable. This would be numbered Building 22.

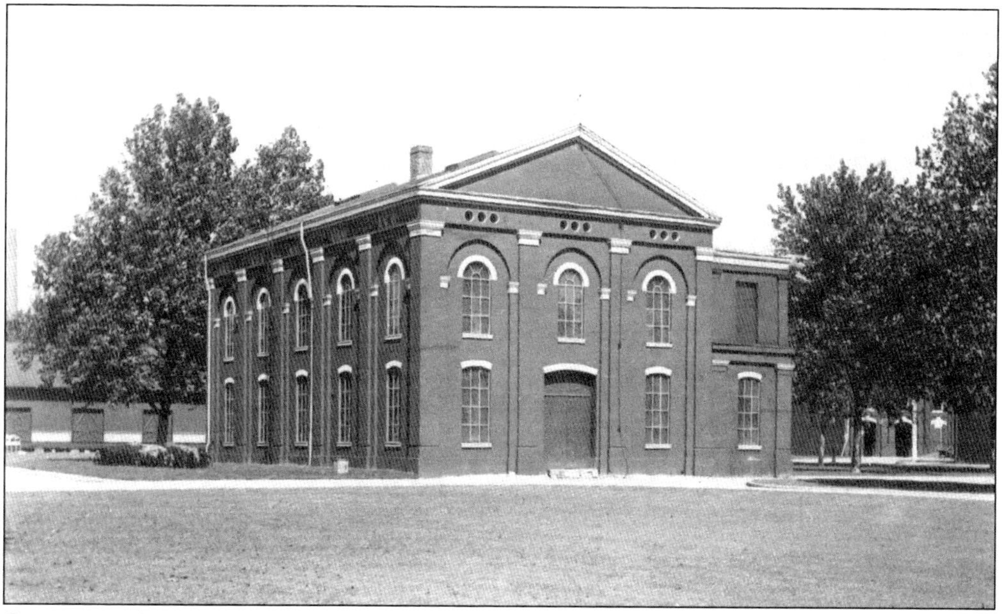

CARPENTER SHOP, BUILT IN 1854. (Courtesy of NIMA) A large, well-equipped carpenter shop was built in 1854, which was also designed by Peck. Constructed of brick and roofed in slate, the 38 by 66 foot, two-story building had two rows of five tall, arched windows on each side, and three across the front and back. The floors were not subdivided, making it easier to organize each for particular projects. A two-story wing of about 14 by 29 feet was built on the north side before the Civil War. The building continued as a carpenter shop until the arsenal closed and may have served as a barracks when the post was converted to cavalry use in 1871. This became Building 3.

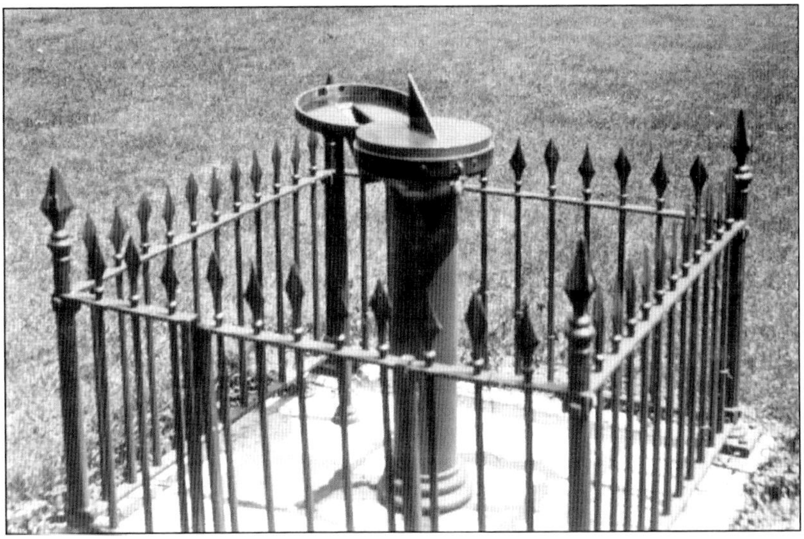

SUNDIAL BUILT BY ARSENAL PERSONNEL, 1859. (Courtesy of NIMA) On December 12, 1859, master armorer N. Engels, machinist A. Schaedel, and engraver W. Hawksley dedicated a sundial, which they had created entirely from spare ordnance materials. It was a scientifically precise instrument, measuring 17 inches in diameter, and was used for many years as the definitive chronometer of the arsenal. Engraved upon it was a poem entitled "The Bird of Liberty," reflecting the patriotic fervor of the day.

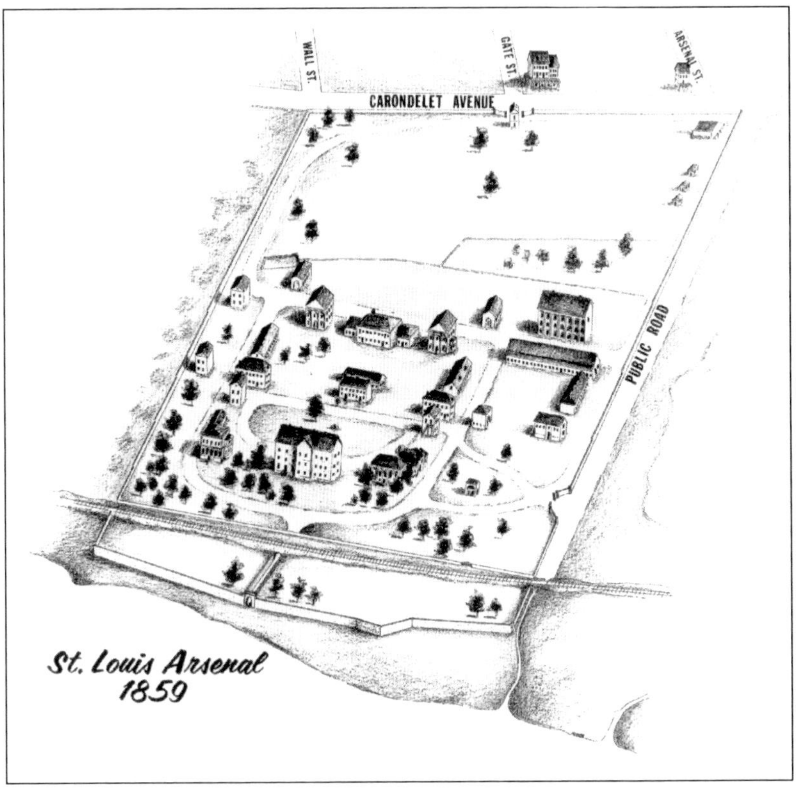

BIRD'S-EYE-VIEW OF THE ARSENAL, 1859. (Courtesy of NIMA) By 1859, the eve of the Civil War, the St. Louis Arsenal boasted more than 25 buildings and a substantial stockpile of arms and ammunition. By this time, the Iron Mountain Railroad crossed the eastern end of the facility and community leaders were urging the war department to abandon the property and subdivide it for private sale. The government agreed to the proposal, but soon it became the most hotly contested property in Missouri as proponents of northern and southern causes fought to control it.

Six

Ordnance & Equipment at the Arsenal (1850s & 1860s)

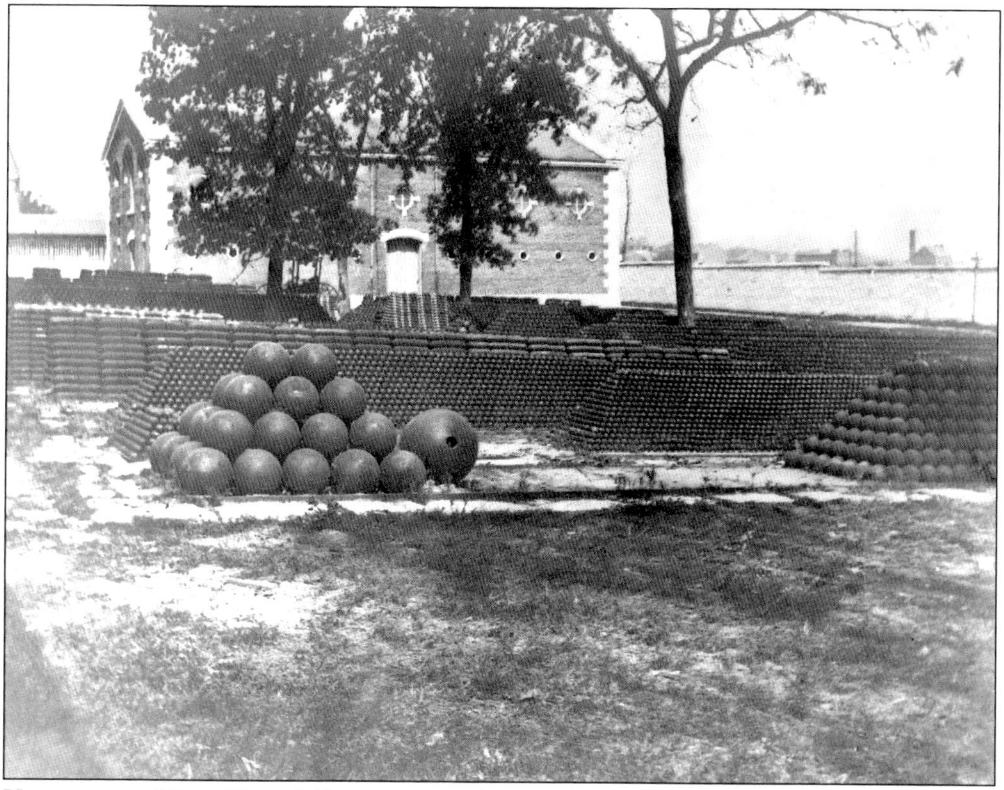

VIEW OF THE "BALL YARD," BOEHL, 1866. (Courtesy of Missouri Historical Society) Just east of the stable building (#20) lay an expansive stretch of ground called the "ball yard." This was just inside the north gate and provided room for stacking thousands of cannon balls according to size and caliber. There were also two long skids on the south side of this area for laying cannon barrels when not mounted on carriages. Great pains were taken to protect these highly corrosive materials from the weather by constantly treating them with oils and preventing water damage. The above image was taken shortly after the war when the arsenal became the major collecting point for munitions from the western theater of operations.

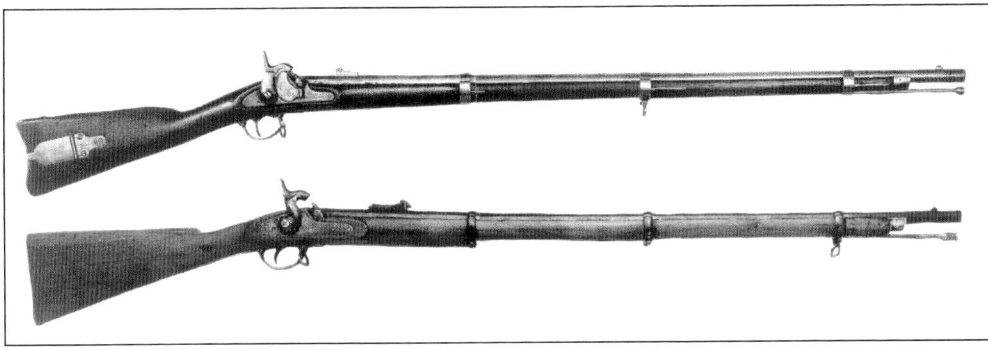

Two Common Muskets Stored at the Arsenal and Issued to Federal Troops. (Courtesy of NIMA) The top weapon here is the 1855 U.S. Model Rifle musket, nearly 30,000 of which were made in various versions at Harper's Ferry and Springfield Arsenals. The St. Louis Arsenal issued several thousand. It featured rifling for the new .58 caliber "Minie ball," a highly accurate rear-mounted sight and an improved percussion system. These were issued primarily to regular troops until political pressures during the Civil War made them available to some state units. The bottom weapon is the 1853 British Enfield musket. Versions of this .58 caliber rifle were produced both in Britain and America for issue to militia units. Many complained that it was an inferior rifle, but more than 16,000 saw service with Union troops and thousands more with Confederates.

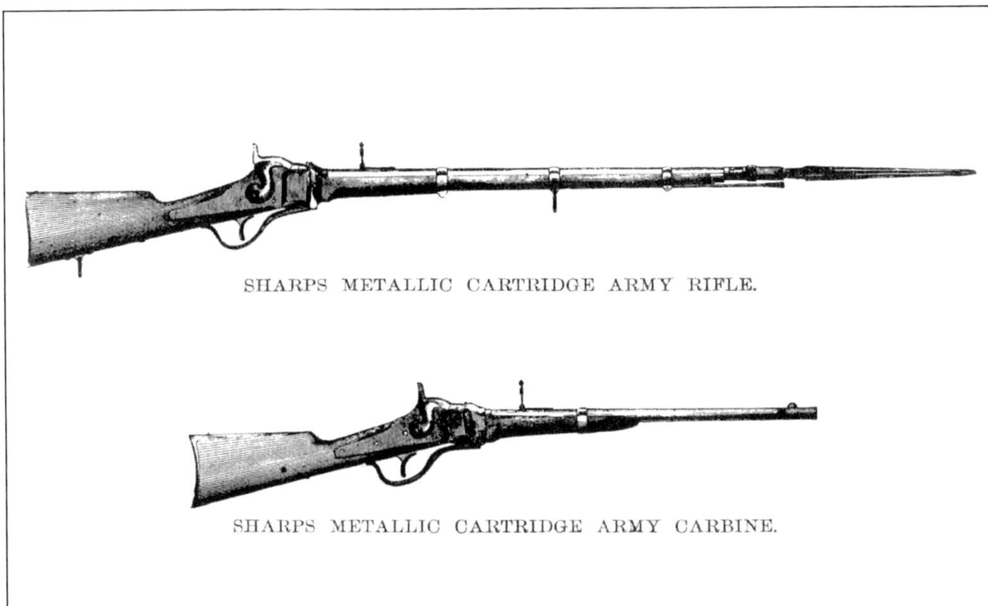

Sharps Contributes Significant Weapons to the Union Cause. (Rywell, SLU Archives) In 1848, Christian Sharps received a patent for a simple but strong breech-loading mechanism, using the trigger guard as a lever. The design evolved during the 1850s into both rifle and carbine versions which fired metallic cartridges with accuracy and high volume. Berdan's "Sharps Shooters" gained fame for the awesome firepower demonstrated with these weapons against the Confederates. Many Union soldiers thought these were the finest breechloaders of the war. More than 9,000 rifles and 80,000 carbines were purchased by the federal government, and more by states and individual units, with many thousand being issued through the St. Louis Arsenal.

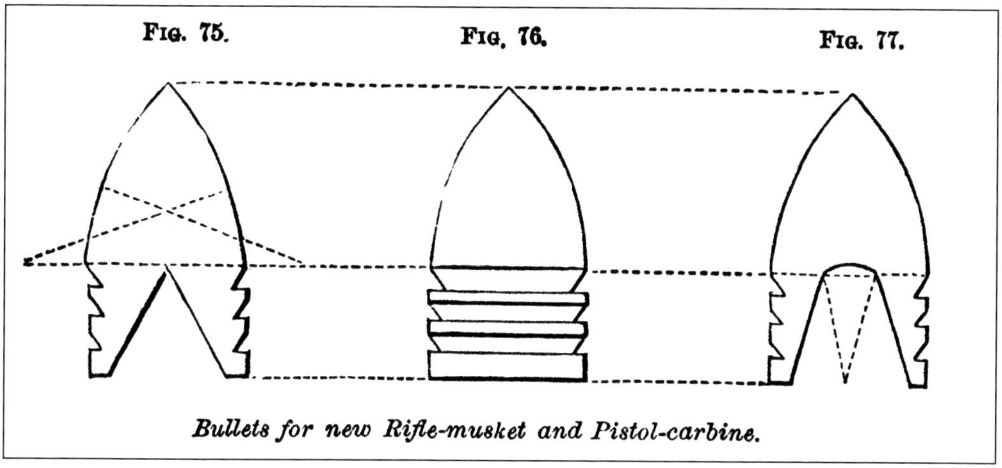

THE "MINIE BALL" BECOMES THE STANDARD ROUND FOR MILITARY FIREARMS. (Gibbon, SLU Archives) In 1849, French officer Claude-Etienne Minie designed a cylindrical bullet with a conical point and a hollow base that could be muzzle-loaded and fired with great accuracy and range (up to a thousand yards) from rifled muskets and pistols. This became the standard bullet of European and American armies in the 1850s and was the primary round used in the Civil War. The St. Louis Arsenal produced and distributed millions of these rounds from the mid-1850s through the Civil War.

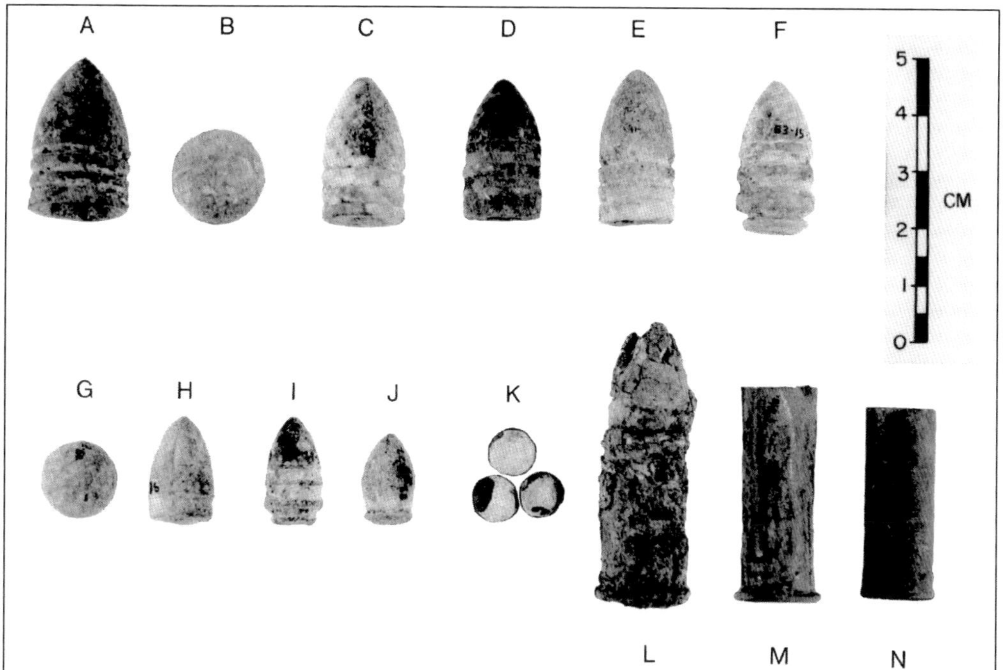

A WIDE VARIETY OF CARTRIDGES WERE EXCAVATED AT THE ST. LOUIS ARSENAL. (Courtesy of William Woods) Nearly 300 small arms projectiles were found during archaeological excavations at the arsenal in 1983–84. Several of these rounds are represented above. They include .69 caliber rifle (A) and musket balls (B); .58 caliber Minie balls (C); .52 caliber Spencer (D) and Sharps rounds (F); .54 caliber "Mississippi" musket balls (E); .44, .36, and .28 caliber pistol balls and a variety of others.

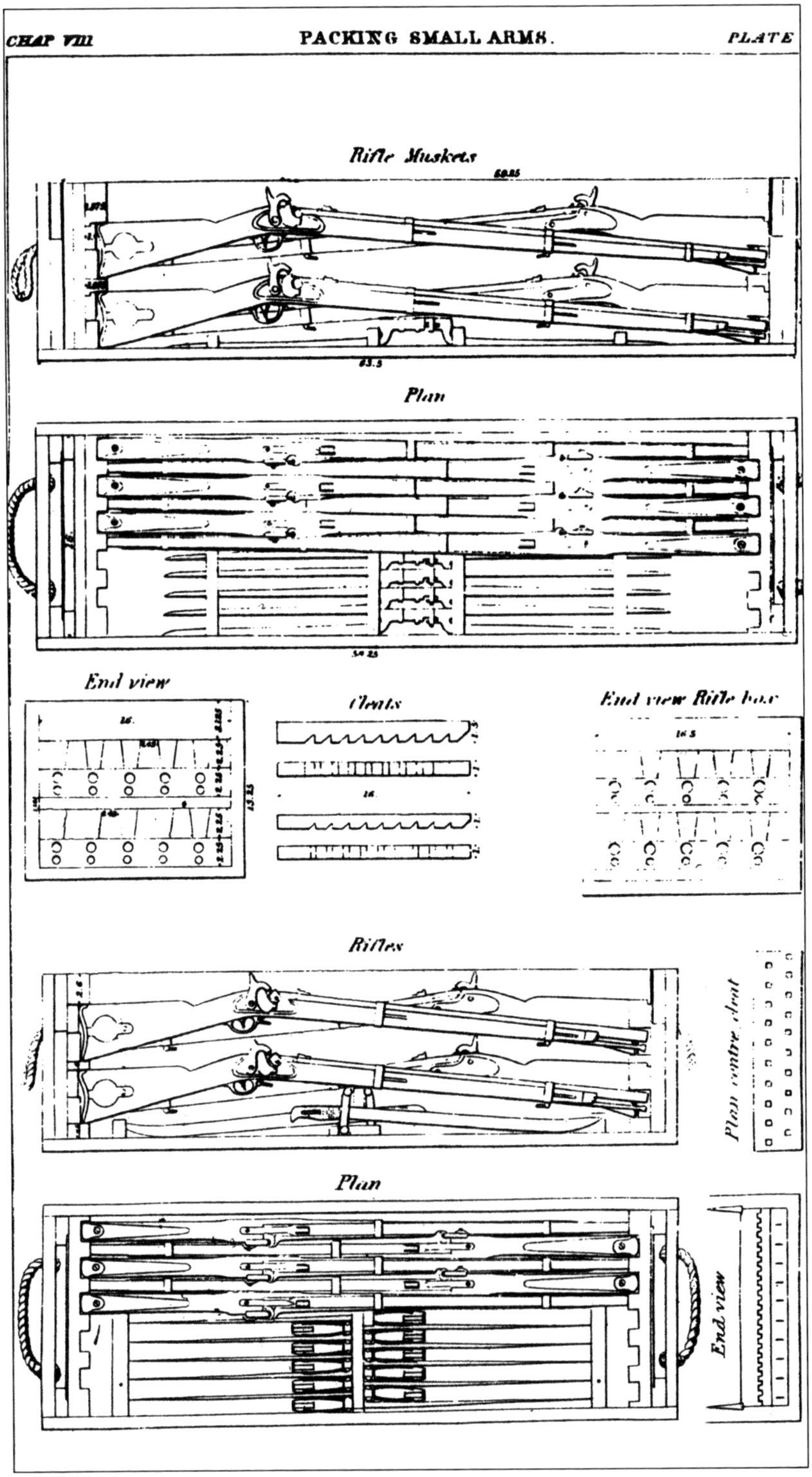

INSTRUCTIONS FOR PACKING SMALL ARMS. (*Ordnance Manual*, 1861, SLU Archives) U.S. small arms were packed with great precision according to strict standards to ensure secure shipment to the issuing point. Boxes were stenciled with the name of the arsenal issuing the weapons.

A PACKET OF .58 CALIBER AMMUNITION READY FOR USE BY FEDERAL TROOPS. (Courtesy of Sweeny's Museum) Cartridges manufactured at the arsenal were bundled in packets of 10, stamped with the year of manufacture (in this case 1864), and were packed with dozens of others in an ammunition crate for shipment to the field. Millions of rounds of ammunition were produced at the arsenal during the war, but only a few have survived to the present.

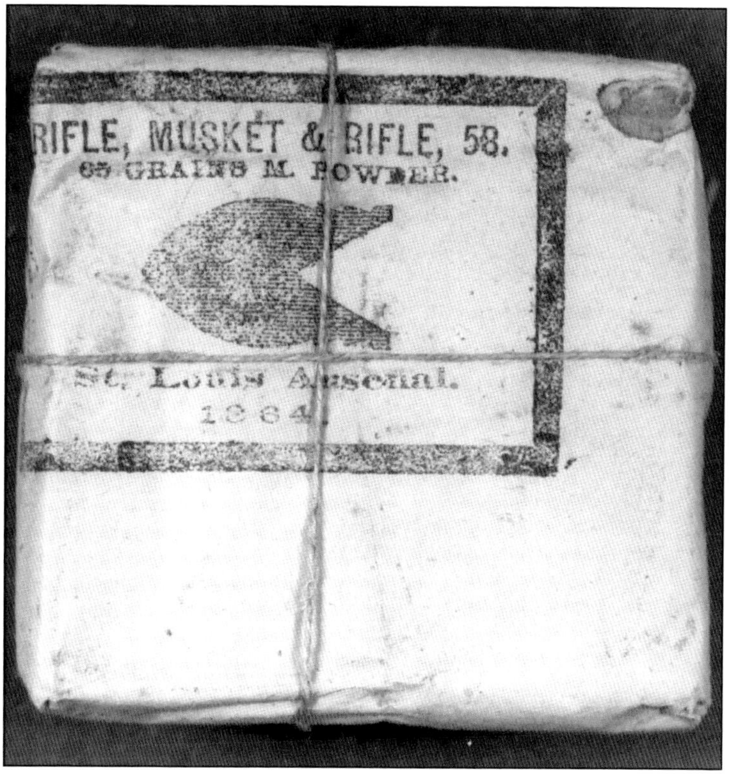

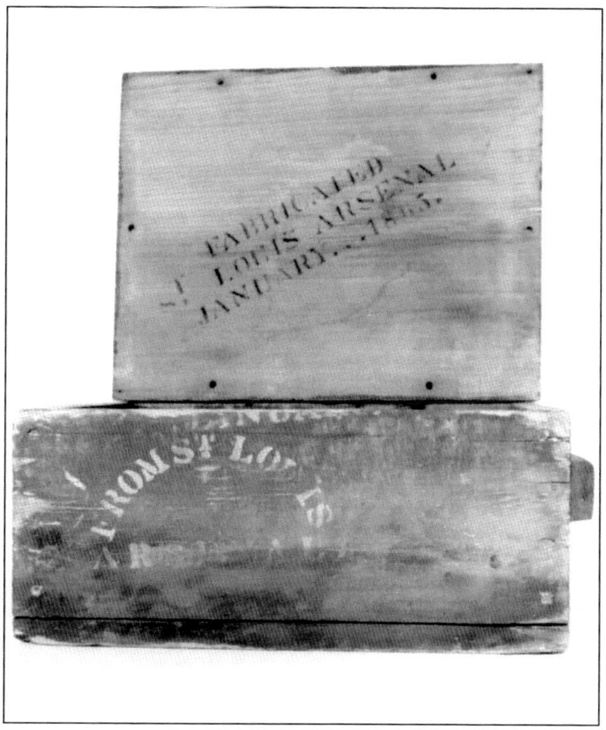

WOODEN PACKING CRATE FOR CARTRIDGES MANUFACTURED AT ST. LOUIS ARSENAL, 1865. (Courtesy of Sweeny's Museum) The only known surviving ammunition crate from the St. Louis Arsenal has happily found a home at Sweeny's Civil War Museum in Republic, Missouri, near the site of Wilson's Creek Battlefield. Dr. Tom Sweeney, founder of the museum, located the ammo box and the above packet of cartridges with an antiques dealer in Montana. Apparently, the cartridges were shipped to the Montana Territory after the war and were never used. They survived among other military surplus items that were auctioned off in later years, and Dr. Sweeney was fortunate enough to discover these products of the arsenal and to return them to their home state.

Fig. 79.

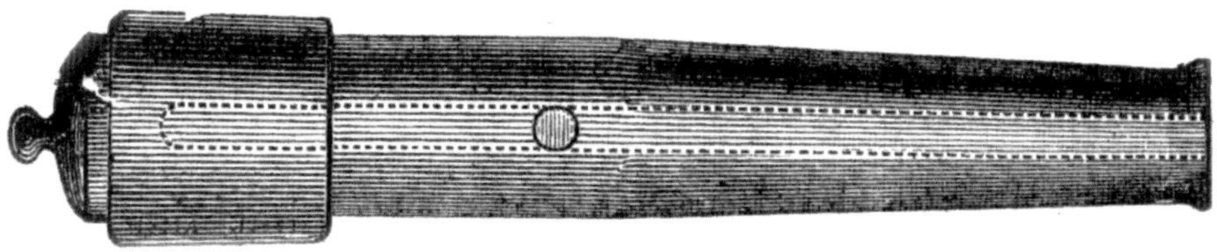

THE PARROTT FIELD RIFLE CAME IN 10- AND 20-POUNDER VERSIONS WHICH USUALLY FIRED SHELL AND CASE SHOT AT GREAT DISTANCE FROM THE ENEMY. (Gibbon, SLU Archives)
Although small arms and ammunition were the primary stock in trade at the St. Louis Arsenal, a significant business was also conducted in artillery, with its attendant carriages and support equipment. Prior to the Civil War this was a very small percentage of the ordnance passing through the arsenal, since western service required more small arms than heavy guns. With the onset of Civil War, however, the arsenal received increasing demands for artillery and heavy ammunition, and these demands were met expeditiously. At the end of the war, so much artillery was returned to the arsenal that it was sold as scrap and much of it melted down to create the underground sewer and water pipes of the growing metropolis of St. Louis.

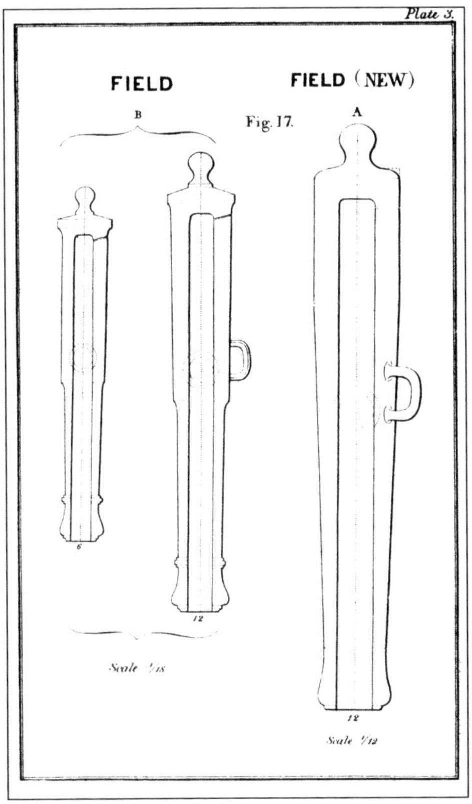

THESE 6- AND 12-POUNDER SMOOTH BORE FIELD GUNS WERE THE "LIGHT" ARTILLERY USED BY UNITS MANEUVERING IN THE FIELD TO ENGAGE ENEMY TROOPS AT CLOSE RANGE. (Gibbon, SLU Archives)

FIG. 83.

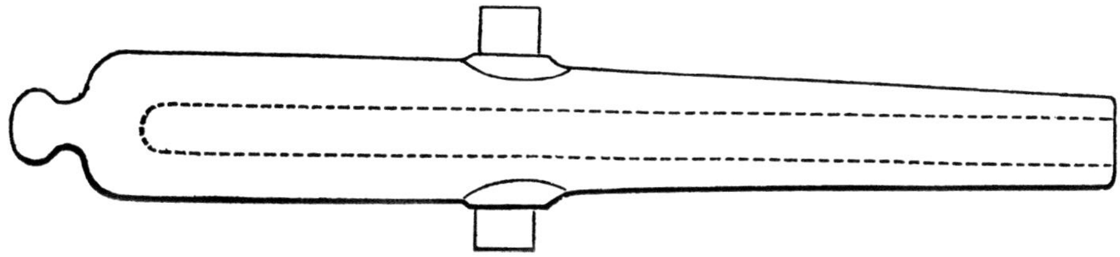

THE 3-INCH ORDNANCE RIFLE WAS A SLEEK, ACCURATE FIELD GUN SUPERIOR TO THE 10-POUNDER PARROTT, USUALLY FIRING THE DESTRUCTIVE HOTCHKISS OR SHENKL SHELLS. (Gibbon, SLU Archives) The older field guns and howitzers, such as those shown at the bottom of these two pages, were made of bronze and fired projectiles as far as 900 to 1600 yards. The more high-powered guns, such as the rifles at the top of these pages, were made of iron and fired at ranges between 1,800 and 2,000 yards. The old smooth bore cannons were effective against troops at close range because they could fire grape and canister rounds. On the other hand, the newer rifles could batter down defenses at long range and fire on troop concentrations long before batteries were within small arms range. This helped to change the face of modern warfare.

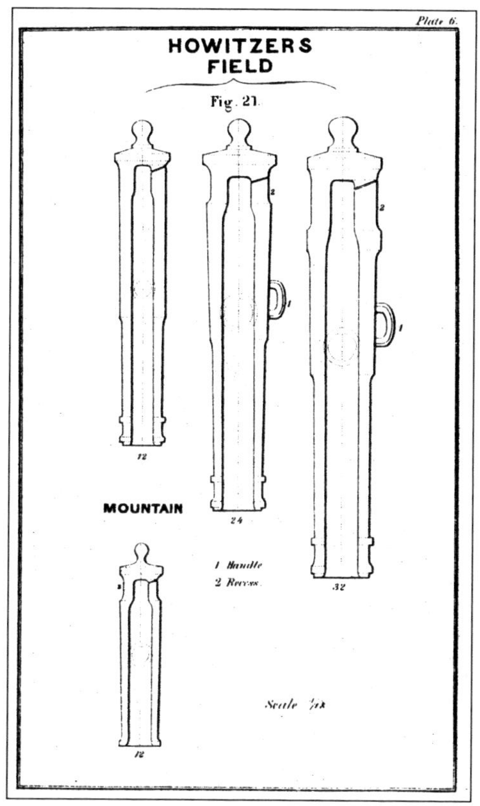

FIELD HOWITZERS WERE DESIGNED TO FIRE SHELLS AND HOLLOW PROJECTILES HIGH OVER ENEMY DEFENSES, CAUSING DESTRUCTION BY THEIR OVERHEAD EXPLOSIONS. (Gibbon, SLU Archives)

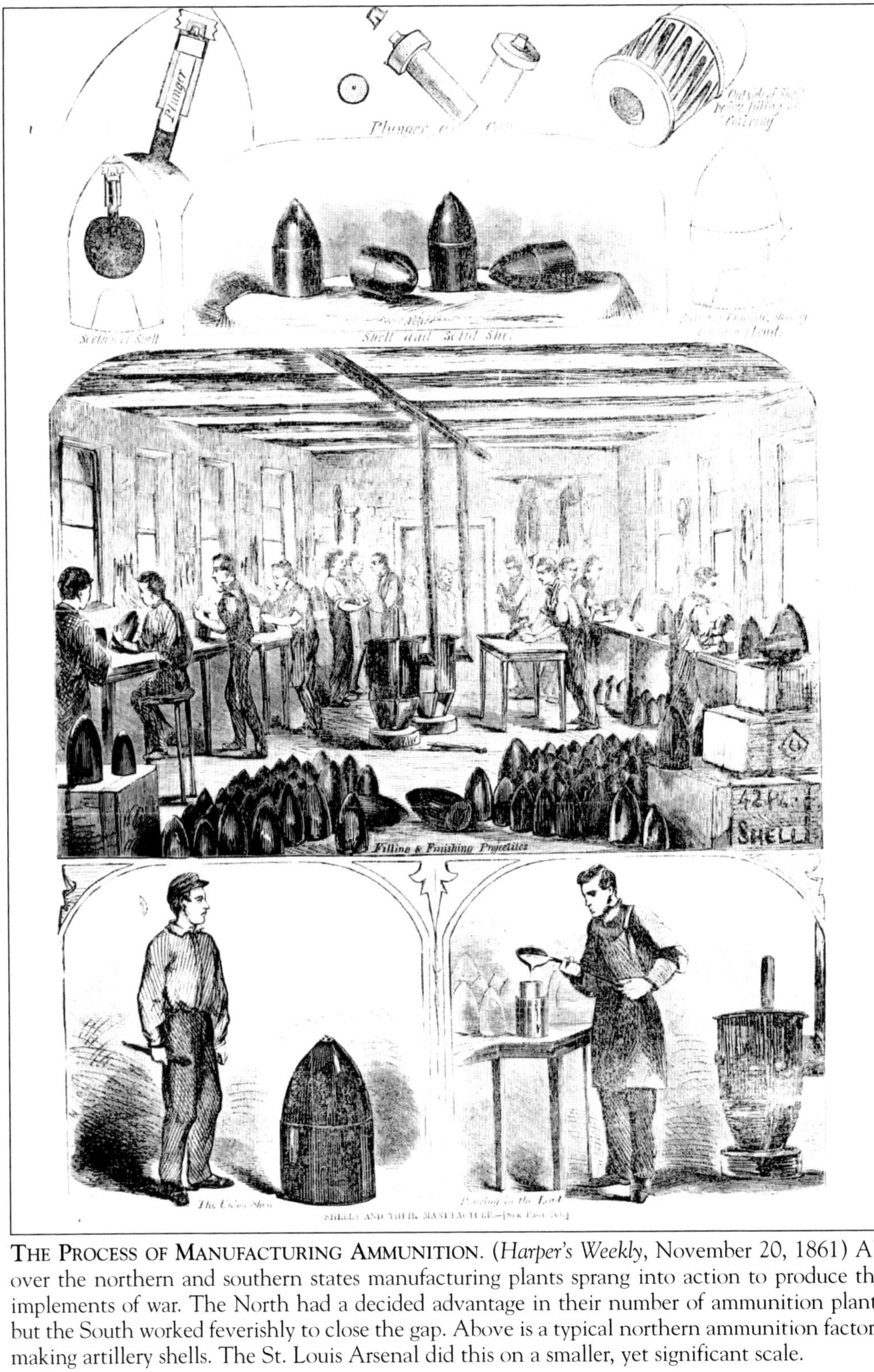

The Process of Manufacturing Ammunition. (*Harper's Weekly*, November 20, 1861) All over the northern and southern states manufacturing plants sprang into action to produce the implements of war. The North had a decided advantage in their number of ammunition plants but the South worked feverishly to close the gap. Above is a typical northern ammunition factory making artillery shells. The St. Louis Arsenal did this on a smaller, yet significant scale.

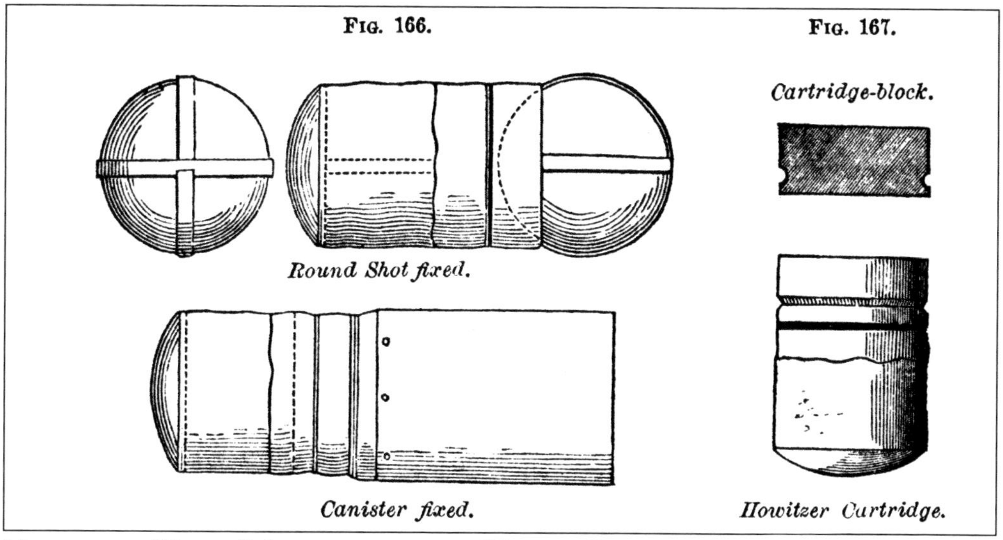

METHODS OF "FIXING" AMMUNITION WITH WOODEN BLOCKS IN PREPARATION FOR FIRING. (Gibbon, SLU Archives) Cannon balls were not fired simply "as is" by ramming them down a gun barrel and setting off a fuse. Rather, they were carefully attached to wooden or metal devices called sabots or cartridge blocks and inserted in the gun tubes with a gunpowder charge beneath the round. This was called "fixed" ammunition. Once the powder exploded it forced the sabot to expand and engage the rifling in the barrel, and this is what gave the round its spin coming out of the barrel. In smooth bore guns the sabot simply helped the round keep its position during loading and firing.

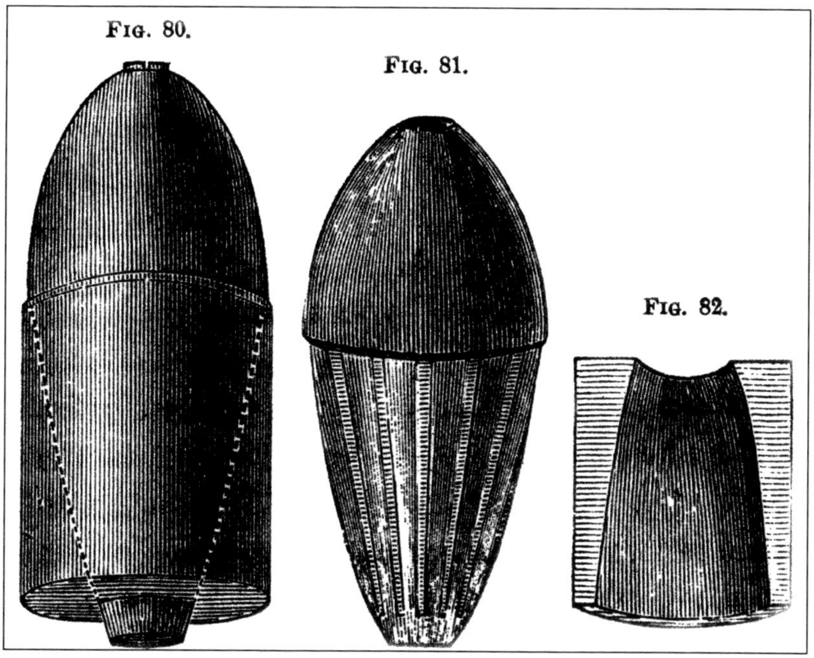

FIXING A SHENKL PROJECTILE WITH A PAPIER-MACHE WAD. (Gibbon, SLU Archives) This is an example of a shell fired from a Parrott gun. The body, which was made of cast iron, terminated in a cone. This was inserted into a papier-mache "wad" which held the round in place in the barrel. When the gun was fired, the force of the explosion forced the wad to expand into the rifling and give the round its proper twist, then the shredded remains of the wad blew free of the round as it left the barrel. This proved to be a very effective device.

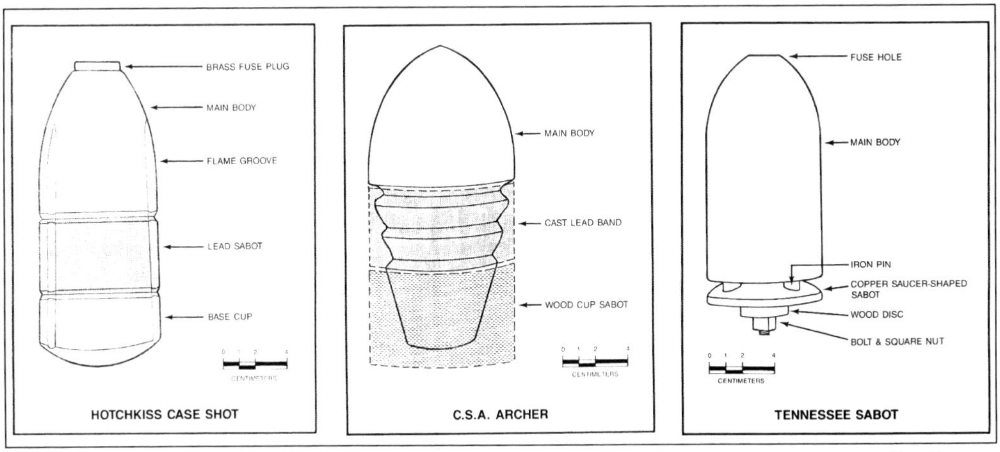

DIAGRAMS OF THREE RECONSTRUCTED ROUNDS FOUND IN EXCAVATIONS AT THE ST. LOUIS ARSENAL. (Courtesy of William Woods) The Hotchkiss Case Shot on the left was probably designed for a 20-pounder Parrott cannon. It had thin walls, iron balls within, and a time fuse. It was designed to detonate over personnel from long range. The CSA archer had a lead ring sabot that was forced into the rifling upon discharge of the gun, giving it the appropriate spin. This projectile is a bolt solid shot whose purpose was to breach fortification walls and buildings. It was designed for use in a 3-inch Ordnance Rifle. The Tennessee Sabot pictured here is very rare. The pins at the base bolted it to a sabot that locked into the rifling during firing. This specimen is a shell, with thick sidewalls, and it was filled with black powder and set to detonate in the air or on the ground. It was designed for a rare Confederate bronze mountain rifle.

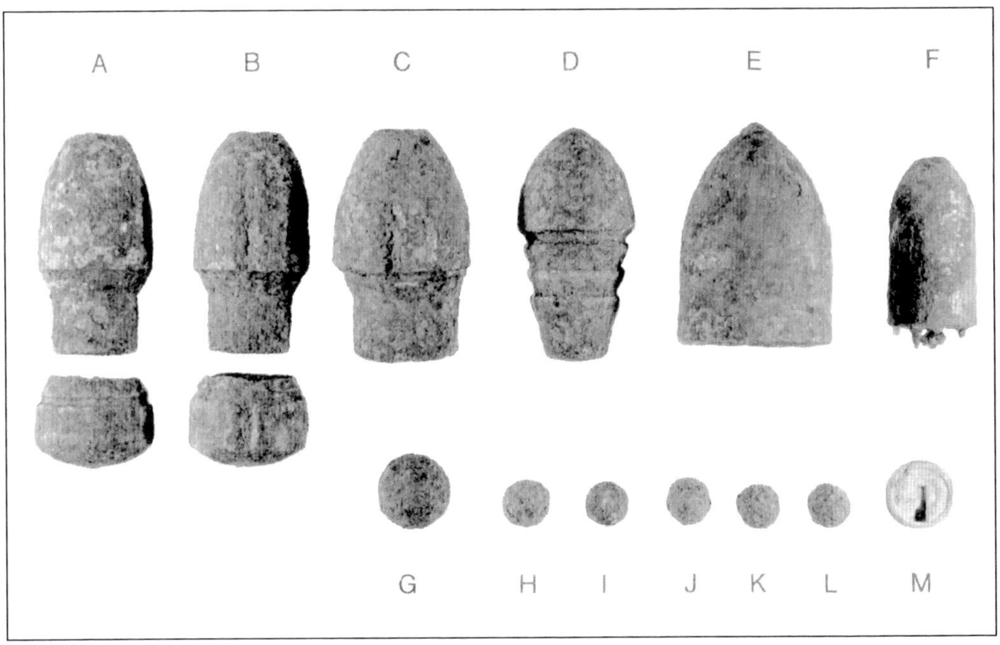

ARTILLERY PROJECTILES EXCAVATED AT THE ARSENAL IN 1983. (Courtesy of William Woods) These include a Hotchkiss Shell with base cup (A), Hotchkiss Case Shot (C) with base cup (B), Archer Shell (D), Read Shell (E), Tennessee Sabot (F), Case Shot or Grape Shot ball (G), Canister balls (H-L), and a Bormann Time Fuse (M).

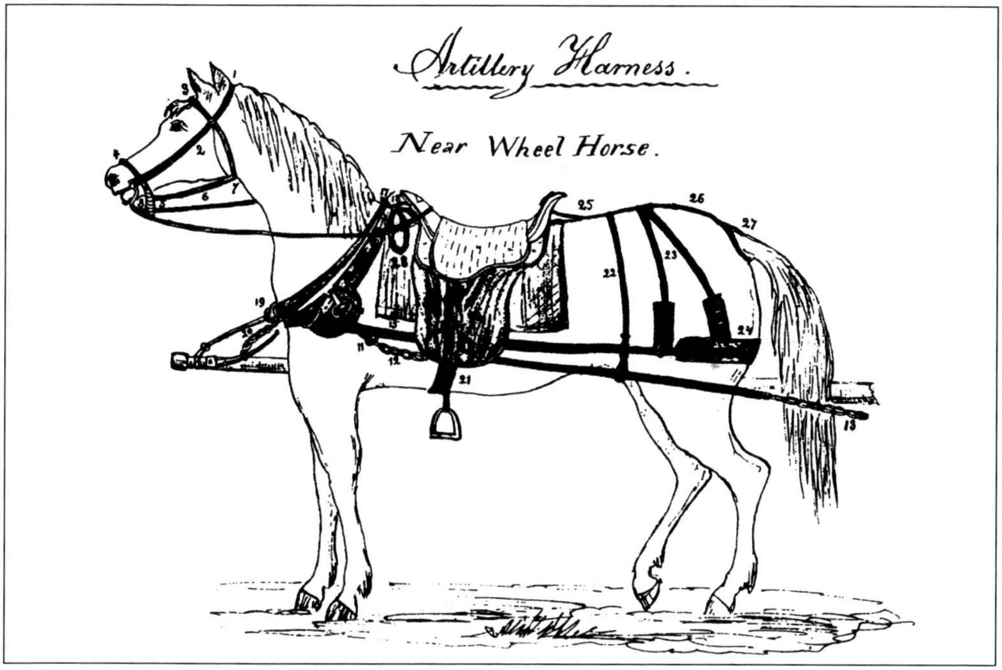

AN ARTILLERY "NEAR WHEEL HORSE" IN FULL HARNESS. (Huebner, SLU Archives) One of the essential "accouterments" stored and distributed by the arsenal was harness for artillery horses. Full sets of harness were prepared and hung with care in designated areas of the artillery sheds. Civil War artilleryman Henry Richard Huebner created a sketchbook of artillery equipment and procedures. He included meticulous drawings of horses in full harness, identifying every detail of halter, bridle, trace, and strap, all of which were undoubtedly stocked and issued by the St. Louis Arsenal.

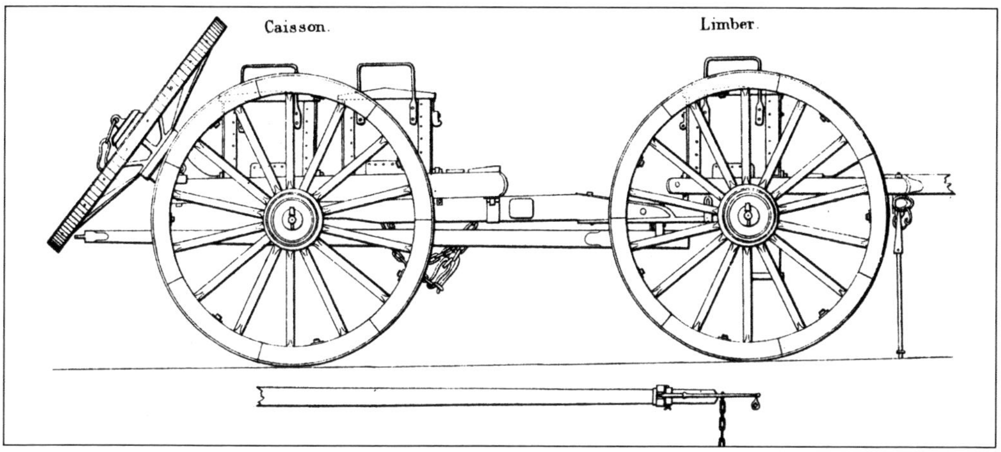

THE CAISSON CARRIES AMMUNITION FOR ONE GUN. (Gibbon, SLU Archives) A caisson was assigned to each gun. It held three ammunition boxes upon which up to nine crewmen could ride on field marches. A spare wheel was attached to the rear of the caisson, which was interchangeable with any broken wheel among the supporting carriages. An extra pole was also carried beneath the vehicle. The limber carried the instruments needed for firing the gun and the ammunition boxes held the specific rounds needed for a given mission. The arsenal was equipped to assemble and repair such caissons.

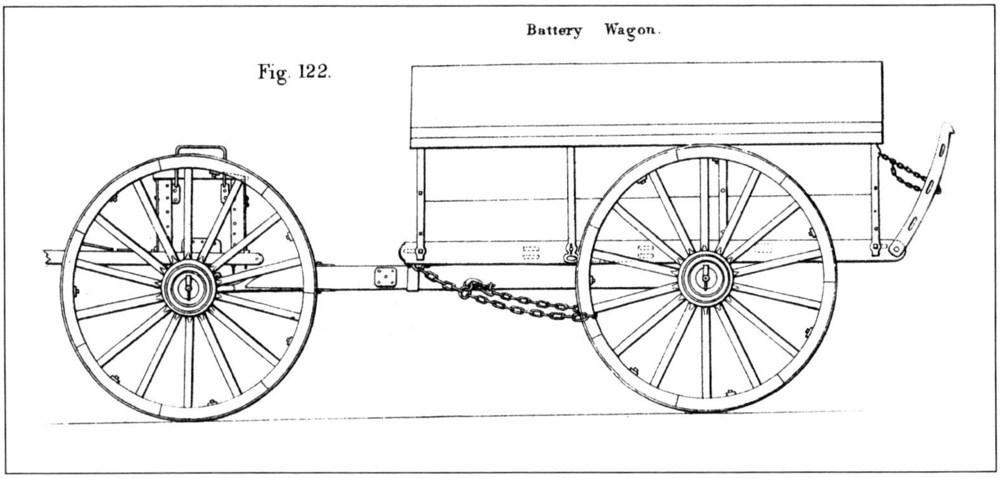

ONE BATTERY WAGON WAS ASSIGNED TO EACH BATTERY OF FOUR OR SIX GUNS. (Gibbon, SLU Archives) The battery wagon was made of pine with canvas stretched over it. It was as maneuverable as all of the other carriages in a battery. Its purpose was to carry carriage-maker's and saddler's tools, spare parts for carriages, harness and other equipment, and raw materials for constructing necessary parts. These also were assembled and repaired at the arsenal.

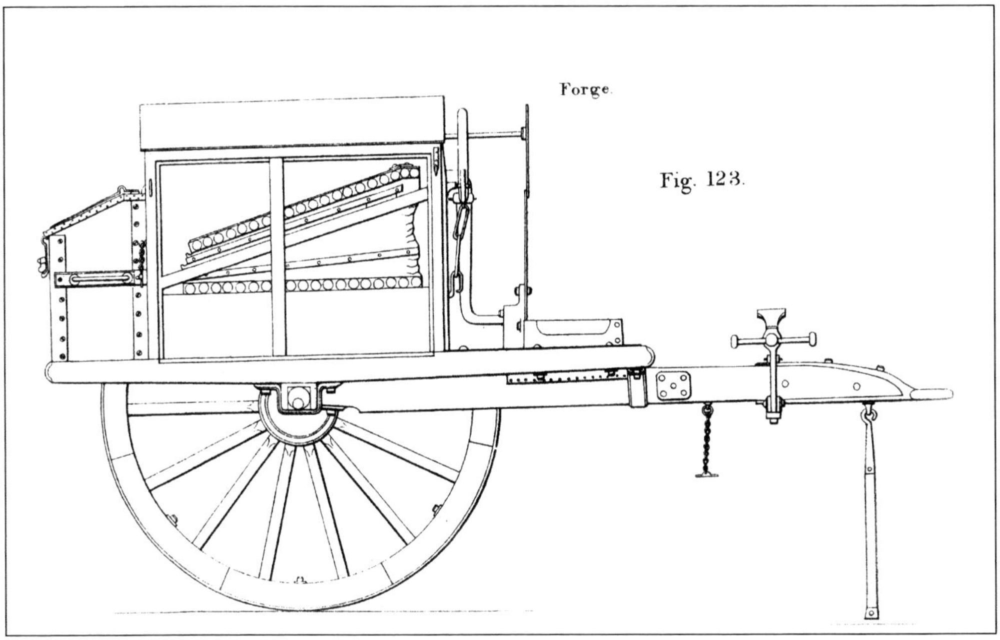

THE TRAVELING FORGE BECAME ESSENTIAL TO MAINTAINING EQUIPMENT AND CARRIAGES IN THE FIELD. (Gibbon, SLU Archives) One of these forges was assigned to each field battery and several others to army support units. They performed an essential task in providing a means of repairing carriages and other battery equipment that became disabled in the rough and tumble environment of the field. Each forge had a bellows and fireplace along with supporting structures. They also carried a coal box full of coal for the fireplace and a limber box which held horseshoes, nails, and spare iron parts for carriages and harness. As heavy as it was, the forge was extremely maneuverable and capable of keeping up with an active battery on the move.

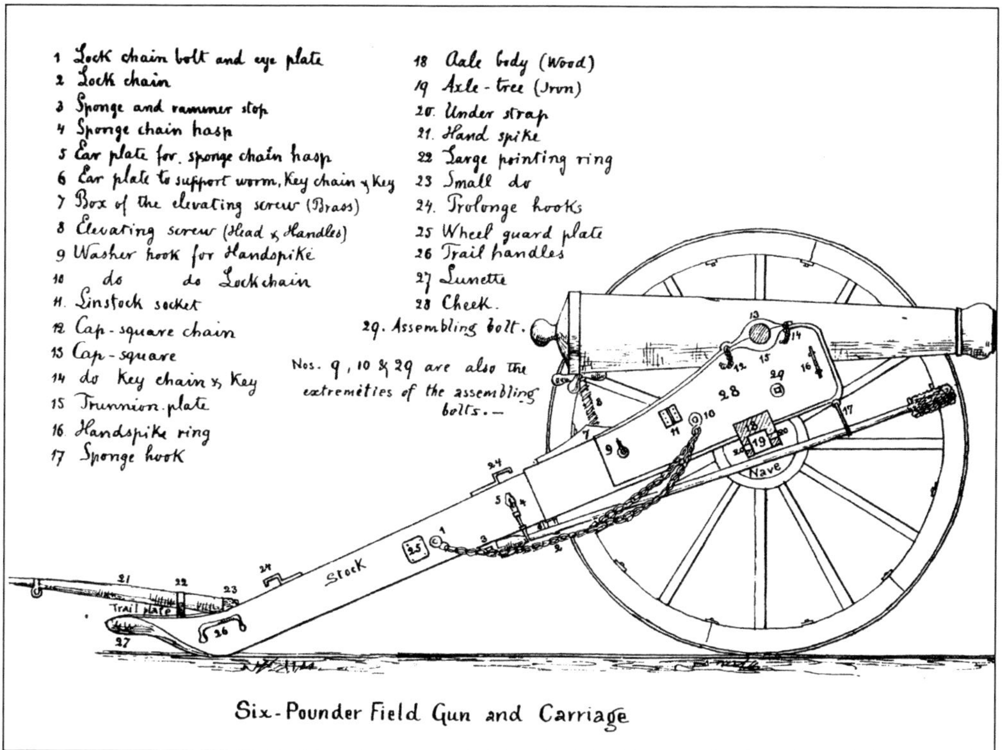

THE GUN CARRIAGE WAS ESSENTIAL TO TRANSPORTING MEDIUM-SIZED GUNS IN THE FIELD. (Huebner, SLU Archives) In combat maneuverability was necessary to give an armed force the advantage over the enemy. The availability of medium-sized field guns proved to be the deciding factor in many close-fought battles of the Civil War. These guns were transported on "gun carriages" that were built to fit their particular size. All supporting equipment matched these carriages to keep up with them in the field. Above we see an excellent rendition of a field gun on a carriage, by artillerist Henry Huebner, carefully identifying all of its parts.

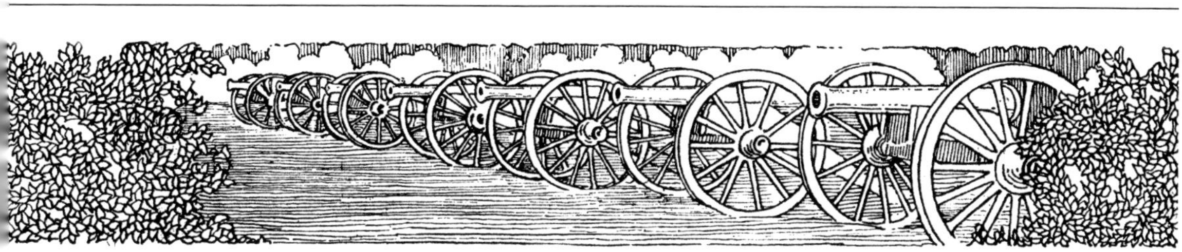

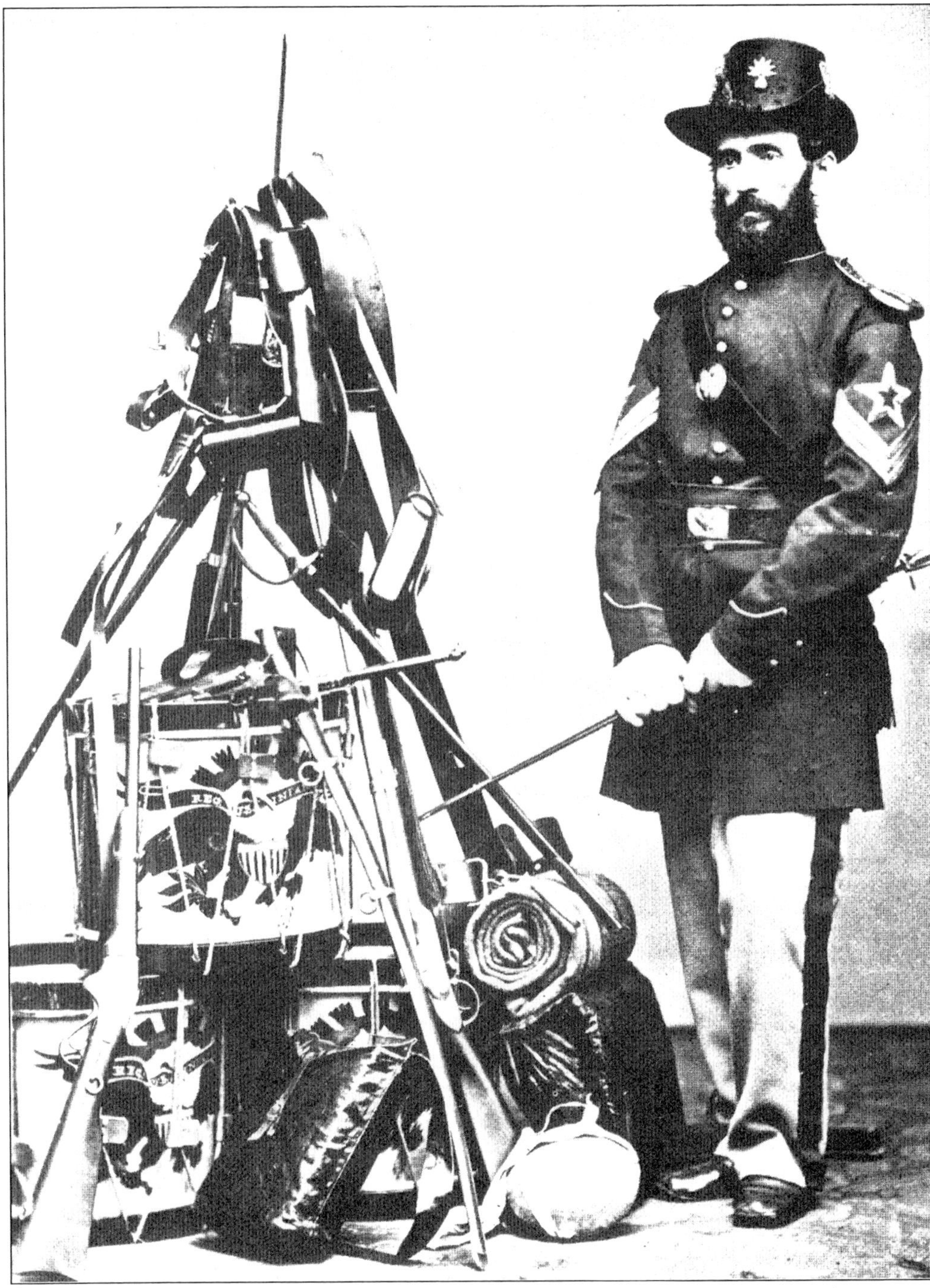

A Sergeant of Ordnance Stands by a Stack of Ordnance Items. (U.S. War Department, 1861, SLU Archives) Near the beginning of the Civil War, the war department issued a series of photographs depicting the uniform styles worn by members of the various branches of the army. The above image depicts an ordnance sergeant with his distinctive uniform and a sampling of some of the equipment issued by ordnance installations. The items in this image would have been commonly seen at the St. Louis Arsenal.

Seven

WAR COMES TO THE ARSENAL (1861–1865)

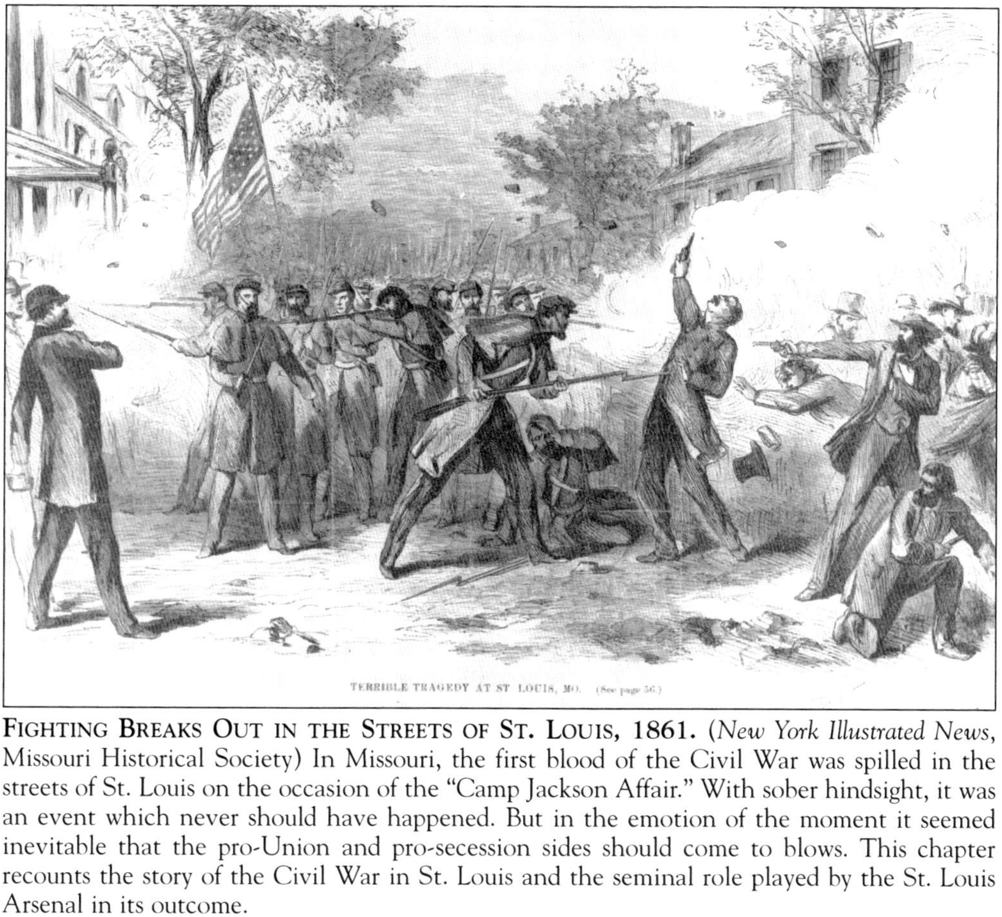

FIGHTING BREAKS OUT IN THE STREETS OF ST. LOUIS, 1861. (*New York Illustrated News*, Missouri Historical Society) In Missouri, the first blood of the Civil War was spilled in the streets of St. Louis on the occasion of the "Camp Jackson Affair." With sober hindsight, it was an event which never should have happened. But in the emotion of the moment it seemed inevitable that the pro-Union and pro-secession sides should come to blows. This chapter recounts the story of the Civil War in St. Louis and the seminal role played by the St. Louis Arsenal in its outcome.

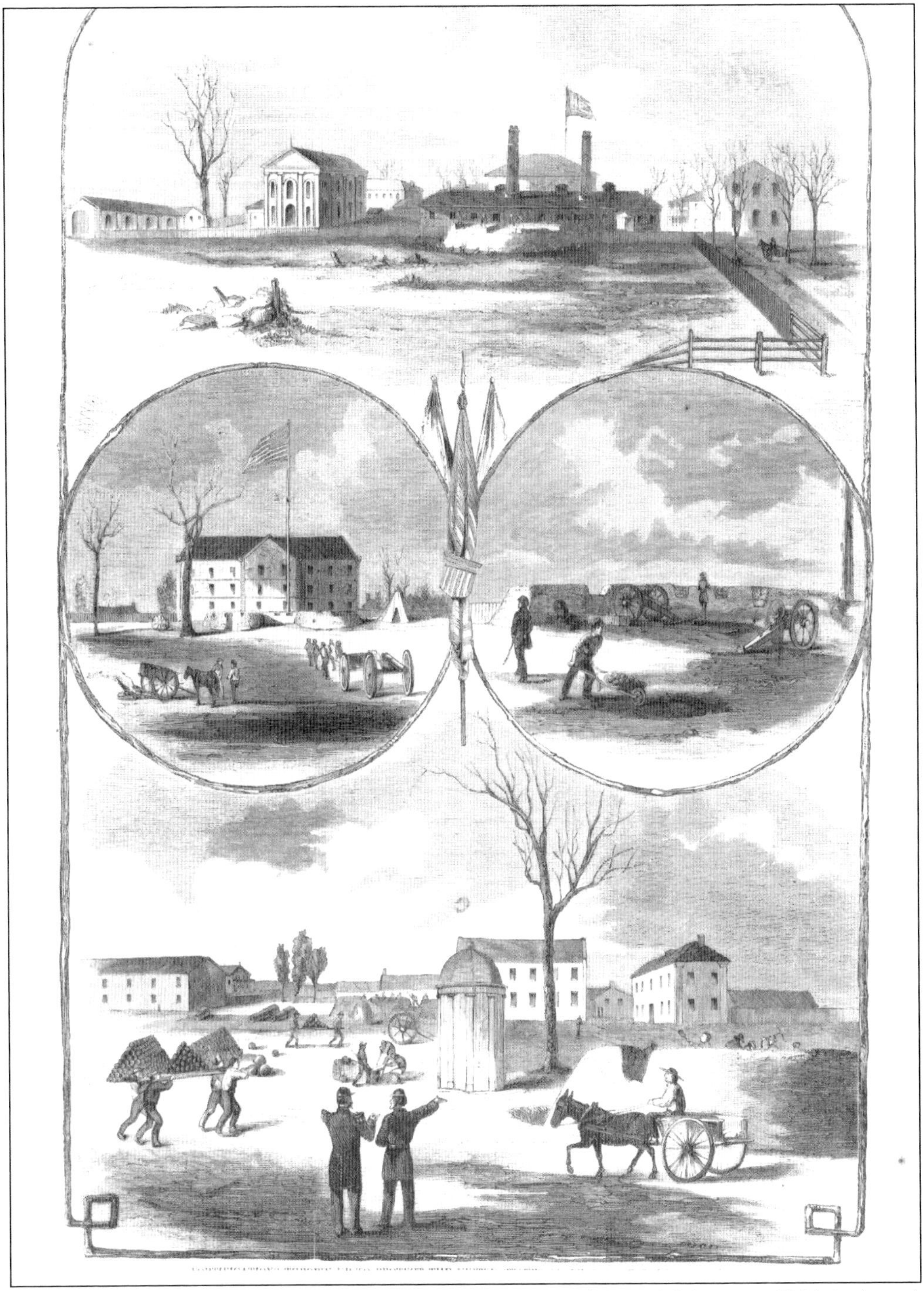

FORTIFICATIONS BEING ERECTED AT THE ARSENAL, 1861. (*Harper's Magazine*, SLU Archives) As soon as news reached St. Louis of the Confederate attack on Fort Sumter on April 12, 1861, efforts were underway by federal authorities to reinforce the U.S. Arsenal at St. Louis and protect it from possible attack by secessionist forces. The above image is a very accurate rendition of measures being taken by the small Union garrison to fortify its defenses.

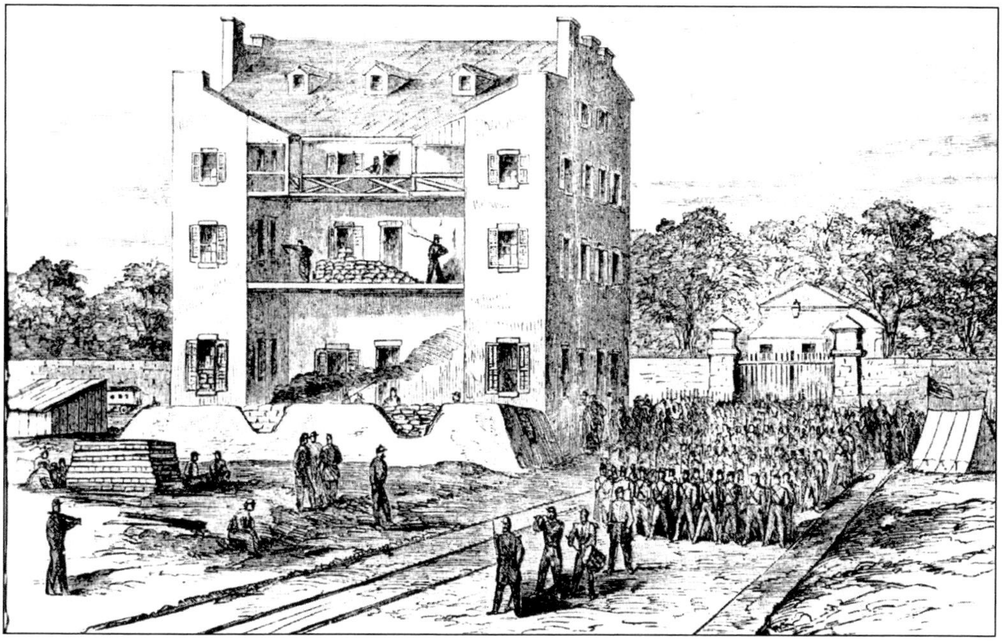

NEW RECRUITS MARCH OUT OF THE WEST GATE OF THE ARSENAL, JULY 1861. (*New York Illustrated News*, SLU Archives) Union volunteers were enlisted at the arsenal by the hundreds each day after the commencement of hostilities. By early May 1861, over 7,000 recruits swelled the ranks of 10 reserve regiments. Fortification of the arsenal grounds was proceeding well and buildings in the immediate vicinity were occupied by Union troops to prevent Confederate sympathizers from gaining access to the installation. The above image depicts new recruits marching out of the west arsenal gate past a fortified house on the northwest corner of Carondelet Road and "Gate" Street. This three-story private dwelling and business served as an external guard house to the main gate in the opening days of the war. The building remained until the 1950s, when it was razed by Anheuser-Busch to build a bottling plant. The image below shows the street scene today from approximately the same vantage point. The building on the left is the bottling plant and the street, which ends at Lyon Park and Broadway Boulevard, is now called Wyoming.

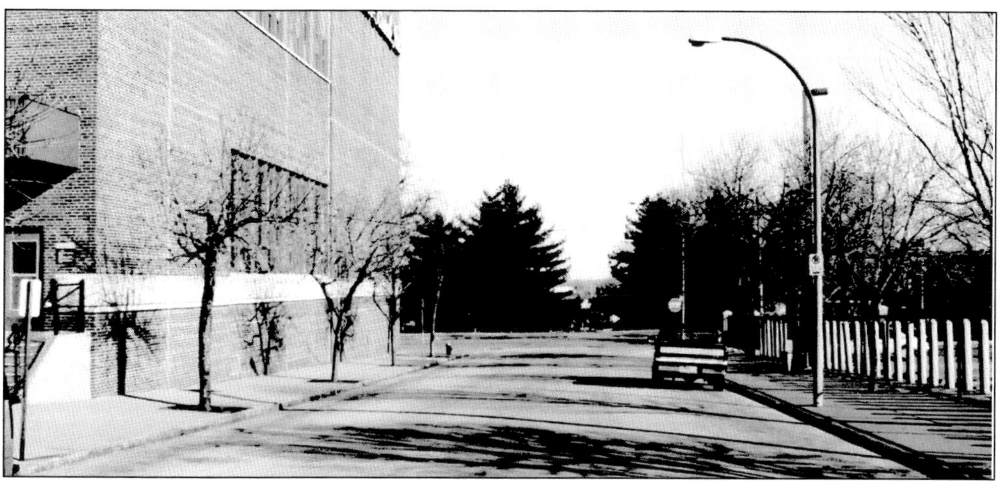

INTERSECTION OF WYOMING STREET AND BROADWAY BOULEVARD, FORMER LOCATION OF THE MAIN WESTERN GATE TO THE ARSENAL. (Photo by the author)

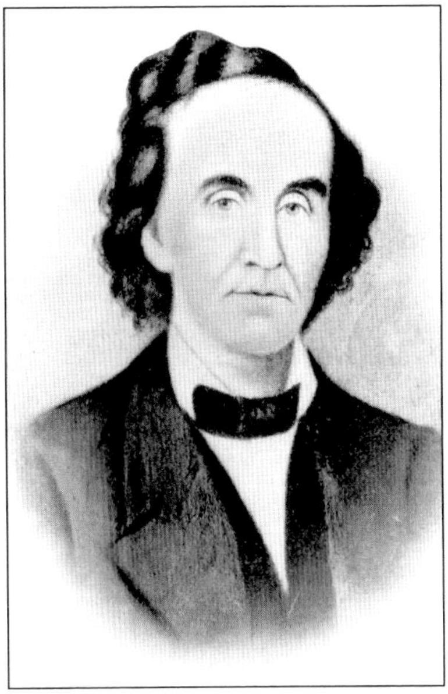

Claiborne Fox Jackson, Governor of Missouri and Ardent Secessionist. (McElroy, SLU Archives) Born in Kentucky, Claiborne Jackson moved to Howard County, the "Boon's Lick" region of central Missouri, at the age of 21. He soon became involved in politics and served as a democrat in both houses of the Missouri legislature. In 1860 he was elected governor of Missouri on the pro-slavery ticket and immediately set about positioning Missouri for secession from the Union. Publicly he advocated neutrality for Missouri, but privately he prepared for war. He mobilized the Missouri State Guard, calling for 50,000 volunteers to resist the coercion of federal troops. In May 1861, the St. Louis District of the Missouri State Guard was assembled for training at Lindell Grove under the command of General Daniel Frost, and the encampment was named "Camp Jackson." After the showdown at Camp Jackson, the governor appointed respected Missouri statesman Sterling Price commander-in-chief of the Missouri Guard. Price was authorized to negotiate the restriction of federal troops to the St. Louis area with Union Commander William S. Harney, but this was little more than a delaying tactic to give the state militia time to mobilize. In June, Jackson and Price met with Harney's replacement, Nathaniel Lyon, and with Congressman Frank Blair to seek a compromise, but Lyon gave Jackson an ultimatum and forced him out of Missouri. Jackson conducted a government-in-exile from Texas and Arkansas, but was replaced as governor of Missouri on July 31, 1861, by Hamilton R. Gamble, a fervent Union man. Jackson died of cancer in Little Rock, Arkansas, the following year and Missouri remained within the Union.

General Sterling Price, Commander of the Missouri State Guard. (Courtesy of John Vollmann) Sterling Price was born in Virginia in 1809, educated at Hampden-Sydney College, and moved to central Missouri with his family in 1831. He ran a hotel and engaged in farming until the outbreak of the Civil War. He also participated in Missouri politics and was elected to the U.S. Congress. He resigned his congressional seat to serve in the Mexican War where he attained the rank of brigadier general for "gallant and meritorious conduct." After the war, Price settled on his farm in Chariton County until being elected governor of Missouri in 1852, an office he performed with great distinction for four years. In the presidential contest of 1860 Price supported the moderate Democrat Stephen Douglas. Although initially opposed to the secession of Missouri, after the fall of Camp Jackson Price accepted appointment as a major general in command of the Missouri Militia and eventually accepted a commission in the Confederate Army. In addition to participating in numerous campaigns outside of Missouri, he led a major invasion of his home state in 1864. After the war, Price moved to Mexico for a short time, but returned to conduct a business in St. Louis where he died in 1867, still highly revered by many Missourians as "Old Pap."

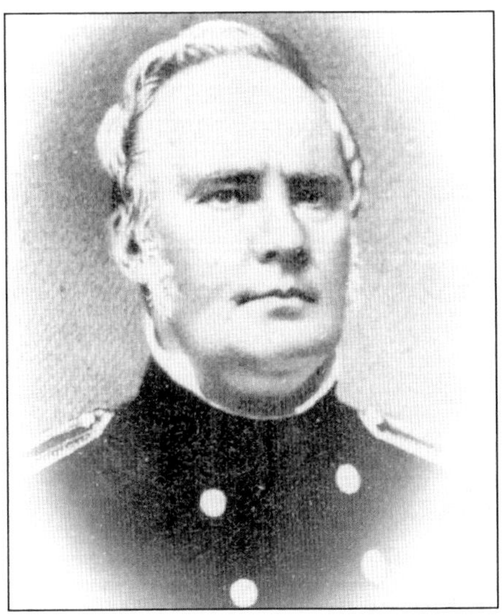

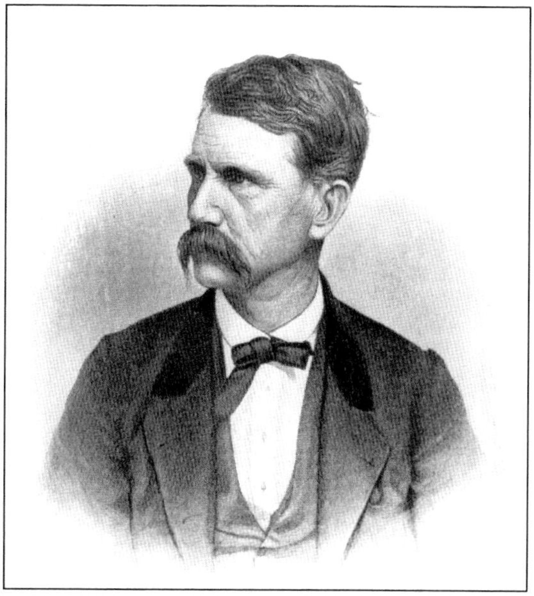

HONORABLE FRANK P. BLAIR JR., LAWYER, SOLDIER, AND STATESMAN, LED THE UNION EFFORT IN MISSOURI. (McElroy, SLU Archives) Frank Blair was born in Kentucky and raised in Washington D.C., where his father was editor of the *Globe* newspaper. After attending Princeton College, he returned to Kentucky where he studied law, then settled in St. Louis in 1843. Blair became an influential lawyer and politician and was an outspoken opponent of slavery. He served in the Missouri legislature from 1852 to 1856, when he was elected to Congress on the Free Soil Party ticket. He became highly influential in the new Republican Party and his brother, Montgomery Blair, was well-placed as postmaster general in Lincoln's cabinet. Frank Blair organized a "Committee of Public Safety" which included Nathaniel Lyon and others rabidly opposed to slavery or secession. Having been supported by the German elements of St. Louis, Blair rallied these ardent Unionists to service in the reserve units raised to counter the Confederate threat. He was elected colonel of the first regiment of volunteers and led his regiment at Camp Jackson. He became brigadier general of volunteers in August of 1861 and was later promoted to major general. He later returned to Congress and was critical of the radical republicanism of the postwar era with its severe treatment of the southern states. Frank Blair died in 1873, a highly esteemed citizen of Missouri.

BRIGADIER GENERAL NATHANIEL LYON, DEFENDER OF THE ARSENAL AND UPHOLDER OF THE UNION. (Courtesy of SLU Archives) There is no name more intimately attached to the memory of the St. Louis Arsenal than that of Nathaniel Lyon. Lyon was assigned to the arsenal in February 1861 at the request of Frank Blair for more federal army support for the defense of this strategic installation. Lyon was a captain in command of a company of the 2nd U.S. Infantry stationed at Fort Riley, Kansas. He was an unconditional Union man and was prepared to defend these principles with his life. He quickly linked up with Blair and other members of the "Committee of Public Safety," conspired to have General Harney removed from command and took command of the troops at the arsenal himself. Lyon raised between seven and ten thousand volunteers for ten reserve regiments in St. Louis. He also led the force that captured Camp Jackson on May 10, 1861, for which he was promoted to brigadier general of volunteers. Lyon pursued the rebellious Missouri Militia across the state until confronting a much larger Confederate force at Wilson Creek. There he was killed on August 10, 1861, leading the Union volunteers in a desperate attempt to drive the Confederates from Missouri. He was the first Union general to die in the war.

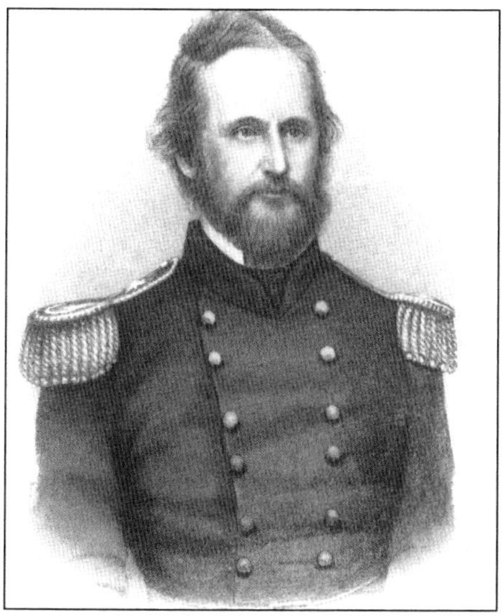

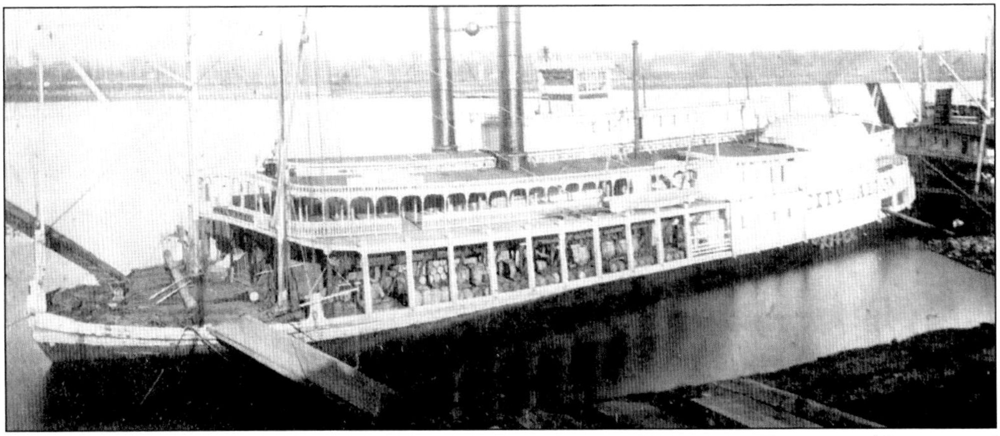

THE STEAMBOAT *CITY OF ALTON* TRANSPORTS ARSENAL WEAPONS TO ILLINOIS. (Courtesy of Missouri Historical Society) On April 24, 1861, Captain James Stokes of Chicago arrived at the arsenal with a requisition from Governor Yates for 10,000 muskets to arm Illinois volunteers. Captain Lyon more than complied with the order, issuing 20,000 muskets, 500 carbines, 500 revolvers, 110,000 cartridges, and a number of cannons, leaving only enough muskets for the new recruits at the arsenal. The *City of Alton* arrived quietly at the arsenal wharf at 11:00 pm on April 26, where arsenal personnel worked feverishly during the night to transport the ordnance through the sally port down to the river. By 2:00 am all was loaded and the steamboat embarked for Alton, arriving three hours later to the delight of Illinois authorities and the ultimate consternation of Confederate sympathizers. Captain Stokes relished his role as "hero of the arsenal" and greatly embellished his retelling of the story.

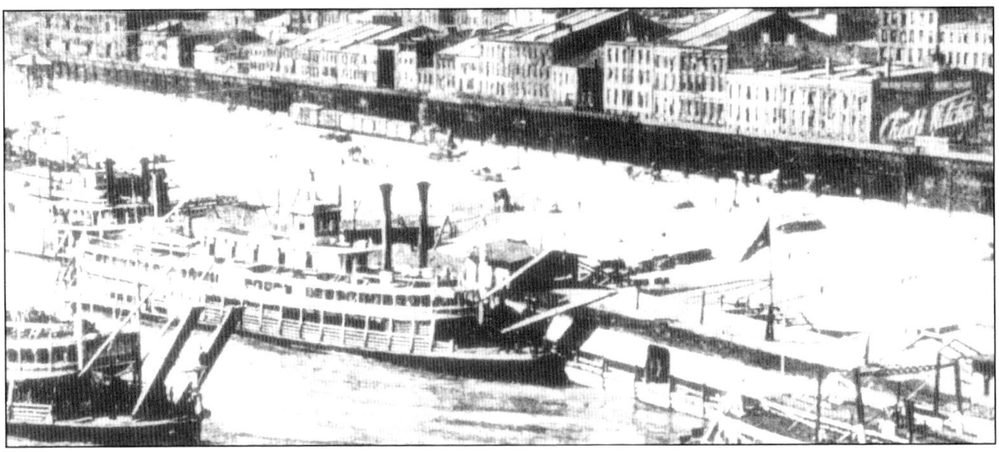

THE ST. LOUIS LEVEE, BUSY WITH STEAMBOAT TRAFFIC. (Courtesy of SLU Archives) Early in May 1861, two captains of the pro-Confederate Missouri Volunteer Militia paid a visit to Jefferson Davis in Montgomery, Alabama. They delivered a request from Governor Jackson for siege guns to be sent to St. Louis to aid in the capture of the arsenal. President Davis concurred and sent the heavy artillery in boxes marked "Tamaroa Marble" to deflect questions about their contents. On May 9, the guns arrived by steamboat at the St. Louis levee and were quickly transported to Camp Jackson. In spite of the attempted secrecy, Union spies quickly informed Captain Lyon of the clandestine operation. Lyon is said to have donned an old woman's dress and veil and proceeded with driver and carriage directly to the encampment where, blending in with other visitors moving about the camp, he soon located the artillery boxes. Returning immediately to the arsenal, Lyon firmed up plans to capture Camp Jackson.

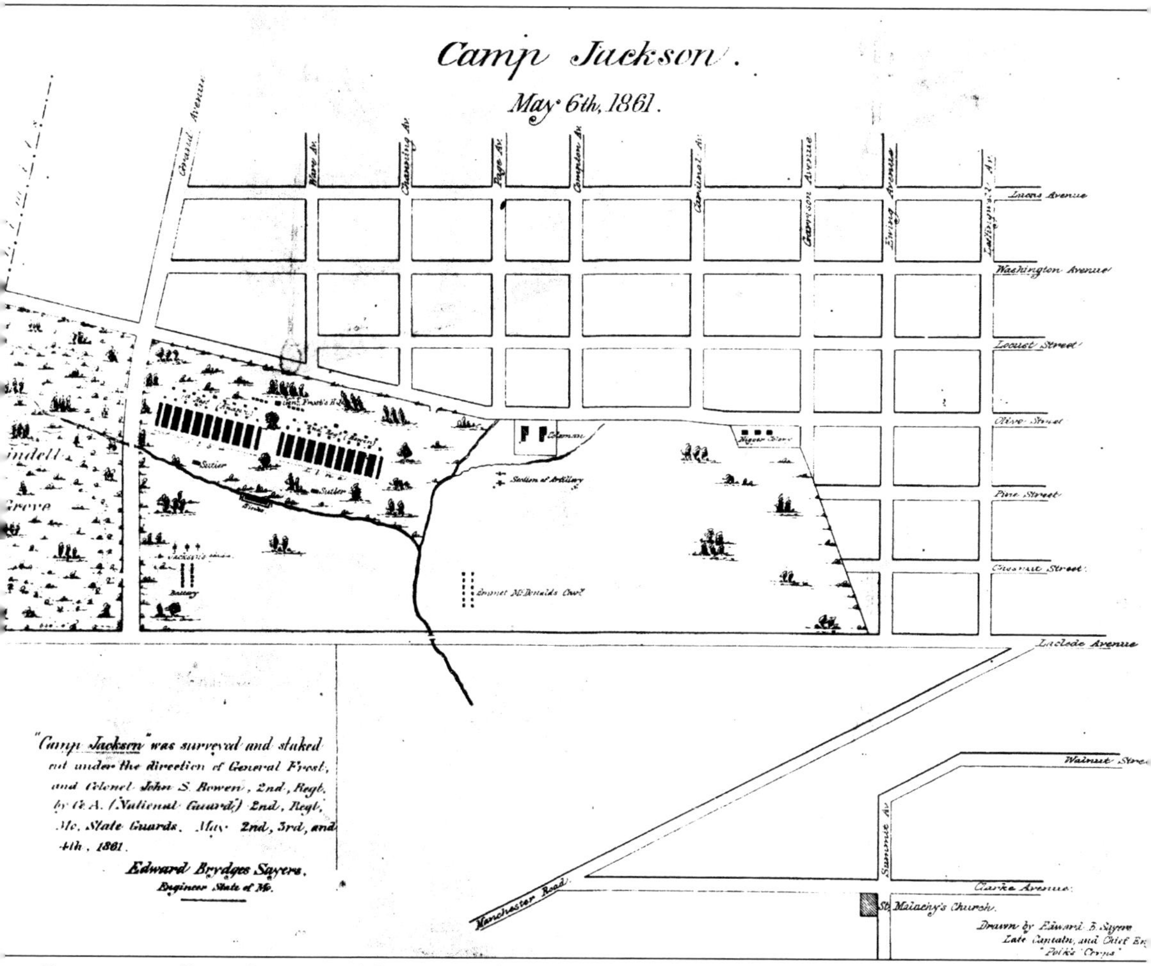

LAYOUT OF CAMP JACKSON, MAY 1861. (Courtesy of Mercantile Library) Prior to the spring encampment of the Missouri Volunteer Militia, the Engineer Corps laid out the bivouac area in Lindell Grove at the point where Olive Street angled toward the northwest. The site was surveyed on May 2–4, 1861, by Edward B. Sayers, an engineer for the state of Missouri. The encampment was named Camp Jackson, after the governor, and its interior streets were said to be named after well-known Confederate leaders. The grounds were fairly flat with Mill Creek running through the center. High ground dominated the site on the north and west sides. Only two houses stood within the area designated for the encampment. The grove was served by the Olive and Market Street railways, though the militia were marched to the spot via Olive Street. The encampment consisted of the First Brigade, which was the largest and best organized militia unit in the state, numbering nearly 1,300 officers and men. Only half of these were in camp, however, since the rest had been assigned to duty in other parts of the state. The brigade was divided into two regiments, the first commanded by Lieutenant Colonel John Knapp and the second by Colonel John S. Bowen. Three cavalry troops and one artillery battery rounded out the brigade.

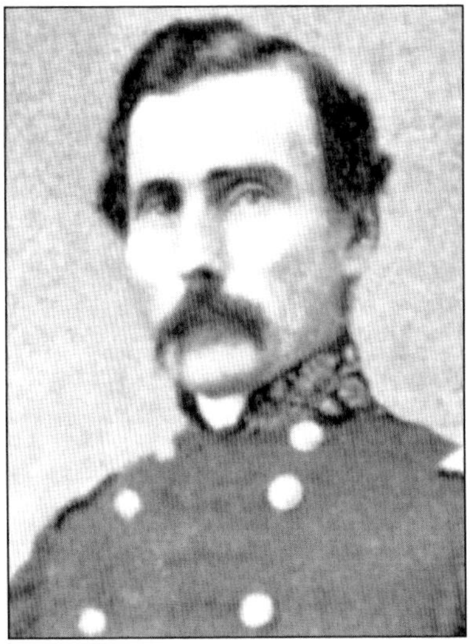

Brigadier General Daniel M. Frost, Commander, First Brigade, Missouri Volunteer Militia. (Miller, SLU Archives) The 37-year-old commander of Camp Jackson was an 1844 graduate of West Point. He had served on active duty for nine years, including two years in the Mexican War, at which time he was breveted for gallantry at the Battle of Cerro Gordo. In 1853 he resigned his commission to enter the lumber and fur business in St. Louis, by which he became quite wealthy. In 1854 he was elected to the Missouri State Senate. When the Missouri Volunteer Militia was formed in 1858 to defend the state against threats from North or South, Frost was appointed brigadier general in charge of the First Military District, which covered St. Louis City and County. He soon joined Governor Jackson in supporting the secession of Missouri from the Union and sought permission to capture the arsenal for the use of the Confederacy. He was in command of Camp Jackson on May 10, 1861, when Lyon and his troops marched on the encampment, demanding its surrender. Recognizing that he was outnumbered ten to one, Frost capitulated to Lyon's demands. He was eventually paroled as a prisoner-of-war, but accepted a commission as brigadier in the Confederate Army in March 1862. He resigned his commission in 1863 in order to care for his wife and family, who had suffered at the hands of pro-Unionists in St. Louis. After the war Frost was repatriated and settled on a farm in St. Louis County. He received many state and federal honors in the post-war years and died peacefully on his farm in 1900.

Colonel John S. Bowen of Carondelet, in the Uniform of the Missouri Volunteer Militia. (Courtesy of Missouri Historical Society) John Bowen was born and raised in Georgia, the fourth of thirteen children. He attended the U.S. Military Academy, graduating in 1853, and was stationed at Jefferson Barracks with the Regiment of Mounted Rifles. He married Mary Kennerly, the daughter of a prestigious St. Louis family which had strong roots in the South. He resigned from the army in 1856 to become an architect and engineer in St. Louis. He and Mary built a home in Carondelet in 1859 (which still stands today with a marker from the Carondelet Historical Society). Bowen served as a lieutenant colonel in the Missouri Militia and was one of the commanders of the Southwest Expedition which saw service on the Kansas-Missouri border in 1860 and '61. As a result of the notoriety gained from this action, Bowen was elected colonel of the 2nd Regiment of the Missouri Volunteer Militia in March 1861. He was in command of this regiment at Camp Jackson on May 10, when it was captured and paroled. Although under parole, Bowen went straight to Richmond, Virginia, and was commissioned a colonel in the Confederate Army. Bowen organized the 1st Missouri Infantry Regiment, CSA, the first Missouri unit in the Confederacy, and moved up through the ranks to Major General. His career ended tragically on July 3, 1863, at the siege of Vicksburg, when fellow St. Louisian, U.S. Grant, forced the Confederate surrender. Bowen died of dysentery 10 days later, or, as one sympathetic admirer noted on the *carte de visite*, pictured on the right, "Bowen he died of grief."

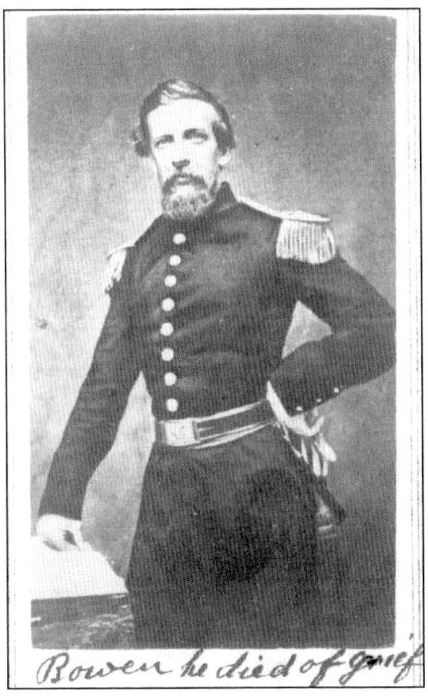

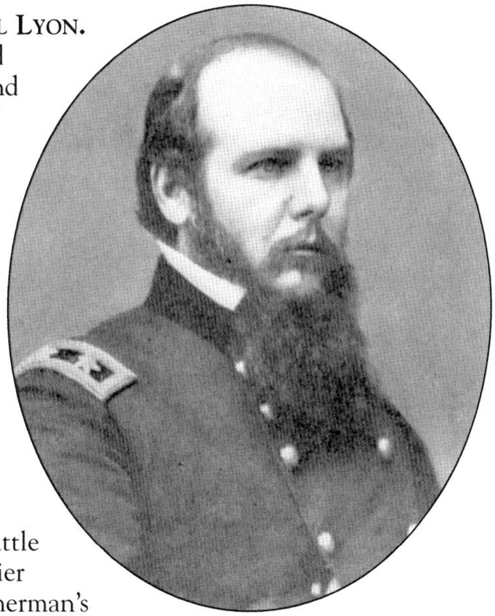

John Schofield, Chief of Staff for General Lyon. (Miller, SLU Archives) John Schofield graduated from West Point in 1853. He served in Florida and taught at West Point before requesting a leave of absence in 1860 to teach physics at Washington University in St. Louis. When the war broke out, Schofield became a mustering officer for the state of Missouri and was eventually appointed a major in the First Missouri Infantry (USA) which he reorganized into an artillery unit. He became chief of staff to General Lyon and was on a sortie for the general at Wilson's Creek when Lyon was killed. In November 1861, Schofield was appointed brigadier general of volunteers in command of all Union militia in the state of Missouri. After involvement in numerous campaigns and defeating General Hood at the Battle of Franklin in 1864, Schofield was made a brigadier general in the regular army. He participated in Sherman's operations at the close of the war and some years later became commander of the army. General Schofield retired to Florida and died in 1906. His most notable contribution to U.S. military history was his recommendation that a naval base be established at Pearl Harbor. The base was built, and a now-famous army barracks in Hawaii was named in his honor.

Captain Thomas W. Sweeny, 2nd U.S. Infantry, as he Appeared at Camp Jackson. (Courtesy of Sweeny Museum) Thomas Sweeny was born in County Cork, Ireland, on Christmas Day in 1820. At age 12, he followed his widowed mother to New York. When he came of age, he enlisted in a local militia unit, which became Company A of the 1st New York Volunteers in the Mexican War. At the Battle of Churubusco he lost his right arm, but chose to remain in the army. In 1848 he was commissioned a lieutenant in the 2nd U.S. Infantry and he remained in that unit until the Civil War. He was promoted to captain in January of 1861 and served under Nathaniel Lyon at the arsenal. After the Camp Jackson Affair, Sweeny was ordered to Springfield, Missouri, to confront the Confederate threat. On July 1, he led an attack on Forsythe, Missouri, and on August 10, was in the Battle of Wilson's Creek, where he was wounded in the thigh. In October 1861, he was promoted to colonel and took command of the 52nd Illinois Infantry. He led the regiment in the Battle of Shiloh where he was again severely wounded. Sweeny was promoted to brigadier general in April 1862 and participated in other battles in the western theater, distinguishing himself in the Battle of Atlanta. After the war he joined the ill-fated Fenian Invasion of Canada, for which he was arrested but then released. He retired as a brigadier general of regulars and died in 1892 in Astoria, New York. A very fine Civil War Museum has been established in his honor at Republic, Missouri, by Dr. Tom and Karen Sweeney.

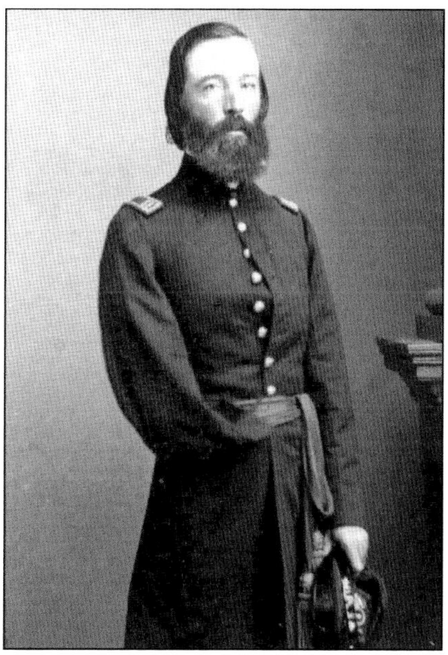

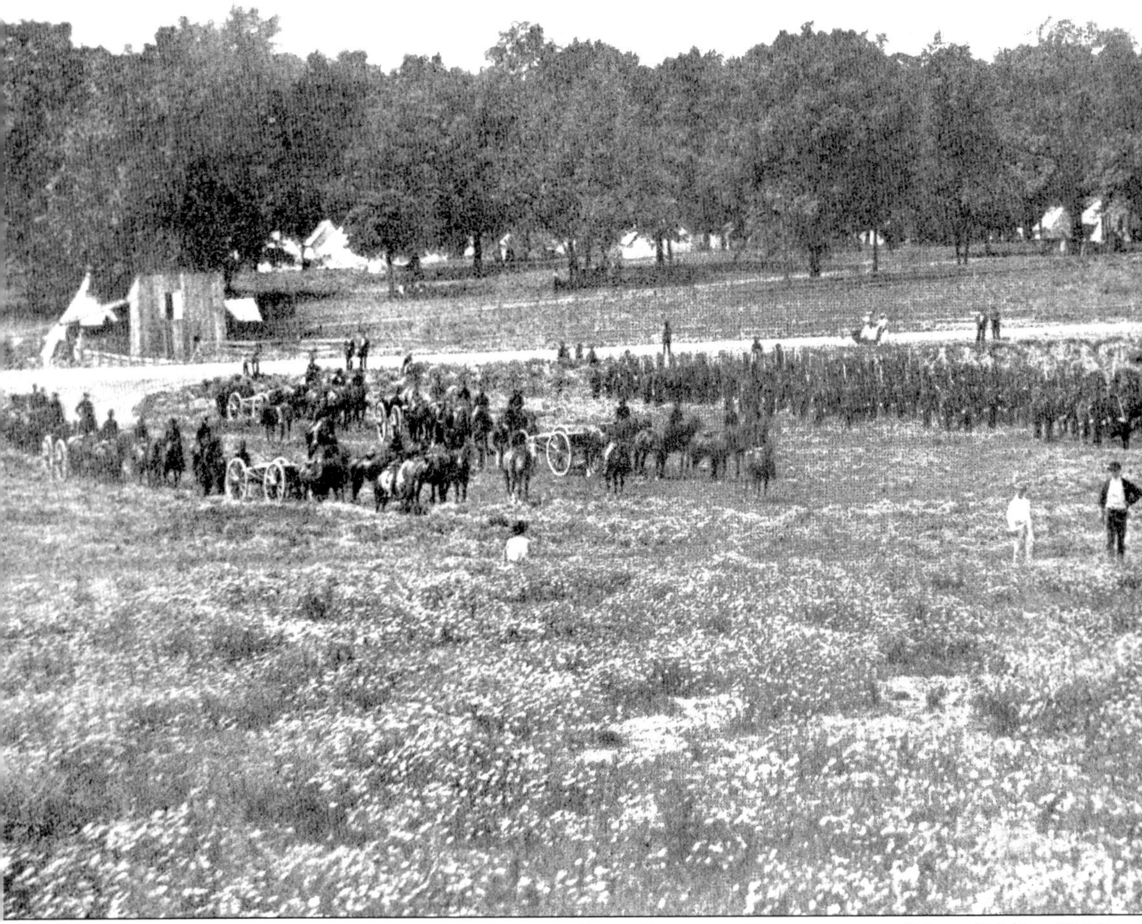

View of Federal Troops on the Site of Camp Jackson Later in the War. (Miller, SLU Archives) Lindell's Grove, on the far western outskirts of the city of St. Louis, was the site of the Camp Jackson encampment in May 1861. After the Missouri Militia was captured and led away from the site, the property remained in federal hands for the rest of the war. Union troops used the site as a drill ground, as seen in the photo above. After the war, the site was subdivided into lots and sold to private citizens. By the 1880s the area was full of homes and businesses. In 1867, Saint Louis University had purchased several acres west of Grand Avenue, across from the former site of Camp Jackson. Between 1884 and 1888 the University constructed buildings on their Grand

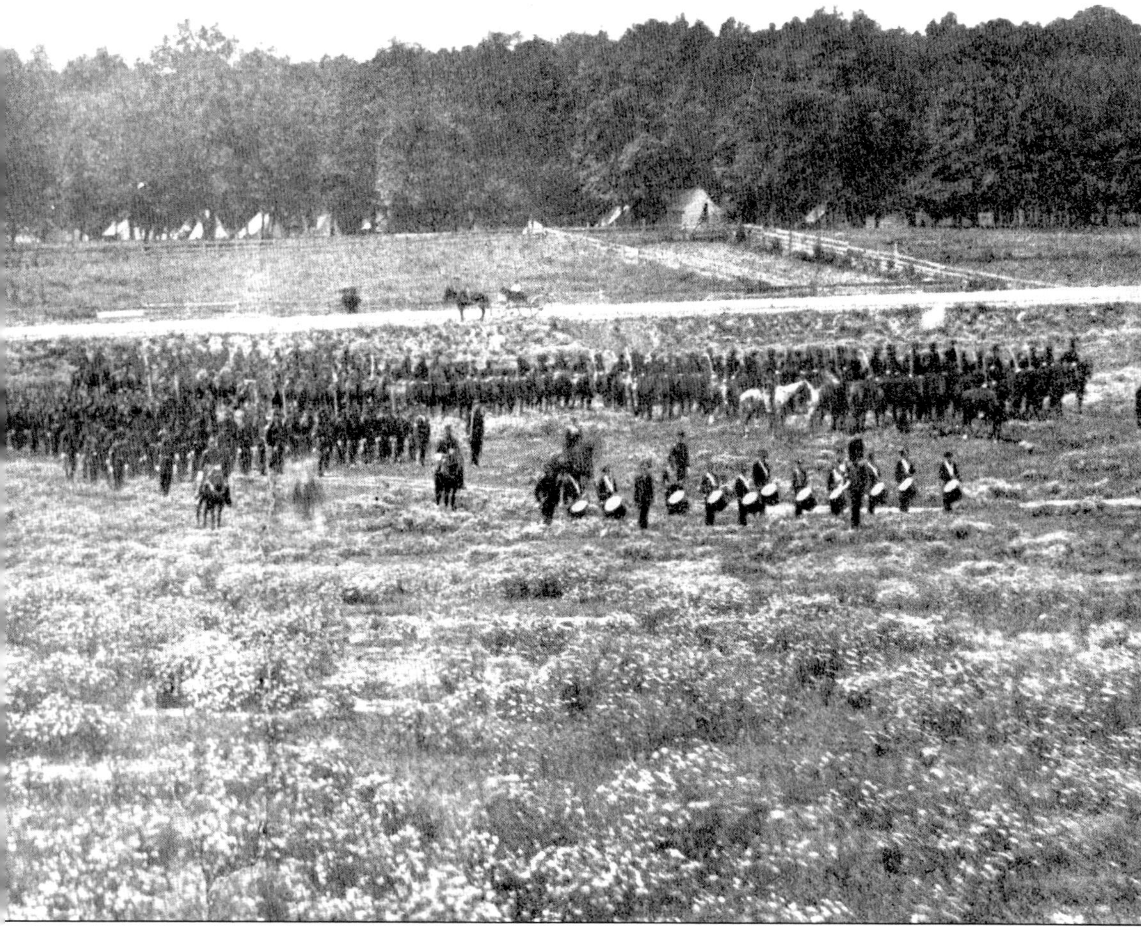

Avenue site until the school owned much of the property for two blocks west of Grand. In 1959, Harriet Frost Fordyce, daughter of General Daniel Frost, gave the university over one million dollars to purchase much of the area formerly occupied by Camp Jackson. The area was called the Mill Creek Development and the university planned to construct several buildings there. Harriet Frost had only one request of the university: that the campus be named Frost Campus after her father. This was done, and a statue of General Lyon which graced the center of the property was removed to Lyon Park. Today, on Frost Campus of Saint Louis University where the statue of General Lyon once stood, a small marker tells the story of the Camp Jackson Affair.

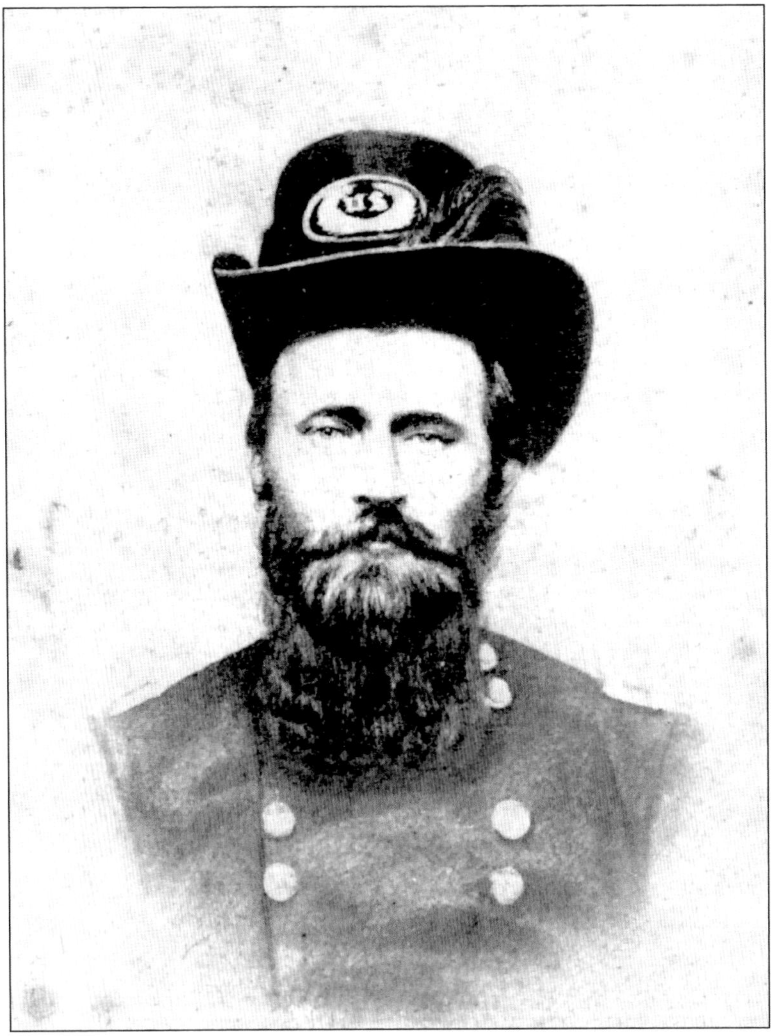

COLONEL ULYSSES S. GRANT, COMMANDER OF THE 21ST ILLINOIS VOLUNTEER INFANTRY REGIMENT. (Courtesy of Missouri Historical Society) When the Civil War broke out in April of 1861, Ulysses S. Grant was a civilian working in his family's leather goods store in Galena, Illinois. With the fall of Fort Sumter, Grant offered his services to the U.S. government in Washington. Despite the fact that he was a West Point graduate and had served 11 years on active duty, there was no response to Grant's offer. Eventually, Governor Richard Yates of Illinois asked Grant to recruit volunteers for ten regiments of Illinois militia. Grant agreed to do so. While he was enlisting a regiment at Belleville, Ilinois, in early May he had a few days free, so he went to visit family and friends in St. Louis. On the morning of May 10, Grant visited the arsenal and greeted Frank Blair who was at the head of his regiment, heading for Camp Jackson. Grant says in his *Memoirs*, "As the troops marched out of the enclosure around the arsenal, Blair was on his horse outside forming them into line preparatory to their march. I introduced myself to him and had a few moments' conversation and expressed my sympathy with his purpose." This was the first time Grant had formally met Blair. He also knew Nathaniel Lyon from West Point and in later western service. The day after the Camp Jackson affair, Grant resumed his recruiting duties in Illinois. On June 17, 1861, Governor Yates appointed him colonel of the 21st Illinois Volunteers and his unit was ordered to southern Missouri. Grant would go on to become the supreme commander of Union armies, accepting the surrender of R.E. Lee at Appomattox Court House in 1865. He would also serve as President of the United States from 1869 to 1877. He wrote his famous *Memoirs* in retirement while suffering from throat cancer, and died in New York on July 23, 1885. He is buried beside his wife, Julia, in a well-known tomb and monument in New York City.

WILLIAM TECUMSEH SHERMAN. (Miller, SLU Archives) One of the curious bystanders at Camp Jackson on that fateful afternoon of May 10, 1861, was William T. Sherman, citizen, who was at the time President of the Fifth Street Railroad, a streetcar company. Sherman had held the job for only a month, having moved to St. Louis from Louisiana when that state seceded from the Union. Sherman became a close friend of the wealthy and influential St. Louisian, John O'Fallon. He also maintained contact with former army colleagues. He states in his *Memoirs*, "I used also to go down to the arsenal occasionally to see Lyon, Totten, and other of my army acquaintance, and was glad to see them making preparations to defend their post, if not to assume the offensive." He writes further, "I remember going to the arsenal on the 9th of May, taking my children with me in the streetcars. Within the arsenal wall were drawn up in parallel lines four regiments of the 'Home Guards,' and I saw men distributing cartridges to the boxes. I also saw General Lyon running about with his hair in the wind, his pockets full of papers, wild and irregular, but I knew him to be a man of vehement purpose and of determined action." The next day, having heard the commotion in regard to Camp Jackson, Sherman, his brother-in-law Charles Ewing, and his son Willie went to the site of the action and observed the prisoners lined up between rows of Union troops. They also witnessed the first gunfire as a drunken civilian fired at the soldiers and the nervous reservists returned fire into the crowd of onlookers. Sherman and his party threw themselves to the ground until the firing subsided, then headed back home with the scene of carnage behind them. Four days later Sherman was called to U.S. service with a commission as colonel of the 13th Regular Infantry. He eventually gained as much fame as U.S. Grant, ending up as general of the army. He died in New York City in 1891 and was buried in Calvary Cemetery, St. Louis.

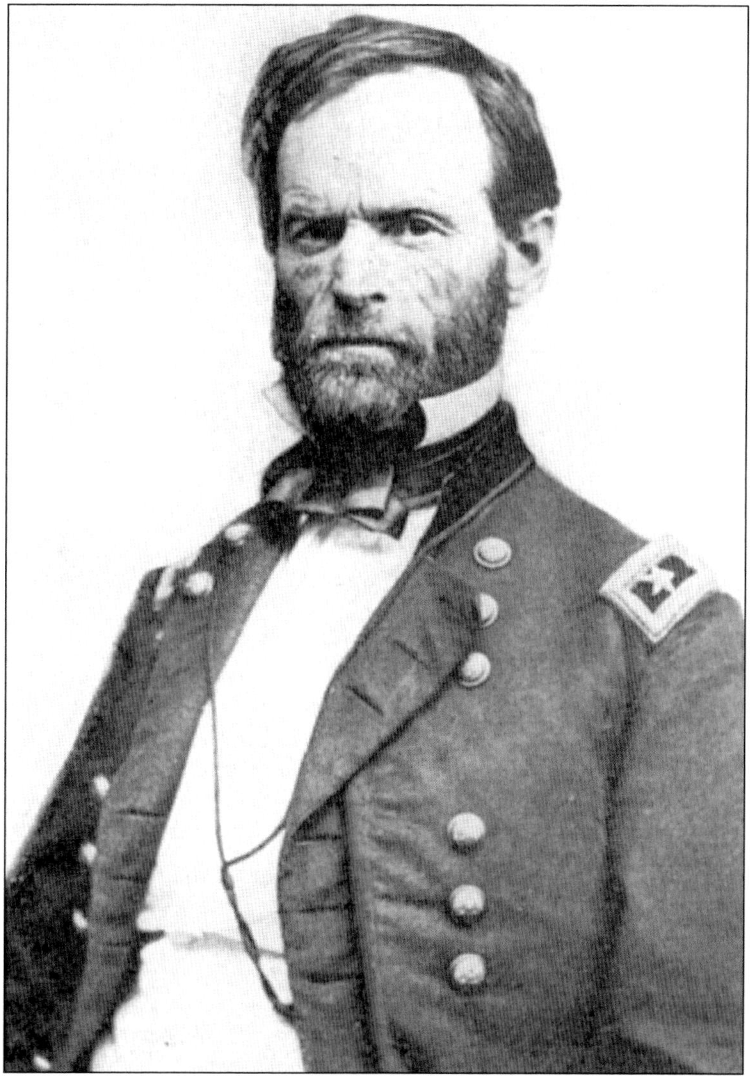

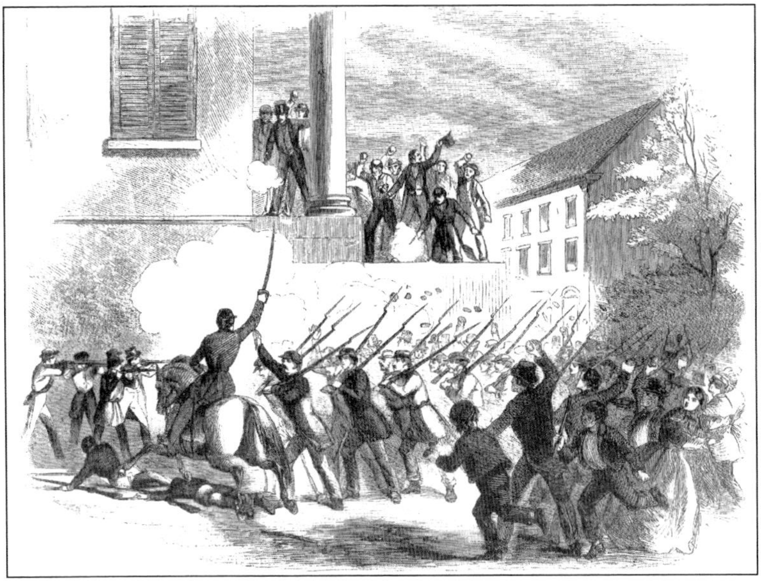

Ambush of New Recruits at 5th and Walnut Streets. (*Harper's Weekly*, June 1, 1861, Author's Collection) On the day after the Camp Jackson Affair, pro-secessionists burned hot with resentment at the demonstration of raw Union power in the streets of St. Louis. The prisoners of Camp Jackson were held overnight at the arsenal and were paroled the next day after taking oaths of allegiance to the Union. In the meantime, the U.S. Reserve Corps continued enlisting 90-day volunteers, most of whom were German immigrants. The 5th Reserve completed its organization at the arsenal early in the evening and marched out of the arsenal, heading for north St. Louis a thousand strong. As they marched west on Walnut Street, between Fifth and Sixth Streets, an angry mob of secessionists confronted them with epithets, throwing stones and dirt. Then, from the vicinity of the front steps of the Second Presbyterian Church, a pistol shot was fired and a soldier fell dead. Soon shots rang out from windows along the street and the panicked soldiers began firing in all directions. Before long, eight people lay dead, including four soldiers, with several others wounded. In the confusion some soldiers had fired into their own ranks. Order was restored by Mayor Daniel Taylor who pleaded with the crowd from the steps of the church, but bitterness continued to seethe on both sides in the conflict.

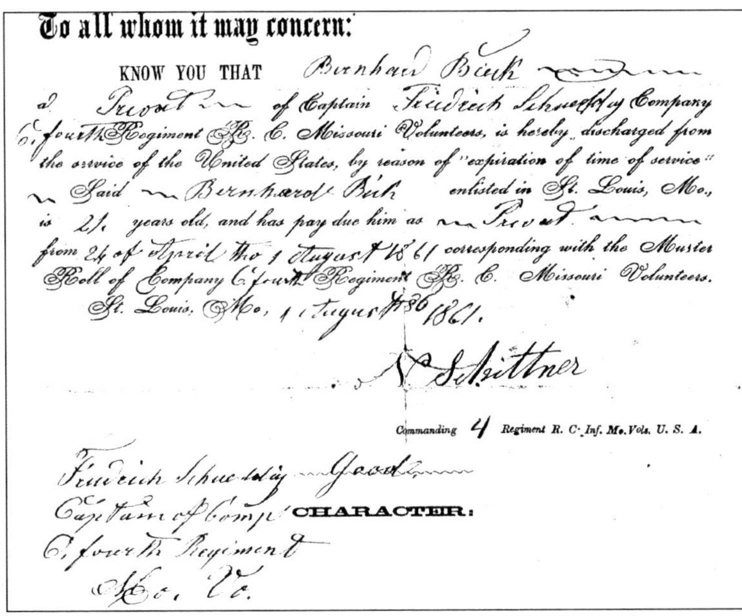

To all whom it may concern:

KNOW YOU THAT Bernhard Bick

a Private of Captain Friedrich Schuchtag's Company C, fourth Regiment R. C. Missouri Volunteers, is hereby discharged from the service of the United States, by reason of "expiration of time of service"

Said Bernhard Bick enlisted in St. Louis, Mo., is 21 years old, and has pay due him as Private from 24 of April to 1 August 1861 corresponding with the Muster Roll of Company C fourth Regiment R. C. Missouri Volunteers.

St. Louis, Mo., 1 August 1861.

N. Schittner

Commanding 4 Regiment R. C. Inf. Mo. Vols. U. S. A.

Friedrich Schuchtag Good

Captain of Comp. CHARACTER:

C, fourth Regiment

Mo. Vo.

Sample Discharge Certificate for a 90-Day Recruit. (Courtesy of John Vollmann) The certificate on the right was issued to Private Bernhard Bick of the 4th Regiment U.S. Reserve Corps, after 90 days of service. Private Bick was present with his regiment at Camp Jackson and later continued his service in central Missouri.

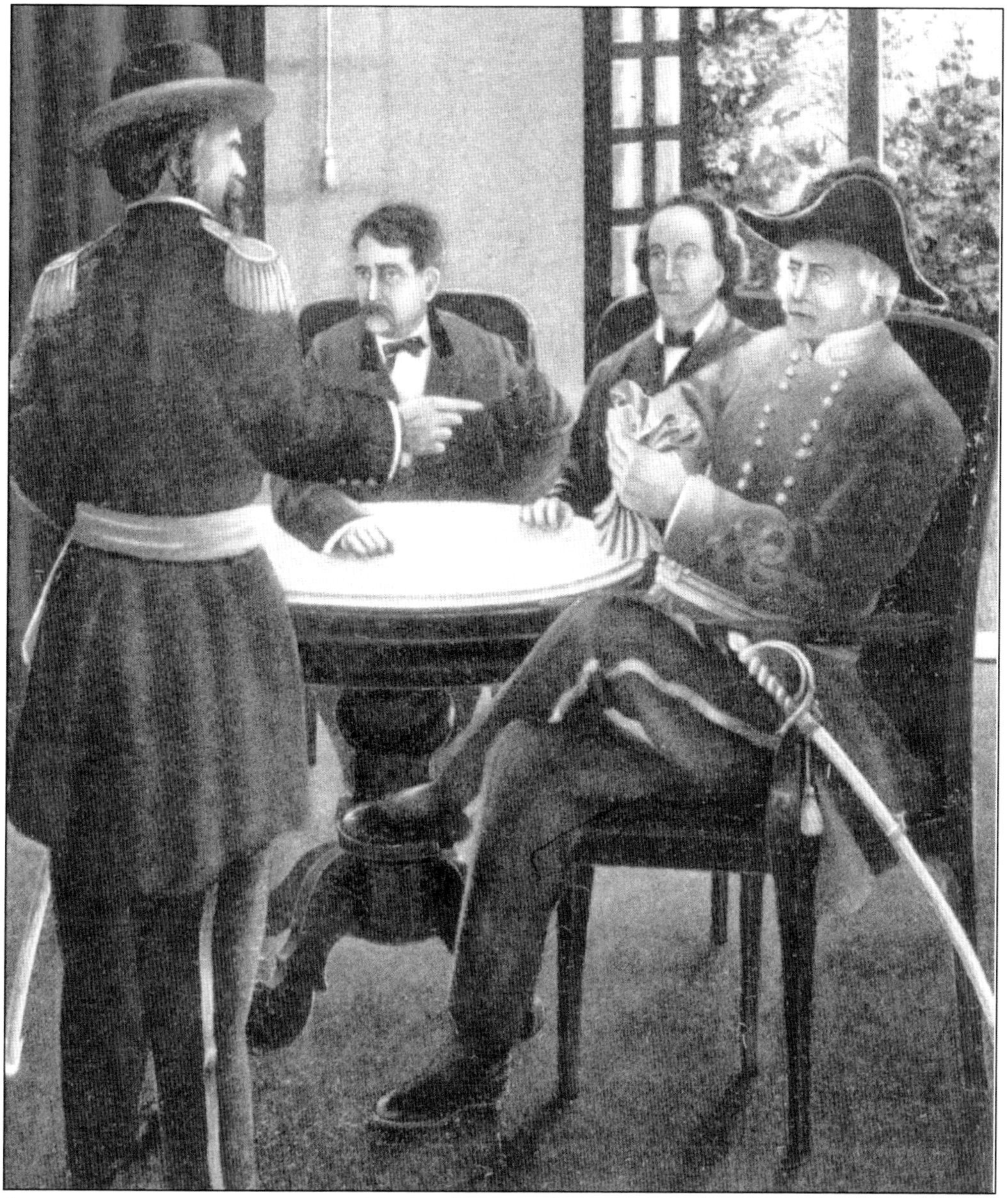

SHOWDOWN AT THE PLANTERS' HOUSE HOTEL. (McElroy, SLU Archives) When General Harney signed a pact with Sterling Price on May 21, pledging that federal forces would not interfere in Missouri affairs as long as Price and his militia kept the peace within the state, Union leaders could no longer trust Harney to protect federal interests in Missouri. By prearrangement with President Lincoln, Frank Blair produced an order relieving Harney of command and General Lyon was assigned to take his place. On June 11, at the request of Governor Jackson, a meeting was held at Planters' House with Lyon, Blair, Price, and Jackson in attendance. For several hours they argued their positions until Lyon is said to have stood up and declared: "Rather than concede to the State of Missouri for one single instant, the right to dictate to my government in any matter however important, I would see you, you, and you, and every man, woman, and child in the state dead and buried. This means War!" With that he stalked out of the room and the Missourians made haste to leave St. Louis. The war was on.

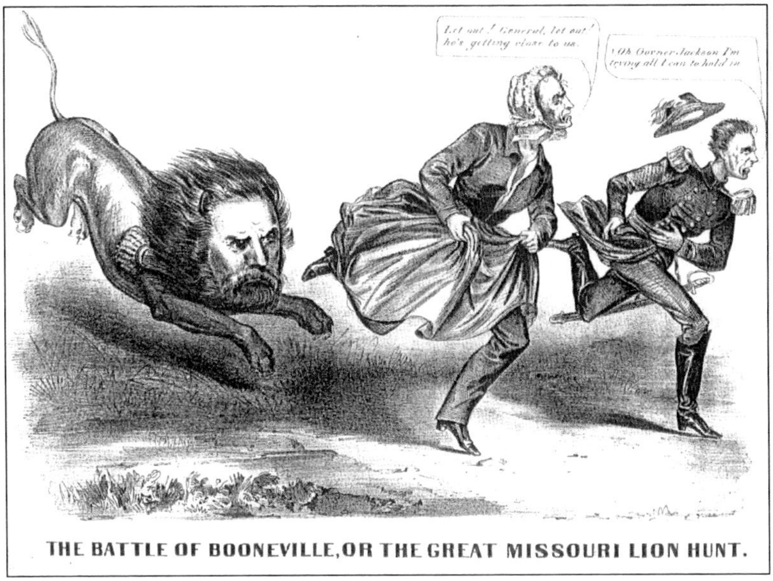

"THE GREAT MISSOURI LION HUNT." (Courtesy of Missouri Historical Society) As Jackson and Price headed west by train to Jefferson City, they paused periodically to cut telegraph wires and to burn bridges in order to slow the anticipated federal advance. On June 15, Lyon led a Union flotilla up the Missouri River to capture the state capital. Jackson and his administration fled to Boonsville to seek the protection of Missouri Guard troops. On June 17, Lyon's force attacked the Missouri Guard at Boonsville and drove them southwest toward Springfield. Union newspapers had a heyday depicting the panicked retreat of the Missouri rebels with Lyon snapping at their heels. All across the north, Lyon was hailed as a hero for his relentless pursuit of the enemies of the Union.

GENERAL LYON MEETS HIS FATE IN THE BATTLE OF WILSON'S CREEK. (Courtesy of SLU Archives) Lyon's expedition began running out of steam as it reached Springfield, so he settled in to re-supply and reinforce for the next stage of his planned attack. Unfortunately, the new commander of the West, John C. Fremont, did not share Lyon's goals and refused to send him the much-needed supplies and reinforcements. In spite of advice to the contrary from his subordinate commanders, Lyon decided to go it alone against rebel forces that outnumbered him at least three to one. Ben McCulloch had entered Missouri from Arkansas with fresh Confederate troops and he linked up with Price near Wilson Creek. Here, on August 10, Lyon attempted a surprise two-pronged attack on the rebel camp. Lyon approached from the north while Sigel attempted to swing around from the south. Although taken by surprise, the rebels rallied and destroyed the federal forces. Lyon himself was killed while leading a desperate charge into a strong Confederate line. The tattered remains of Lyon's army retreated to Springfield, but they had so bloodied the rebels that there was no counter-attack, and this Union defeat turned out to be the first step in saving Missouri for the Union.

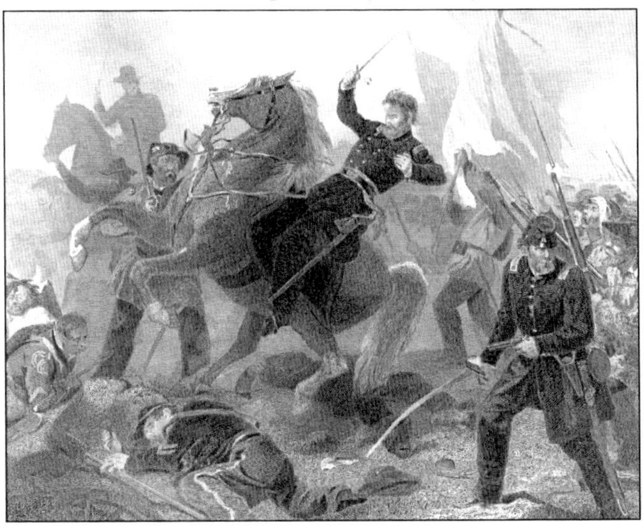

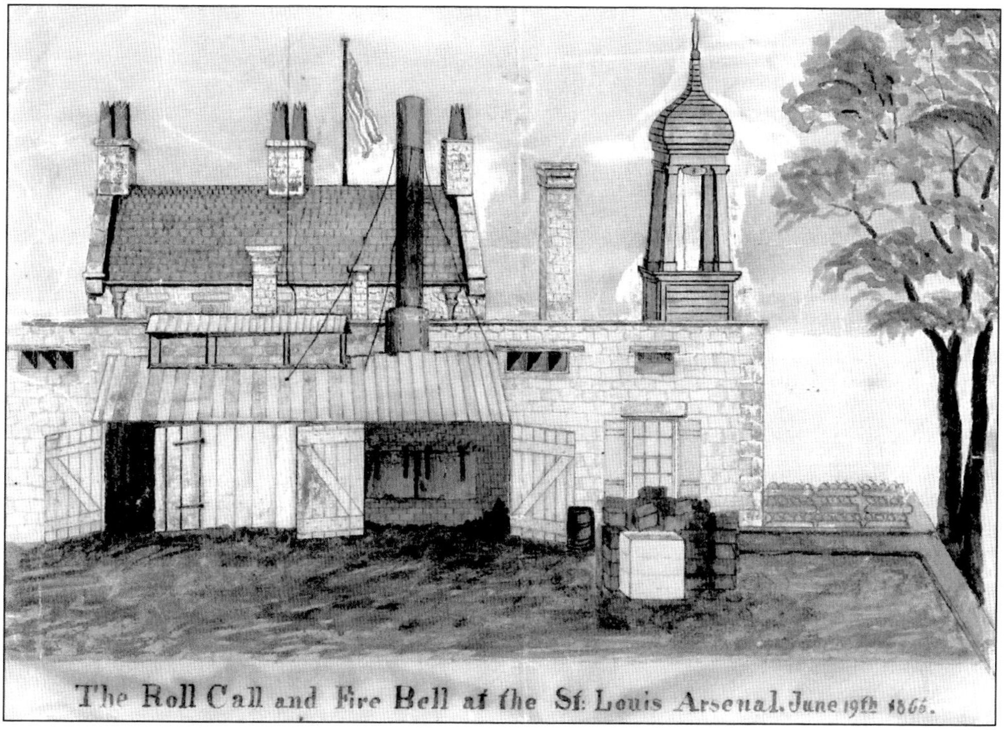

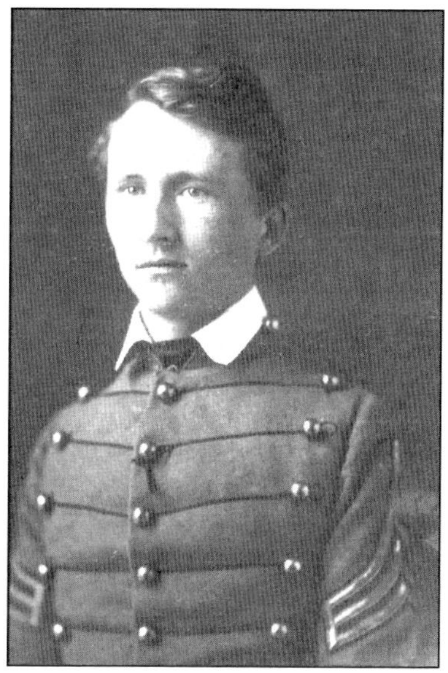

FIRE BELL AT THE ST. LOUIS ARSENAL. (Courtesy of Missouri Historical Society) Back in St. Louis, the work continued unabated to fortify the arsenal. After Wilson's Creek, however, the viable secessionist threat receded and the St. Louis Arsenal once again became the hotbed of ordnance activity. Hundreds of troops and civilians worked around the clock to provide the arms and ammunition required by the insatiable appetites of the armies of the West. One young soldier stationed at the arsenal exercised his artistic talents painting scenes around the arsenal. In the above watercolor we see the fire bell which was used on several occasions to summon personnel to extinguish fires that threatened the volatile contents of the arsenal.

CADET ADELBERT R. BUFFINGTON, YOUNGEST OFFICER AT THE ARSENAL. (Courtesy of West Point) Adelbert Buffington graduated from West Point in the fateful spring of 1861, the month after war broke out at Fort Sumter. Buffington was assigned to the Ordnance Branch, was sent for a month of training "in the field," and then was posted to the St. Louis Arsenal. Buffington arrived on June 8, just a month after the Camp Jackson Affair, and was very quickly introduced to the duties of an ordnance officer at war. He remained at St. Louis for a year and four months, through the most trying period of the arsenal's history. In October 1862, Buffington was assigned to field duty, and a year later to "special duty," which usually meant service at the ordnance headquarters in Washington D.C. In later years Buffington would serve at several ordnance installations, including Watervliet, and would rise to the rank of Lieutenant Colonel, serving late into the nineteenth century.

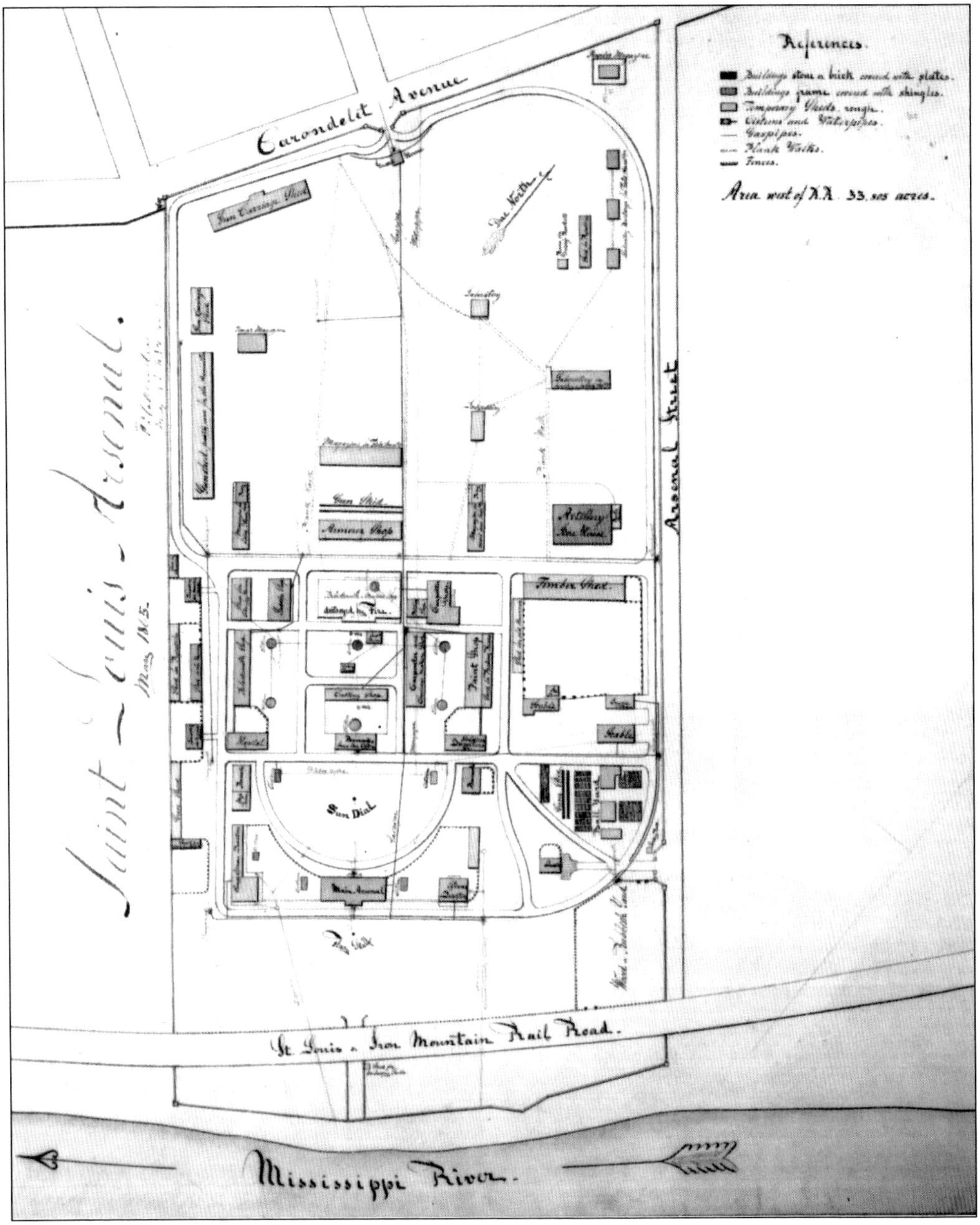

SITE PLAN OF THE ST. LOUIS ARSENAL IN 1865. (Courtesy of the National Archives) As the war came to a close in the spring of 1865, the Ordnance Department was already giving thought to which of its arsenals would continue in operation and which would be closed down. The department ordered a thorough drawing of the St. Louis Arsenal, depicting all of the buildings on the premises, whether permanent or temporary. Captain Franklin D. Callender, post commander, provided the excellent drawing shown above. It is clear from the site plan that the arsenal complex grew a great deal through the demands of the war, but once the armaments of war had been turned in and the armies disbanded, there would no longer be a need for an arsenal at this location. Six years after the war, the arsenal was disbanded and the installation began life anew as a cavalry recruitment post.

Eight

New Life for the Arsenal (1865–1996)

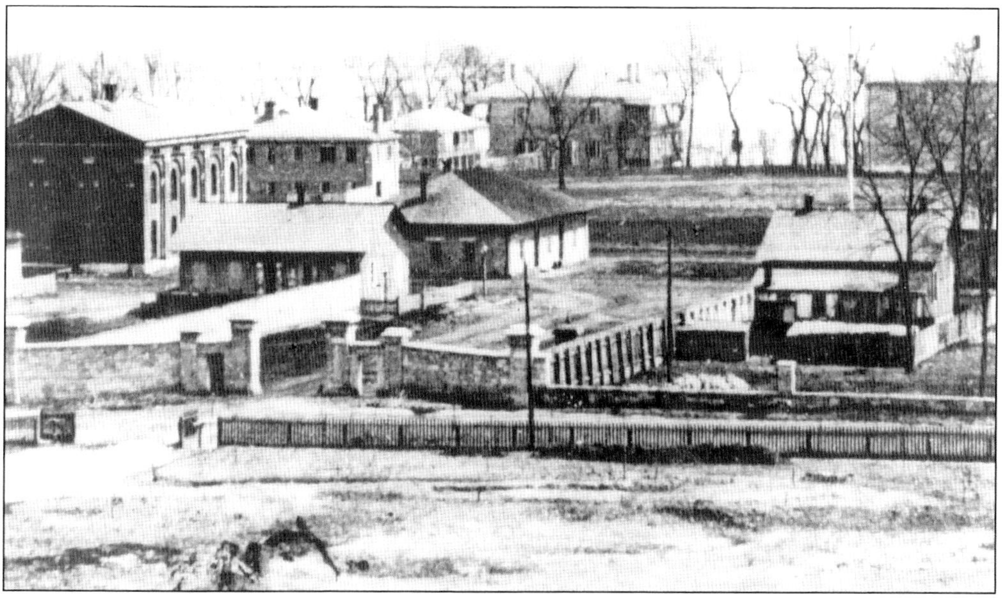

View of the "New" Arsenal as its Mission Changes After the War, c. 1872. (Courtesy of NIMA) After the Civil War, the St. Louis Arsenal served as a major demobilization point for the armies of the West. Thousands of small arms, hundreds of artillery pieces, and millions of rounds of ammunition were turned in to the installation. This included captured Confederate ordnance. Most of the cannons and many small arms were sold for scrap. In fact, foundries in the St. Louis area bought up staggering amounts of scrap iron to mold pipes for the expanding city sewer system. The federal government decided to transfer the ordnance function of the arsenal, first to Jefferson Barracks, then to Rock Island, Illinois. The arsenal was converted to a cavalry recruitment post on January 16, 1871, and was named the St. Louis Depot. In 1873, the name was changed to St. Louis Barracks. It turned out to be unsuited to that purpose, so in 1879 it became the St. Louis Clothing Depot. From 1884 to 1923 it was a general quartermaster depot and from 1923 to 1952 it served as a medical depot. It had made a complete transition from producer of ordnance to producer of medical supplies. Although the name and function of the installation changed many times over the years, old habits die hard and it continued to be known as "The Arsenal" for generations after that designation ceased to be accurate.

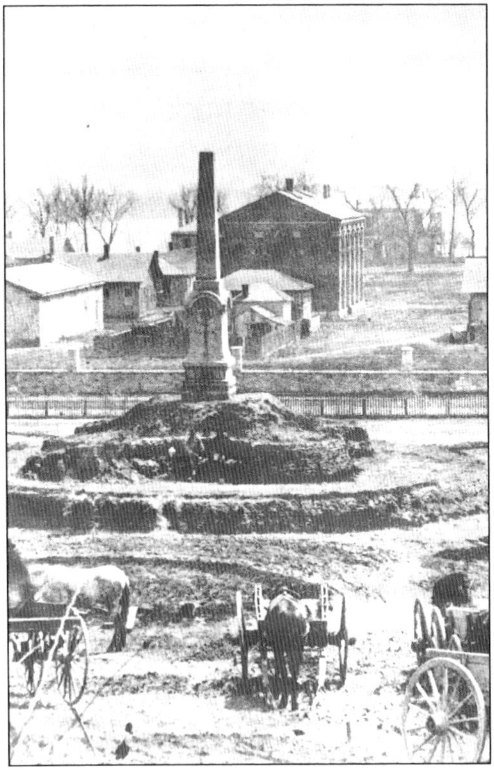

CONSTRUCTION OF GENERAL LYON MEMORIAL IN LYON PARK, 1874. (Courtesy of NIMA) It was clear, after the war, that the new installation would require less physical space than the old arsenal, so two changes were made in the use of the property. In 1871, all of the arsenal property west of Second Street was ceded to the City of St. Louis on the condition that a city park be created there with a fitting monument to honor General Nathaniel Lyon. The city agreed to this condition and nearly 10 acres between Second Street and Carondelet Road (soon to be renamed Broadway) were transferred to the city. A new Second Street was constructed in front of the installation and a new wall and gateway were installed. The above image shows the Lyon monument under construction close to the new front gate. Secondly, in 1882, all of the land between the railroad tracks and the river front was transferred to the Army Corps of Engineers so a service facility could be constructed on the site. This comprised about 5 acres, leaving the installation with about 22 acres of usable space.

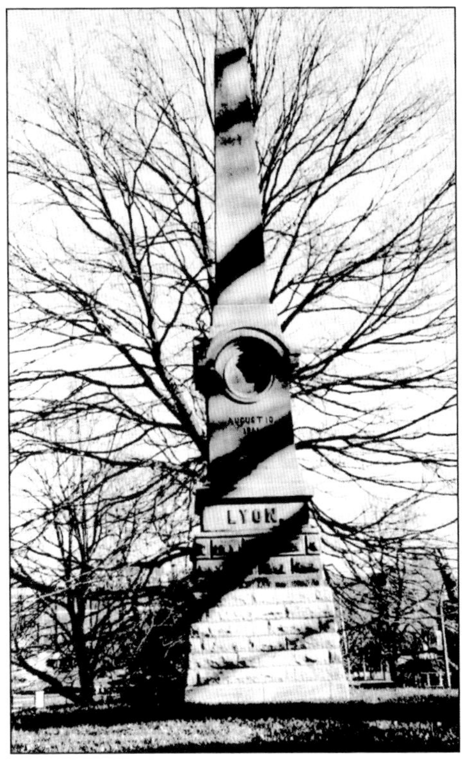

MONUMENT TO NATHANIEL LYON IN LYON PARK, 2001. (Photo by the author) The monument to General Lyon was in the shape of an obelisk, with his name carved above the limestone base, and the date of his death, August 10, 1861, above his name. Originally, brass engravings are said to have been mounted in the circular depressions half way up the monument, but they have long since been removed, perhaps by vandals. At times in the past, ornate gardens were planted around the base of the obelisk, but today only grass remains. Another monument to the general was erected in 1960 after being transferred from the Mill Creek Development, the former site of Camp Jackson. That statue was placed in the northwest corner of the park, on the former site of the small powder magazine and directly across Broadway from the Anheuser Busch complex.

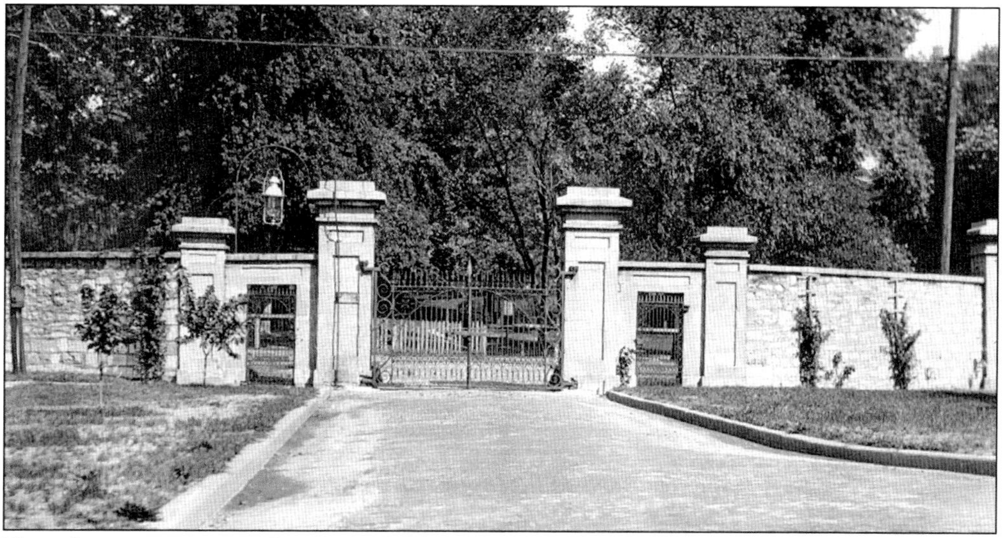

NEW GATEWAY AT THE CENTRAL ENTRANCE TO THE INSTALLATION, C. 1905. (Courtesy of NIMA) When the property for Lyon Park was separated from the installation, a new street had to be constructed running north-south in front of the post. This was named Second Street. In the approximate middle of the block, the above gateway was built. Its design appears identical to the old north gate which was built in 1847 (see page 64) and may, in fact, have been the very same gateway moved to this new position. The above image shows the gate as it looked from inside the installation; Lyon Park is in the background. The gateway was later dismantled and moved to Jefferson Barracks. The image below shows the view just inside the gate, looking into the installation with the gateway to the rear of the photographer. Building 4 is on the left, 5 is on the right, and 14 is the center building seen in the distance. Buildings 4 and 5 are actually the remaining wings of the old armory building (see page 43) which burned down in 1863. These were salvaged and converted to independent use.

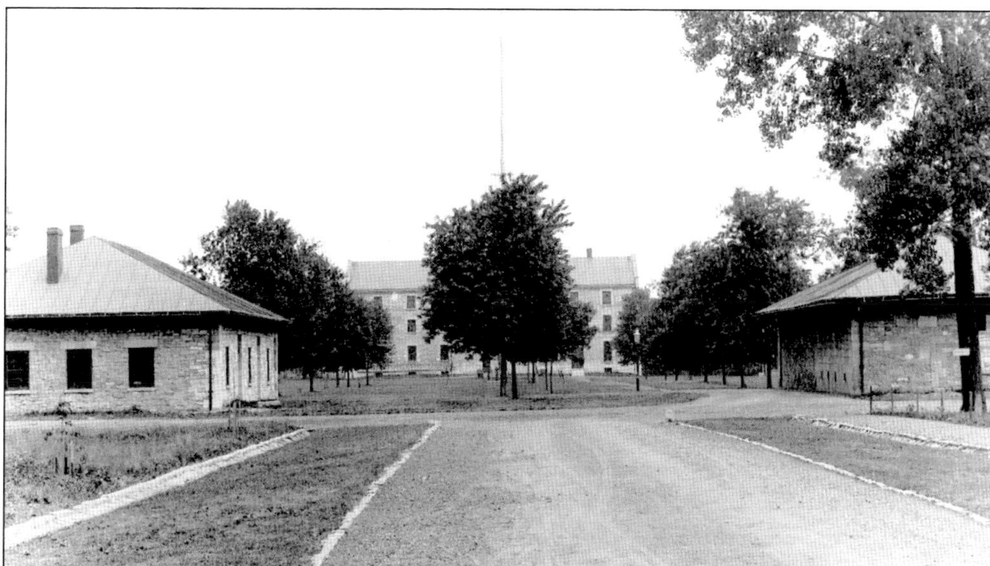

VIEW OF THE INSTALLATION AS SEEN FROM INSIDE THE MAIN GATE, C. 1905. (Courtesy of Missouri Historical Society)

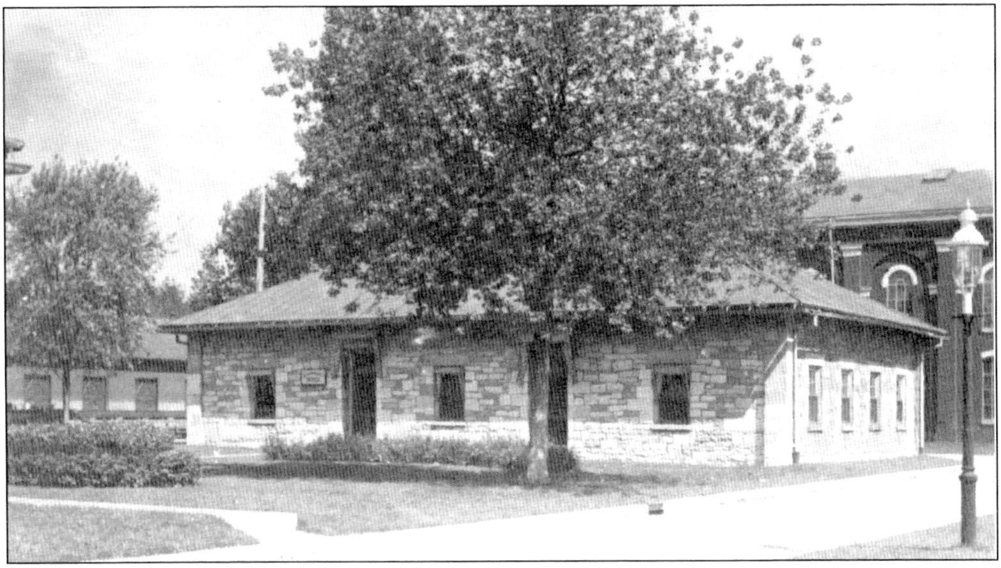

BUILDING 4—QUARTERMASTER OFFICE, C. 1905. (Courtesy of NIMA) This former north wing of the armory complex was remodeled after the Civil War and was used as a warehouse or administrative office in the late 19th century. From 1905 to 1918 it served as the quartermaster's office and later as a cafeteria for officers and civilians. In the mid-1920s it was again remodeled into a civilian family quarters. It became an enlisted family quarters after the Air Force took over in 1952. After Defense Mapping Agency Aerospace Center (DMAAC) took over in 1972, it served as the office of the inspector general. Under the National Imagery and Mapping Agency (NIMA) the Defense Investigative Service (DIS) and personnel security are housed here.

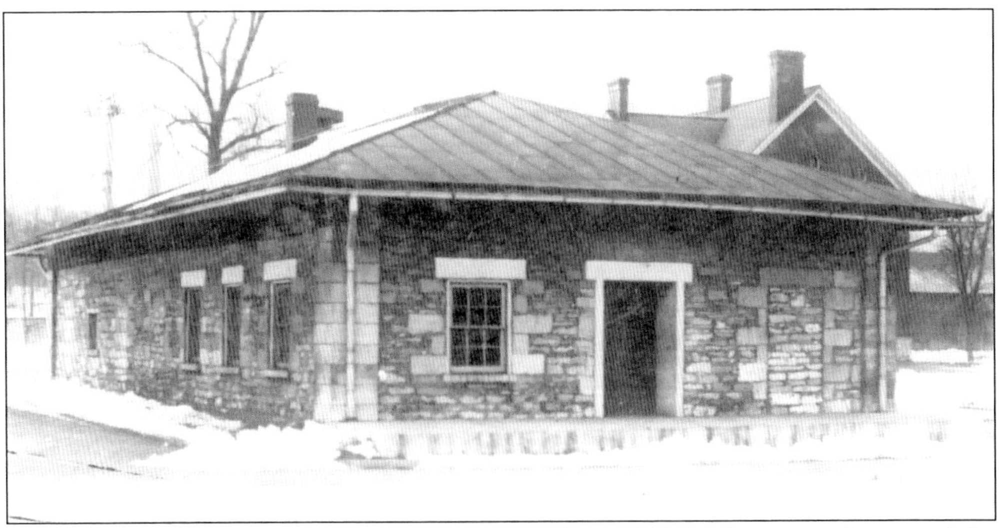

BUILDING 5—WAREHOUSE, C. 1905. (Courtesy of NIMA) The former south wing of the armory complex was remodeled after the fire and served several different functions. It is thought to have been used as a jail facility for some years and in the 1890s it was a clothing warehouse. In 1906 it was converted to a stationery warehouse and under the medical depot it was used to store medical supplies. Its uses are unknown under the Aeronautical Chart and Information Center (ACIC) from 1952 to '72. DMAAC used it for administrative offices after 1972. Today it houses the credit union for NIMA personnel.

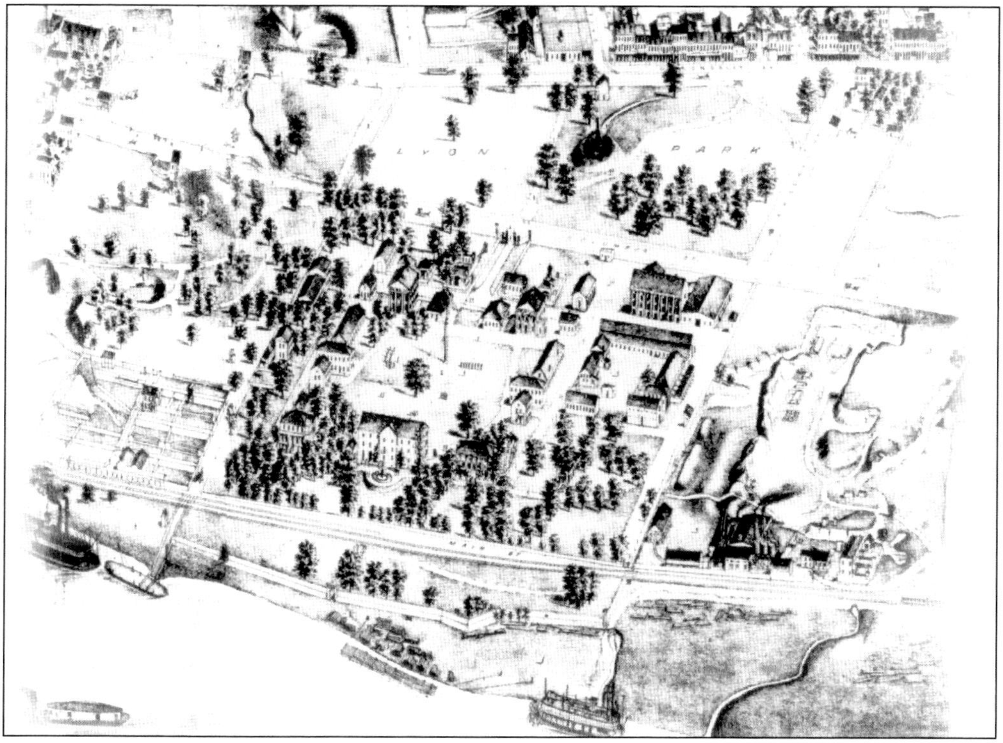

BIRD'S-EYE-VIEW OF THE INSTALLATION IN 1874. (Courtesy of NIMA) This is an artist's rendition, based on a drawing in Hyde and Connor's Atlas of St. Louis. It shows the installation soon after it had been converted to a cavalry recruitment post and shortly after completion of the construction of Lyon Park. By this time many of the buildings in use during the Civil War have been razed. Note that the river front is still largely undeveloped.

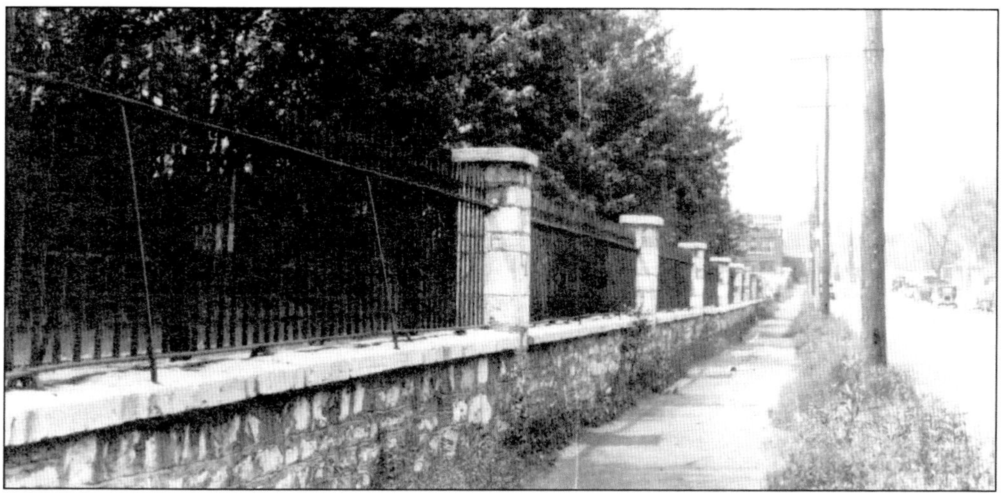

ARSENAL WALL ON SECOND STREET, LOOKING SOUTH. (Courtesy of NIMA) The new wall built along Second Street had a limestone base and wrought iron fencing. Because the function of the installation was primarily that of a depot, it no longer required the heavy protective wall that was necessary for an arsenal. This new design was also more attractive and in keeping with the pleasant atmosphere of Lyon Park.

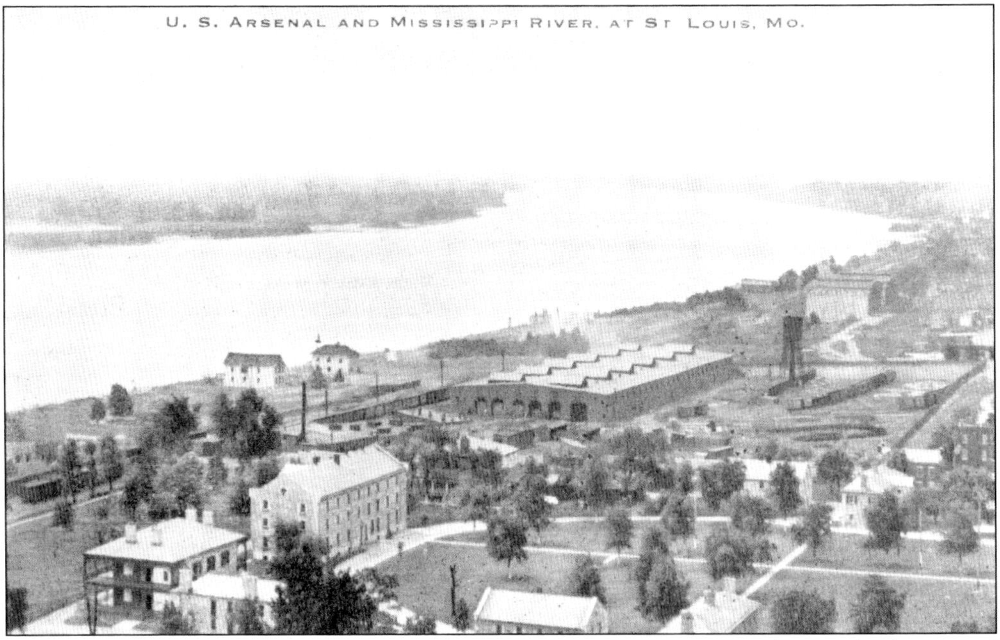

POSTCARD AERIAL VIEW OF THE INSTALLATION, C. 1910. (Courtesy of NIMA) The arsenal was a popular subject of postcards early in the twentieth century. Above is a postcard from approximately 1910 which shows the attractive grounds of what is still referred to as the U.S. Arsenal. This image was made just a few years before the construction of the large, unsightly, but militarily functional quartermaster building (#36). In the background of this image can be seen the building and grounds of the American Car Company, manufacturer of railroad cars.

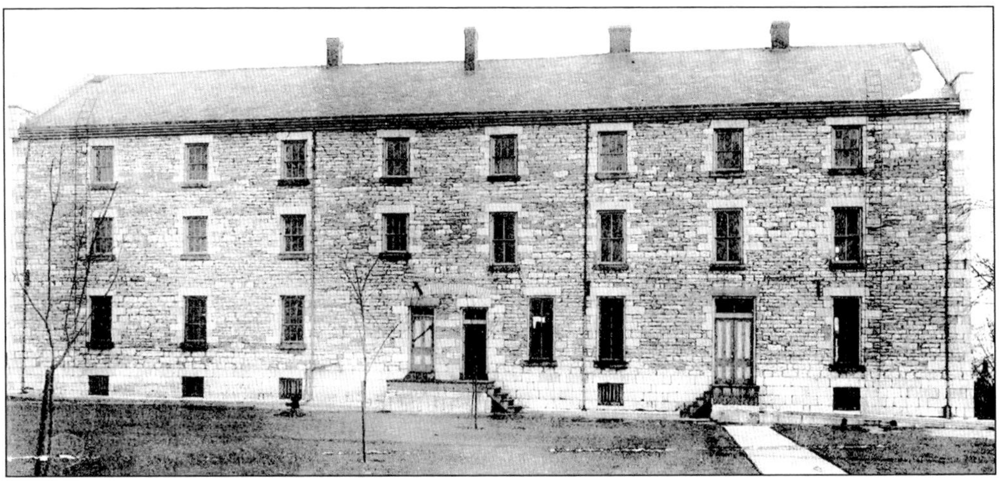

BUILDING 14—MAIN ARSENAL BUILDING AS SEEN FROM THE WEST, C. 1905. (Courtesy of Missouri Historical Society) This building witnessed a world of change in its 98-years of existence. During the Civil War it served as a small arms arsenal. After the armaments were transferred out, the building was used for various types of storage. In the 1890s, for instance, it stored furniture, boots, and shoes, a sad decline from the proud old days when it symbolized the bastion of Union strength. In its final years under the medical depot, it held medical supplies. In 1918 the hulking quartermaster building was constructed just east of the Old Arsenal, between it and the river. The new overshadowed the old, and in 1926 the Old Arsenal building ceased to exist.

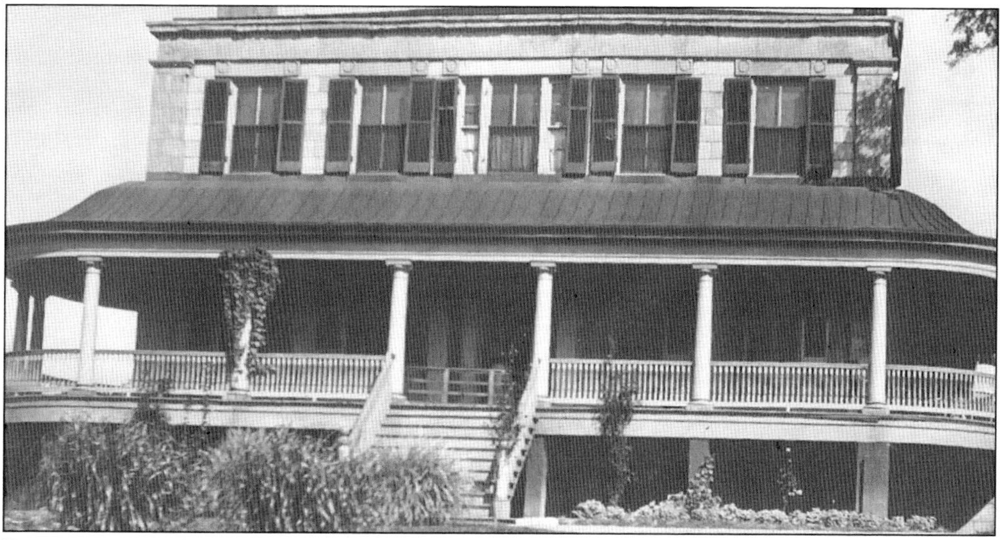

BUILDING 13—COMMANDER'S QUARTERS, C. 1905. (Courtesy of NIMA) The commander's quarters continued serving the housing needs of arsenal commanders and their families until 1906, when Building 25 was constructed. The ornate and well-appointed quarters was the site of many weddings and special functions in the life of the arsenal. From the wide verandah on the east side of the house observers could watch the Mississippi boat traffic. But as time passed, the railroads became more active, increasing the noise and pollution along the waterfront, and the St. Louis Car Company produced railroad cars and parked them in front of the arsenal wall, all of which detracted from the aesthetic view. When Building 25 was constructed, Building 13 became a regular officers' quarters. In 1914 part of the second floor was damaged by fire and was repaired the next year. But with the construction of the quartermaster building just east of the edifice, the old commander's quarters was doomed. It was torn down in the winter of 1919.

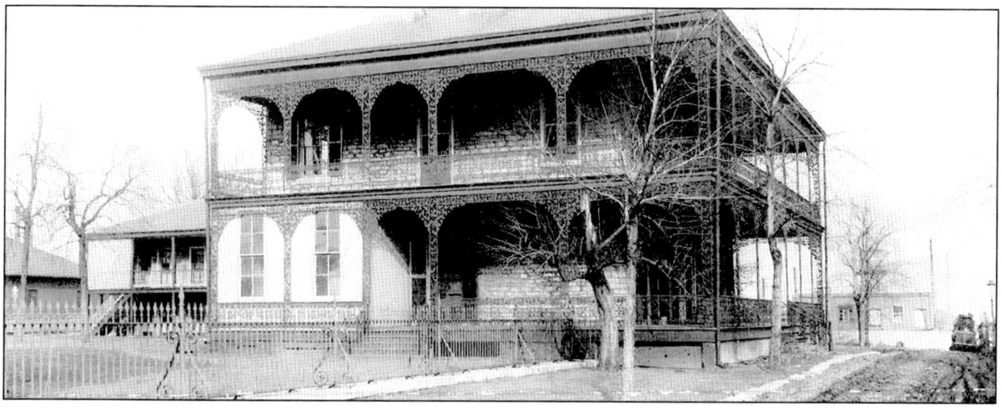

BUILDING 15—OFFICERS' QUARTERS, AS SEEN FROM THE SOUTHEAST, W.C. PERSONS, PHOTOGRAPHER, C. 1905. (Courtesy of Missouri Historical Society) This building was originally the one-and-a-half-story Arend Rutgers residence, built about 1819, and the first building to be inhabited after the war department purchased the grounds. It housed single and married officers and their families. Apparently, after the Civil War, the building was remodeled into a full two-story dwelling with wide, ornate verandas on two floors, surrounding three sides of the structure. The image above shows a wrought-iron fence enclosing the yard and an unpaved street running on the east side of the house. In the later years civilian employees lived in the building. It was torn down in the winter of 1919 at the same time the commander's quarters were razed.

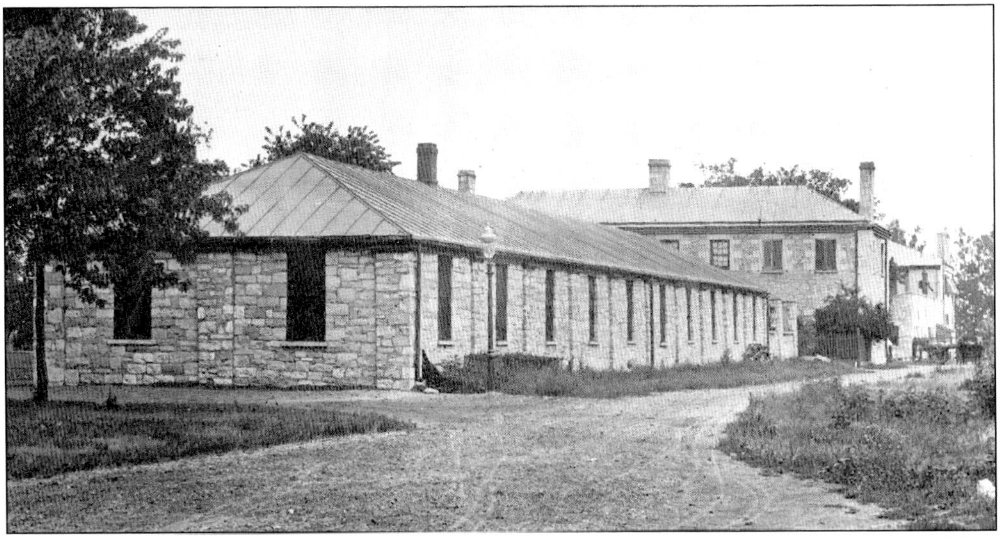

BUILDING 9—WAREHOUSE, C. 1905 (Courtesy of Missouri Historical Society) This building began as the south timber shed but was later remodeled with stone walls to serve other functions. During the Civil War it was a blacksmith shop. After the arsenal operations moved, this building was converted to a warehouse. During the 1890s lumber was stored there and later, quartermaster and medical supplies. In the above image, the old hospital building can be seen, positioned at a 90-degree angle, behind Building 9. Today the building has been extensively remodeled to house Human Resources and has been renumbered 12C.

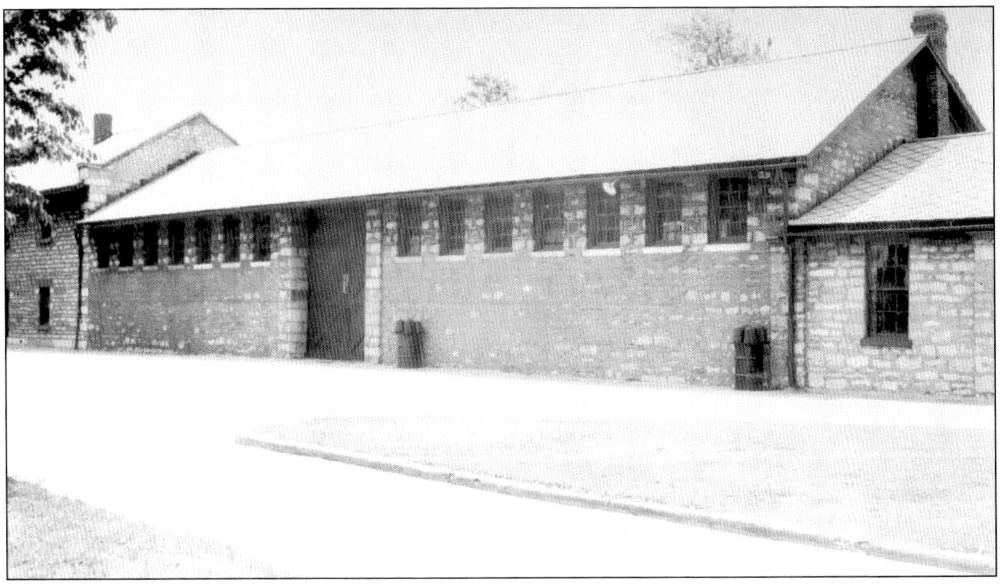

BUILDING 9E—WAREHOUSE BUILT FROM REMAINS OF THE OLD HOSPITAL, C. 1920S. (Courtesy of NIMA) When the old hospital, Building 10, was torn down in 1919, government workers salvaged stone, brick, lumber, window frames, and glazed sash and used them to build a new addition connecting the east end of building 9 with the west end of building 12. This new addition was designated 9E. It measured 29 by 100 feet and was used as a warehouse. Record keepers for the installation proudly recorded that this structure was built "without additional cost to the government."

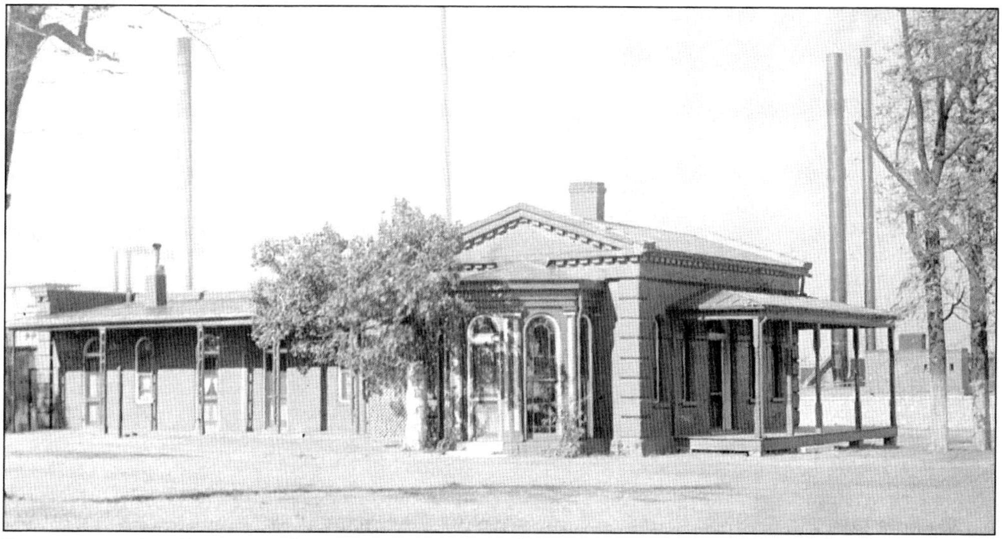

BUILDING 17—CIVILIAN QUARTERS, C. 1905. (Courtesy of NIMA) When the north gate of the arsenal was moved after the Civil War to the west side of the post, a wall was built in its place and there no longer remained a purpose for retaining a guardhouse at this location. For a while it served as the post adjutant's office. Then, an east-west extension was built on the west side of the original building, measuring 62 by 14 feet and the complex was converted to an officers' quarters. Later, in the early twentieth century, this became the dwelling for one civilian employee and his family. With the construction of Building 36, this building was also demolished in the winter of 1919.

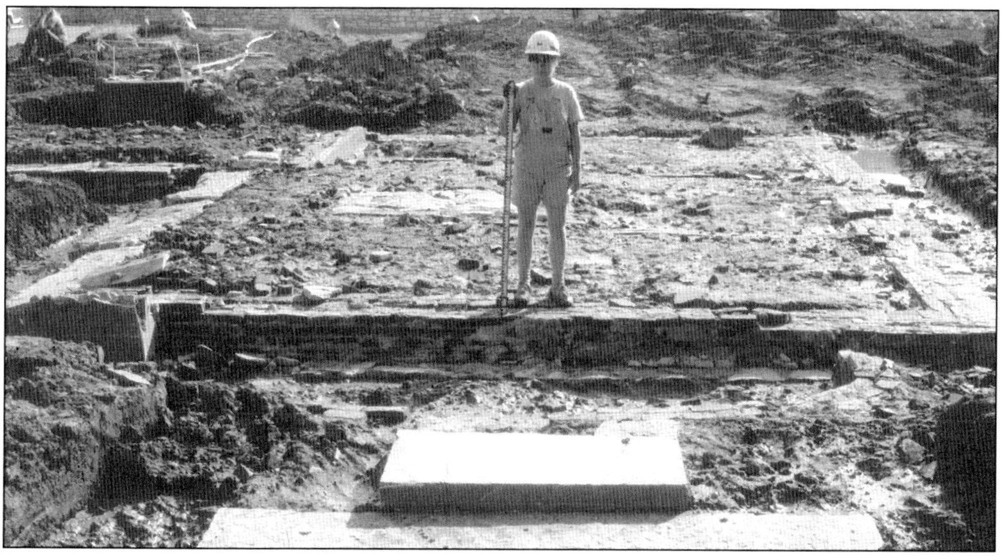

ARCHAEOLOGICAL ASSISTANT, POLLY SHARP, STANDS ABOVE THE EXCAVATED PORCH OF BUILDING 17, 1983. (Courtesy of William Woods) When the archaeological team from Southern Illinois University at Edwardsville conducted excavations on the arsenal property in 1983, they came across the well-preserved foundation of building 17. In fact, a cistern associated with the building yielded highly significant cultural artifacts. In the image above, SIUE student Polly Sharp stands over the excavated porch of Building 17. She is facing south, with the arsenal wall seen in the background.

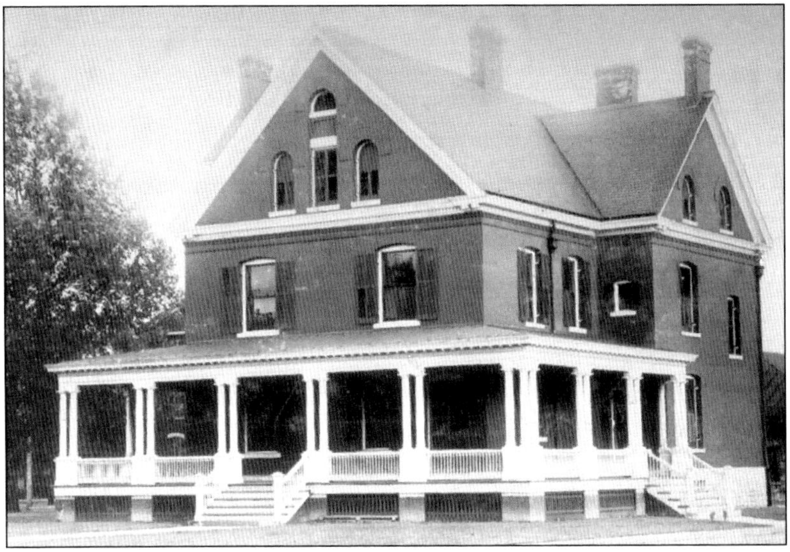

BUILDING 25—NEW COMMANDER'S QUARTERS, C. 1910. (Courtesy of NIMA) In 1906 a new commander's quarters was built just southeast of the front entrance to the installation. Anheuser-Busch contributed the construction in exchange for passageway of the Manufacturer's Railroad along 2nd Street. The new quarters was made of brick at a cost of nearly $20,000. It had a concrete basement and three spacious floors and the roof was covered with slate. One of the more attractive features was the large porch which wrapped around the north, west, and south sides of the house. Strangely, the house was not popular as a commander's quarters; most commanders desired to live at Jefferson Barracks where they would have more contact with other military families. In 1917 it was altered to provide office space for the quartermaster. Thereafter, it served for a time as the personnel office, as the inspector general's office, and then, beginning in the 1960s, as the public affairs office.

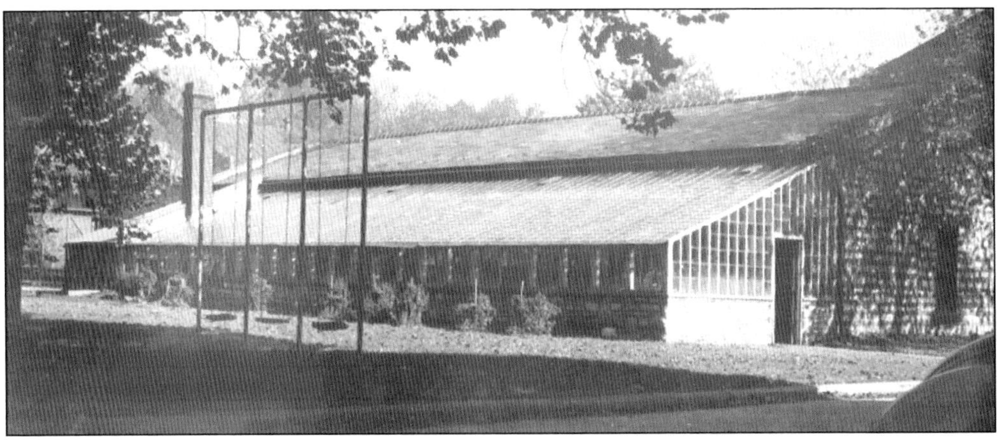

GREENHOUSE ON THE SOUTH SIDE OF BUILDING 2, C. 1930S. (Courtesy of NIMA) In 1919, with the demolition of so many buildings on the arsenal grounds, ample amounts of salvage materials were available for reuse. An enterprising employee of the Quartermaster Depot conceived of the idea to build a greenhouse using much of the glass and stone salvaged from the buildings. So a lean-to greenhouse was built on the south side of Building 2 where there would be plenty of sunlight year-round. It measured 19.5 by 85 feet on the outside and provided 1,280 square feet of space in which to practice the horticultural arts. Attractive shrubbery was planted alongside the greenhouse and a swing-set for employee children was erected nearby. The greenhouse fell into disuse after the Air Force took over the installation and personnel apparently lost interest in the "greening" of the arsenal.

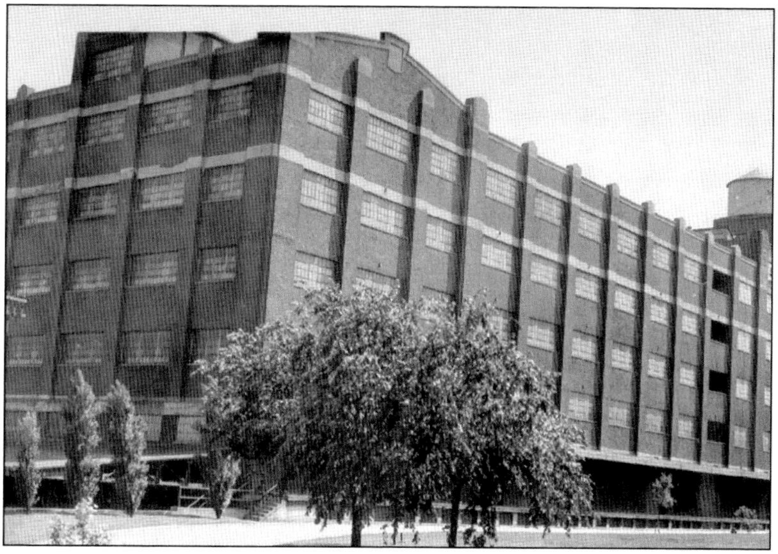

BUILDING 36—MAIN QUARTERMASTER WAREHOUSE, C. 1930S. (Courtesy of NIMA) In 1918 the quartermaster department saw fit to build a gigantic warehouse designed to meet the needs of the modern army much more efficiently than the quaint old buildings left from another era. They designed and built a five-story office and warehouse measuring 104 by 607 feet at a cost of over $1.3 million. It was placed just east of the line of buildings 13, 14, and 15, and west of the railroad tracks. A spur line came in to the loading docks of the warehouse to enhance the loading process. The rear of the building overlooked the Mississippi and blocked the view for the rest of the installation buildings. After the quartermaster left, the medical department used the building, then it was converted to use for aerial chart and map making. It has since been expanded in two large sections by the Defense Mapping Agency Aerospace Center.

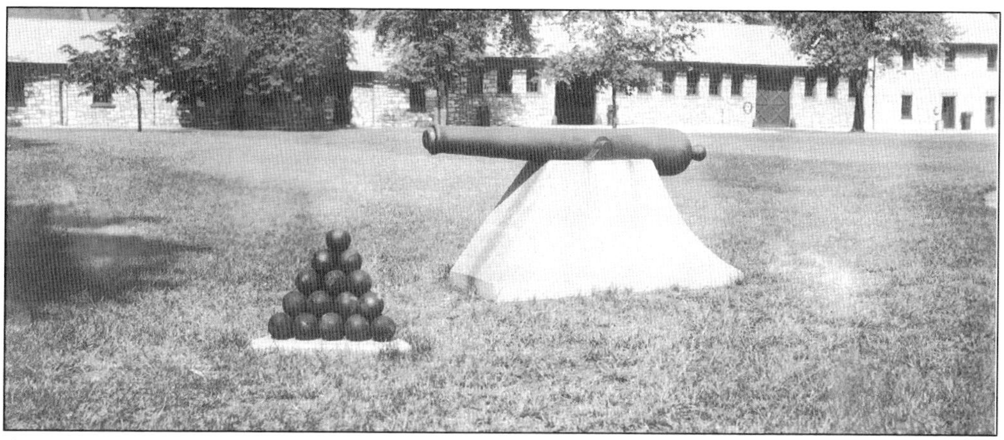

CANNON ON CONCRETE MOUNT, C. 1930S. (Courtesy of NIMA) When Colonel Mathew A. Reasoner took command of the medical supply depot in 1930, he was surprised and grieved to see that there was no physical memory of the arsenal preserved on the site to remind later generations of the significance of the struggle for the Union which had been waged here. Not a cannon or cannonball remained to show the original function of this place. So Reasoner assiduously researched the history of the arsenal, beautified the grounds, and purchased old cannons to set at strategic places in memory of the purpose for which this place had been created. He did not have access to actual cannon balls, so he had concrete replicas made and painted black and piled next to cannons mounted on concrete platforms. It was not a perfect memorial, but it hearkened back to the days of glory more effectively than anything else that had been done.

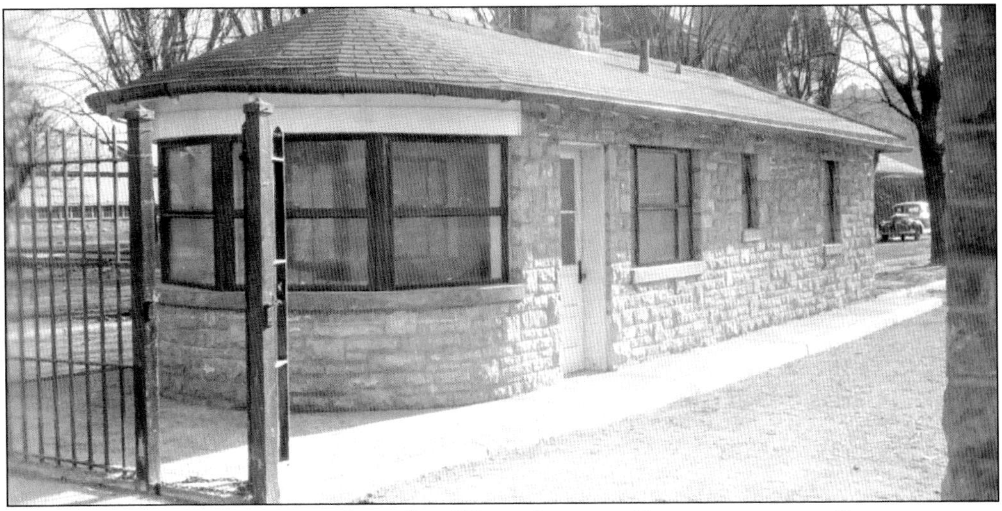

BUILDING 39—NEW "WATCH HOUSE" AT WEST-CENTRAL ENTRANCE TO THE INSTALLATION, 1941. (Courtesy of NIMA) The St. Louis Medical Depot was located at the Old Arsenal site from 1923 to 1952. In 1941, the large western gateway was dismantled and moved to Jefferson Barracks. A new entrance was constructed on Second Street south of the old one, just southwest of Building 25, and a new "watch house" was built to control access to the installation. Another small entrance continued in use at the northwest corner of the post. The new watch house measured 12 by 44 feet and was constructed at a cost of $3,913. It consists of a small watch room and office, a locker room, and lavatory.

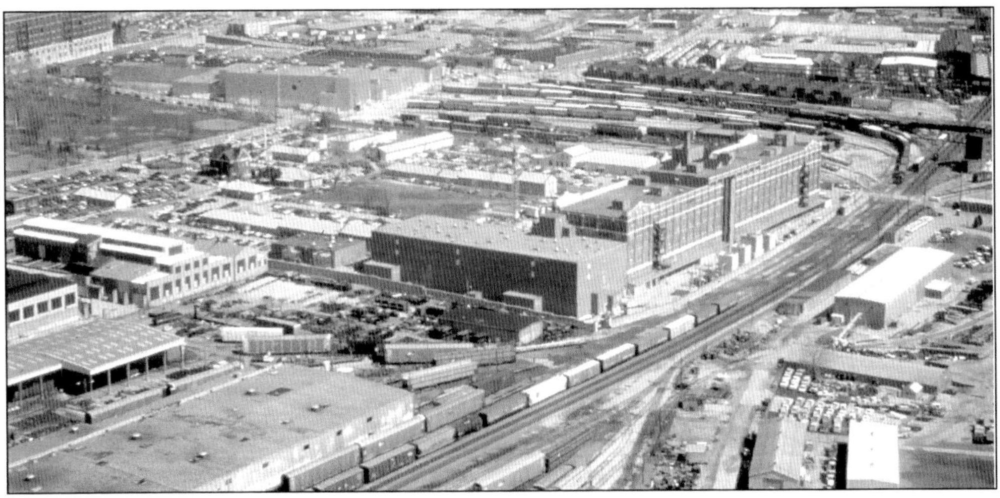

AERIAL VIEW OF THE DEFENSE MAPPING AGENCY AND ARMY CORPS OF ENGINEERS SERVICE BASE, C. 1983. (Courtesy of NIMA) By the 150th anniversary of the founding of the arsenal, the old fort had evolved, along with the city of St. Louis, beyond the wildest dreams of its founders. It had witnessed a dozen cycles of war and peace, had experienced the results of wise decisions and foolish lack of foresight, yet it had survived and contributed liberally to the nation's defense. Today the installation still stands, with the St. Louis Arsenal a proud part of its heritage. Its legacy has not been forgotten because of the dedicated women and men who have worked tirelessly to preserve its memory. But its mission has changed and its will to contribute to the nation's defense continues unabated. In the final chapter we shall see how the present generation has achieved the goal of remembering the past while moving forward to serve the future.

Nine

The Arsenal Today

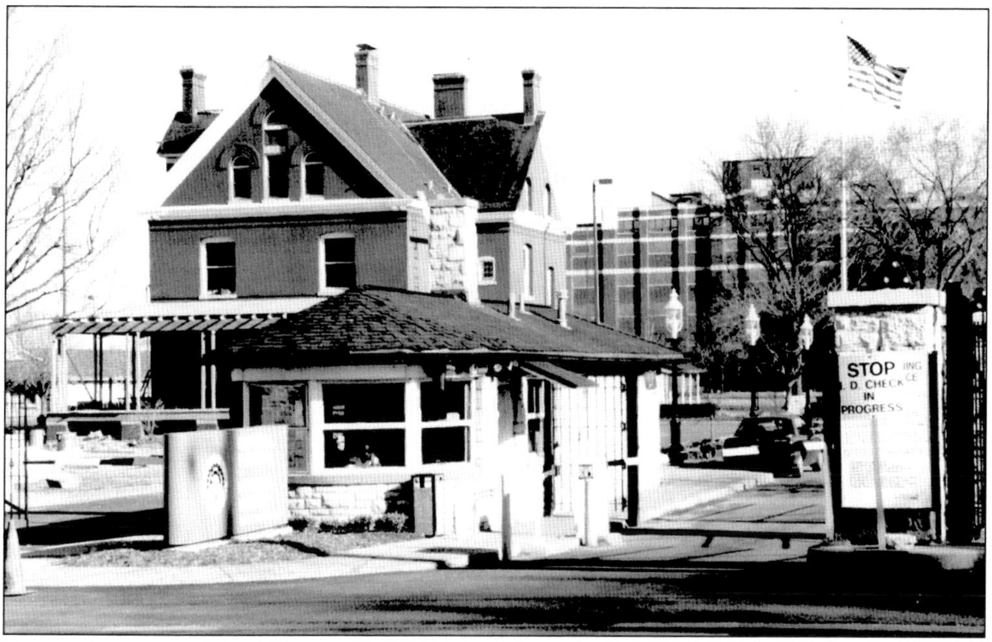

Front Gate and Main Guardhouse to the Installation, 2001. (Photo by the author) In 1996 the National Imagery and Mapping Agency (NIMA) was formed through the merger of the Defense Mapping Agency, the Central Imagery Office, the Defense Dissemination Program Office, and the CIA's National Photographic Interpretation Center, along with related programs of other government agencies. NIMA's stated mission is to provide "timely, relevant, and accurate imagery, imagery intelligence, and geo-spatial information in support of national security objectives." NIMA's major facilities are in Bethesda, Maryland; northern Virginia; Washington D.C.; and St. Louis, Missouri. Once again, the arsenal site has become integral to the nation's security interests through the active operations of NIMA. Yet the historical heritage of this site continues to be remembered and promoted through an active historic preservation program.

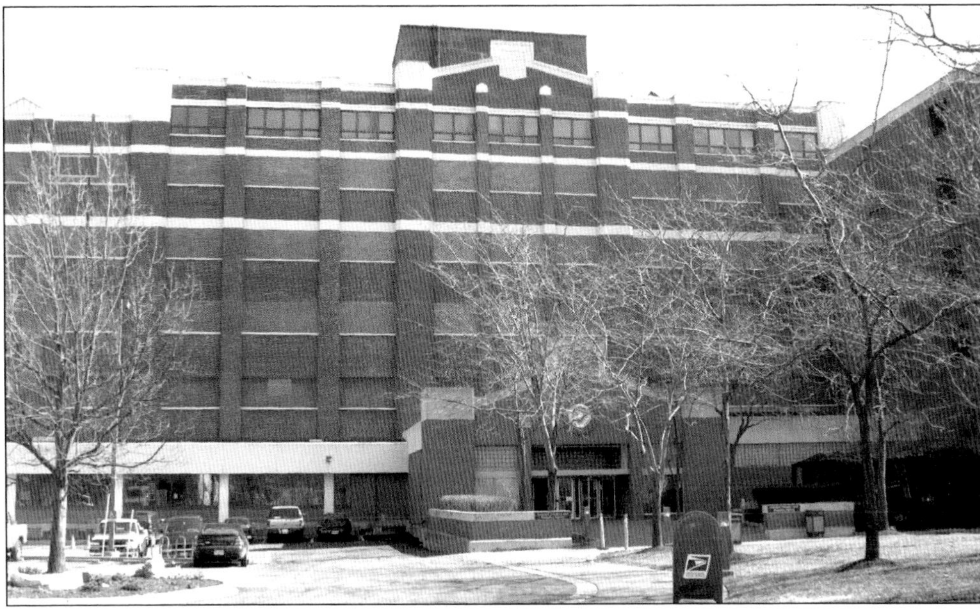

FRONT ENTRANCE TO BUILDING 36, NIMA HEADQUARTERS IN ST. LOUIS, 2001. (Photo by the author) When Building 36 was constructed in 1919, it was designed as a vast warehouse for the Army Quartermaster Corps. Over the years, the building's functions have evolved as it has been updated to meet specific requirements of the Medical Supply Depot, the U.S. Air Force Chart and Information Center, the Defense Mapping Agency, and now the National Imagery and Mapping Agency. The need for a highly secure and multifaceted facility capable of producing the latest in cartographic and digital products has necessitated the most extensive renovation of the old building. Two new wings (designated sections D and E) have been added to the complex in the past 20 years.

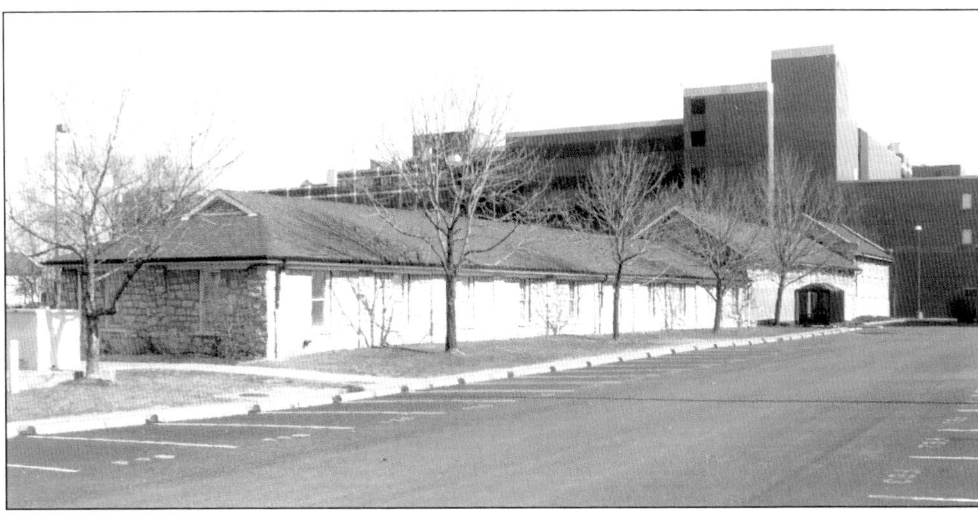

BUILDING 12 COMPLEX WITH BUILDING 36 IN THE BACKGROUND, 2001. (Photo by the author) The complex of structures now designated building 12, originally consisted of buildings 9, 9E, and 12. Today this complex houses several of the Human Resources offices of NIMA. Building 36 rises in the background with its new additions seen in the upper right. A parking lot now covers the area formerly occupied by enlisted housing (Buildings 8 and 11).

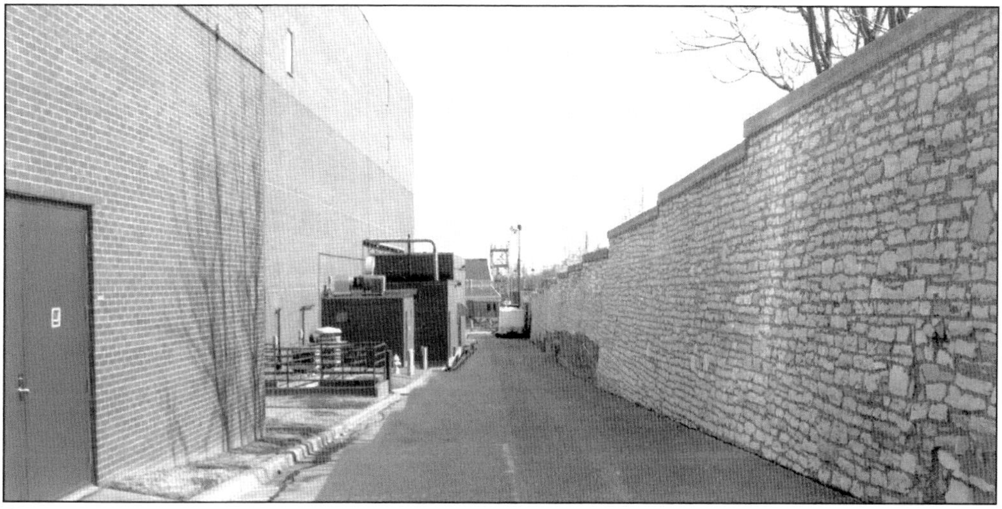

CONTRAST OF OLD AND NEW, 2001. (Photo by the author) Remnants of the old arsenal still stand beside the latest construction on the NIMA site. In the image above, the old 1845 wall stands in opposition to the newest addition on building 36. Air conditioning units on the left cool the massive facility today whereas the large stone buildings formerly depended upon open windows, high ceilings, and a fresh breeze to remain habitable in the sultry summer heat.

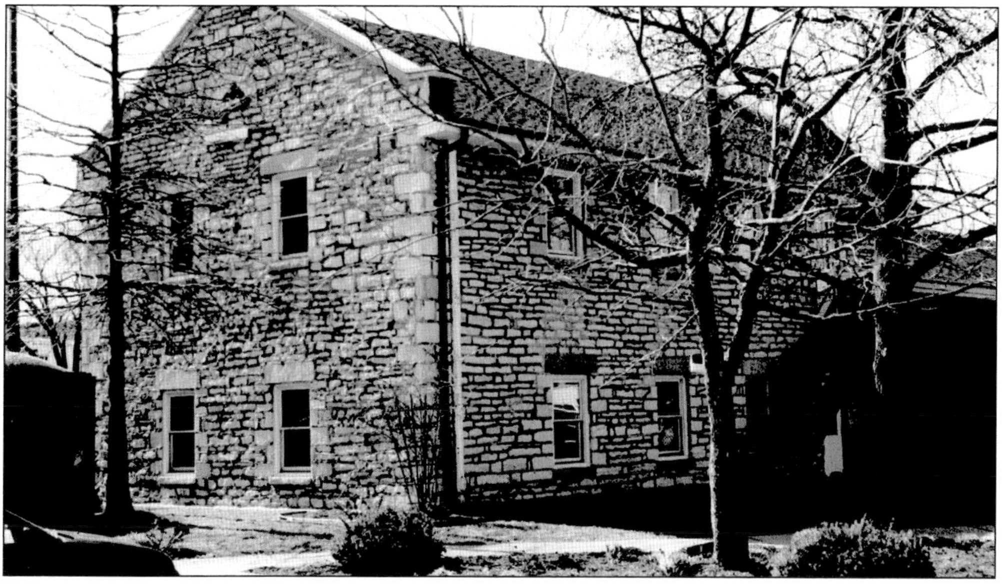

BUILDING 18—INSTALLATION ENGINEERING OFFICE, 2001. (Photo by the author) The St. Louis Arsenal site was enrolled on the National Register of Historic Places on January 17, 1975. Since that time the Historic Preservation Office has endeavored to document the history of the site and to renovate many of its pre-Civil War features. One of the major challenges of this program has been to preserve the architectural integrity of the site while maintaining its functionality for the organization's present mission. So with Building 18 above, for instance, we can admire the meticulous detail of the 1830 stonework on this original carriage-maker's shop, while the current occupants utilize the remodeled interior for the installation engineering offices. (It may be of interest to note that this particular view of the rear of the building depicts details of its structure not seen in most historic photographs.)

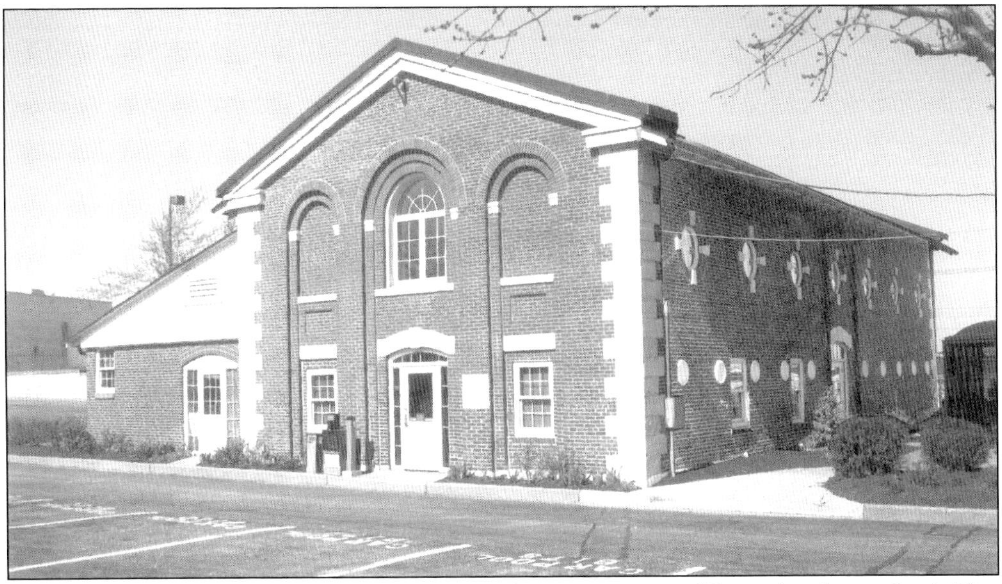

BUILDING 20—NIMA HUMAN RESOURCES CENTER, 2001. (Photo by the author) This building was constructed in 1852 as the main stable and continued in that role well into the twentieth century. In 1910 and 1917 a brick annex was built onto the west side of the building to accommodate 10 horses, bringing the number of horses housed in the structure to nineteen. After World War II it was used for maintenance offices and equipment storage. Today, in its thoroughly renovated state, it serves as a human resources building. The exterior is reminiscent of its days as a stable while the interior is a fully appointed office building.

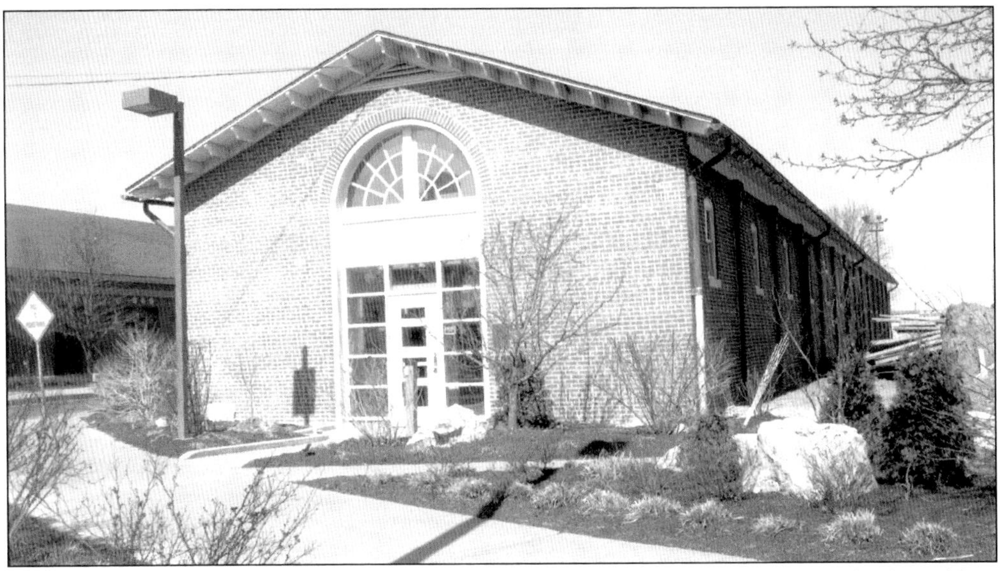

BUILDING 22—NIMA COLLEGE AND TRAINING CENTER. (Photo by the author) Building 22 has experienced a long and varied history. Constructed as a long, narrow, open-air timber warehouse around 1853, it was enclosed with brick in 1892 to become a general storeroom and electric sub-station. It has recently been extensively remodeled and is now the center for NIMA training where employees may take classes or pursue independent study in their specialties and learn new skills for advancement.

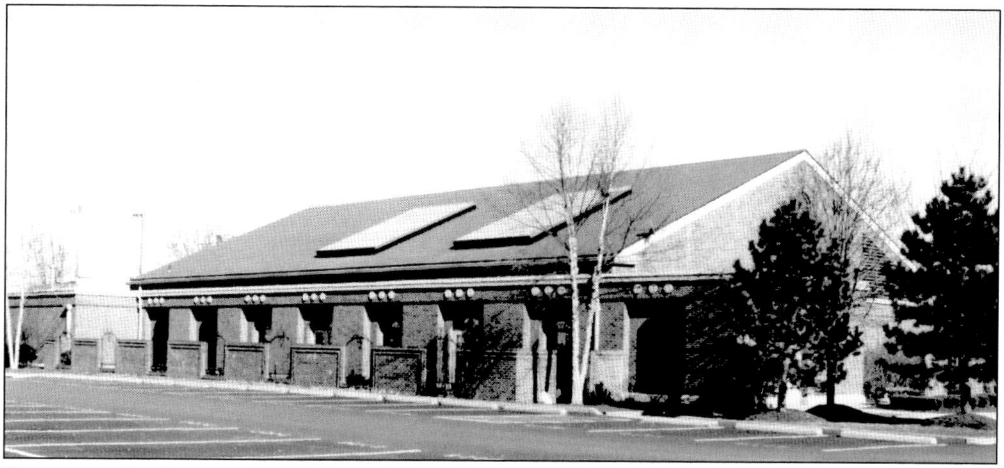

BUILDING 1—INSTALLATION DINING HALL, 2001. (Photo by the author) This building has probably experienced more major renovation than any other on the installation. Built in 1850 as a three-story artillery storehouse, it became a warehouse after the Civil War. The upper two floors were judged too weak to hold any substantial weight in 1939, so they were abandoned. After World War II, under Air Force administration, the top two stories were razed and the bottom story was reconfigured into a cafeteria with a stucco exterior. Under DMAAC, the building was completely remodeled as a spacious dining facility in a style architecturally similar to the original artillery storehouse.

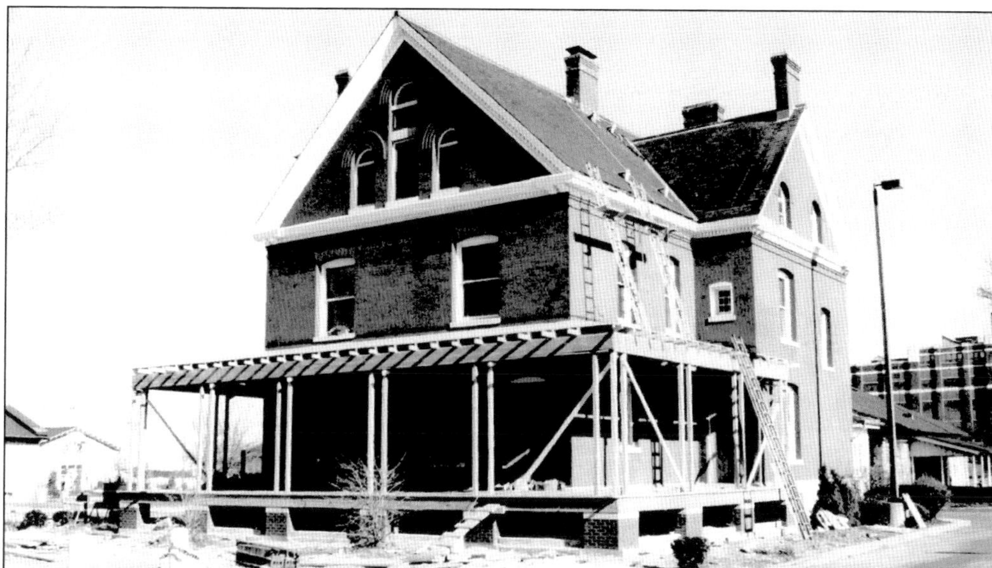

HISTORICAL RENOVATION OF THE PORCH ON BUILDING 25, 2001. (Photo by the author) As indicated earlier, this building served as a commander's quarters for only a short time. Thereafter it provided administrative space for various offices. In 1926 the original wooden porch was replaced with a concrete porch and brick columns. In the spring of 2001 the brick and concrete structure was removed and replaced with a wooden one in the original style, in keeping with principles of the National Register of Historic Places. It is hoped that all of the pre-Civil War buildings will eventually receive appropriate historical renovation. At this time all of the early buildings are identified with descriptive historical markers.

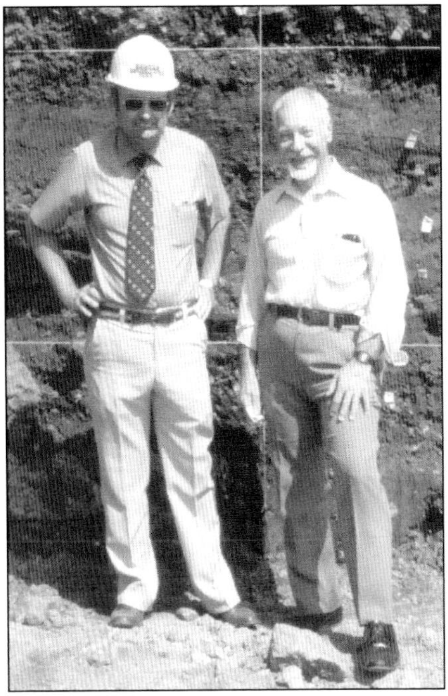

DMAAC Public Affairs Officer and Historian Observe Archaeological Work on Old Arsenal Grounds, 1983. (Courtesy of William Woods) David Black (left), DMAAC public affairs director and Richard Barnard, DMAAC historian, view progress of the 1983 archaeological excavation at the arsenal site. Black held positions in public affairs from 1968, when the installation was under the Air Force, to 1988, when he transferred to Washington D.C. with DMA. Richard Barnard served for many years under the Air Force and DMAAC as cartographer, historian, and technical librarian. He was known as a "walking encyclopedia" of information on the arsenal, having studied and written articles on it throughout his career. Both Black and Barnard were instrumental in arranging for the dig and were gratified in its results. The present generation owes a great debt of gratitude to these men for keeping the memory of the arsenal alive.

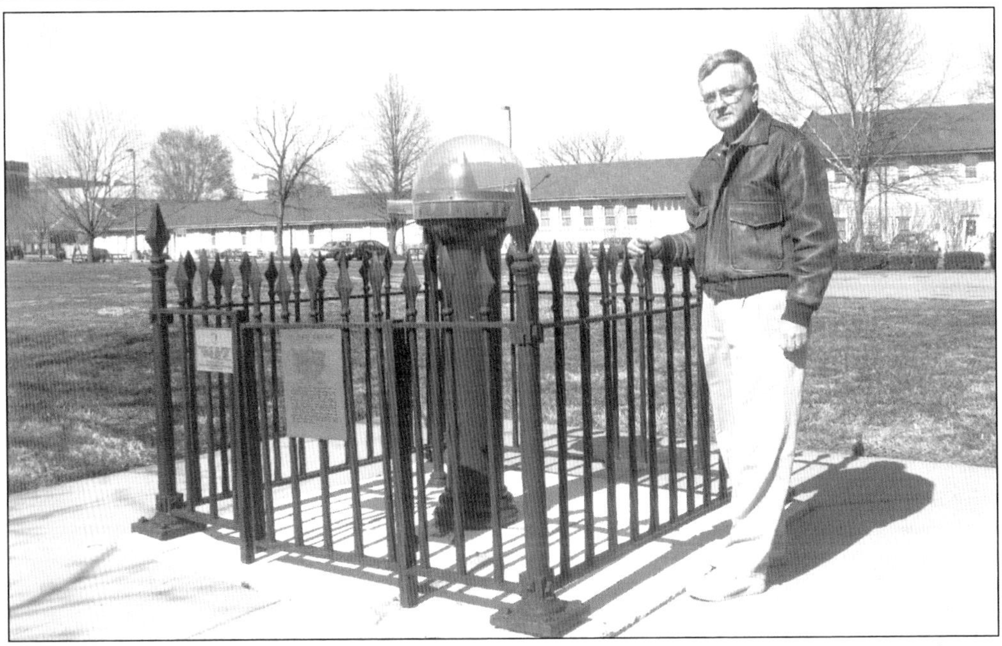

James Mohan, NIMA Public Affairs Officer, Leads a Tour of Old Arsenal Sites, 2001. (Photo by the author) James Mohan first came to work for the graphics department of the Defense Mapping Agency in 1978. Two years later he transferred to public affairs where he became deputy to Director David Black. In 1988 Mohan became DMAAC's public affairs officer and took on additional responsibilities as historic preservation officer. Since then he has worked tirelessly to promote the historic heritage of the St. Louis Arsenal and has become the acknowledged expert on all things pertaining to the site. For more information on the St. Louis Arsenal, call the Public Affairs Office at 314-263-4142.

Selected Bibliography

Black Hawk. *Life of Black Hawk*. Boston: 1834. Reprint, State Historical Society of Iowa, Iowa City, 1932.

Buel, J.W., ed. *Louisiana and the Fair: An Exposition of the World, Its People and Their Achievements*. St. Louis: World's Progress Publishing, 1904.

Dusenbery, Benjamin M. *Monument to the Memory of General Andrew Jackson*. Philadelphia: Walker and Gillis, 1846.

Fayel, William. "Arsenal." In *Encyclopedia of the History of St. Louis*. Eds. William Hyde and Howard L. Conard. St. Louis: Southern History, 1899.

Fremont, John Charles and Jessie Benton Fremont. *Memoirs of My Life: Including in the Narrative Five Journeys of Western Exploration*. 2 vols. Chicago: Belford, Clarke and Co., 1887.

Gibbon, John. *The Artillerist's Manual*. 2nd ed. New York: Van Nostrand, 1863. Reprint Dayton, OH: Morningside, 1991.

Giddings, Joshua R. *The Exiles of Florida*. Columbus, OH: Follett, Foster and Co., 1858.

Grant, Ulysses S. *Personal Memoirs of U.S. Grant*. New York: Webster, 1885 and 1886. James M. McPherson, ed. New York: Penguin Books, 1999.

Guernsey, Alfred H. and Henry W. Alden. *Harper's Pictorial History of the Civil War*. New York: Fairfa Press, 1866. Reprint Crown Publishers, 1977.

Henry, Robert Selph. *The Story of the Mexican War*. New York: Bobbs-Merrill, 1950.

Huebner, Henry Richard. *Civil War Artillery Manual*. Indiana Civil War Centennial Commission. Indianapolis: Indiana Historical Society, 1962.

Iverson, Howard E. "The History of the St. Louis Arsenal: 1826–1861." Master's Thesis. Department of History, Washington University, St. Louis. 1963.

Madaus, H. Michael. *American Longarms*. A Warner Collector's Guide. New York: Warner Books, Main Street Press, 1981.

McElroy, John. *The Struggle for Missouri*. Washington D.C.: National Tribune Co., 1909.

Miller, Francis T., Editor-in-Chief. *The Photographic History of the Civil War*. 10 vols. New York: Review of Reviews, 1911.

Phillips, Christopher. *Missouri's Confederate: Claiborne Fox Jackson*. Missouri Biography Series. William E. Foley, ed. Columbia, MO: University of Missouri Press, 2000.

Piston, William Garrett and Richard W. Hatcher III. *Wilson's Creek: The Second Battle of the Civil War and the Men Who Fought It*. Chapel Hill: Univ. of North Carolina Press, 2000.

Primm, James Neal. *Lion of the Valley: St. Louis, Missouri, 1764–1980*. 3rd ed. St. Louis: Missouri Historical Society Press, 1998.

Reasoner, Mathew A. "The Old St. Louis Arsenal which is Now the St. Louis Medical Depot." Non-published manuscript. Missouri Historical Society, St. Louis. 1934.

Rombauer, Robert J. *The Union Cause in St. Louis in 1861: An Historical Sketch*. St. Louis: Nixon-Jones Printing, 1909.

Rywell, Martin. *Sharps Rifle: The Gun that Shaped American Destiny*. Union City, TN: Pioneer Press, 1979.

Sherman, William T. *Memoirs of General William T. Sherman*. 2 vols. New York: Appleton, 1875.

Thomas, Dean S. *Cannons: An Introduction to Civil War Artillery*. Gettysburg, PA: Thomas, 1985.

United States War Department. *Revised Regulations for the Army of the United States, 1861*. Philadelphia: George W. Childs, 1862. Reprint Smithsonian Institution, 1961.

Vogelgesang, Ernest John. "History of the St. Louis Arsenal: 1861–1877." Master's Thesis. Department of History, Washington University, St. Louis, 1963.

Warner, Ezra J. *Generals in Blue: Lives of the Union Commanders*. Baton Rouge: Louisiana State University Press, 1992.

Warner, Ezra J. *Generals in Gray: Lives of the Confederate Commanders*. Baton Rouge: Louisiana State University Press, 1987.

Wild, J.C. and Lewis F. Thomas. *The Valley of the Mississippi Illustrated*. St. Louis: Republican, 1841–42. Reprint, St. Louis: Joseph Garnier, 1948.

Williams, Joyce A., et al. *Archaeological Investigations at the St. Louis Arsenal Site*. (March 1985)

Winter, William C. *The Civil War in St. Louis: A Guided Tour*. St. Louis: Missouri Historical Society Press, 1994.

Photo Credits

I am deeply indebted to several individuals and institutions for making images available for this book. Due to the limited space for captions, abbreviated titles have been used throughout the book to identify the contributor of each image. The abbreviated forms are listed below, along with a more complete form in keeping with the requirements of each contributor.

CARONDELET HISTORICAL SOCIETY: From the Carondelet Historical Society, St. Louis, Missouri
MERCANTILE LIBRARY: From the collections of the St. Louis Mercantile Library at the University of Missouri-St. Louis
MILITARY HISTORY INSTITUTE: From the collections of the Military History Institute, Carlisle Barracks, Carlisle, Pennsylvania
MISSOURI HISTORICAL SOCIETY: From the Department of Photographs and Prints, Missouri Historical Society, St. Louis, Missouri
NATIONAL ARCHIVES: From the Special Media Archives Services Division, Maps and Plans Group, National Archives at College Park
NIMA: Images used with permission of the Public Affairs Office, National Imagery and Mapping Agency, St. Louis, Missouri
SLU ARCHIVES: From the Saint Louis University Archives, Pius XII Memorial Library, St. Louis
SWEENY MUSEUM: From the collection of Dr. Tom and Karen Sweeney, General Sweeny's Museum, Republic, Missouri
JOHN VOLLMANN: From the private collection of Mr. John Vollmann, St. Louis, Missouri
WASHINGTON UNIVERSITY: From the Becker Medical Library, Washington University School of Medicine, St. Louis, Missouri
WATERVLIET MUSEUM: Museum of the Big Guns Archives, Watervliet Arsenal, Troy, New York
WEST POINT: From Special Collections or the Museum of the United States Military Academy
WILLIAM WOODS: Images used with permission of Dr. William I. Woods, Professor and Contract Archaeologist, Southern Illinois University at Edwardsville (SIUE)

Acknowledgments

Although I have listed institutions who contributed to this project, I would like to direct special thanks to individuals not already mentioned, who went out of their way to be helpful: John Waide, Saint Louis University Archivist; Ted Stahl, Jonathan Grimm, and the IMC staff of Saint Louis University; Jim Mohan and Jane Wilkinson, National Imagery and Mapping Agency; Ellen Thomasson, Dennis Northcott, and the staff of the Missouri Historical Society; Jennifer Davis Heaps and Michael Musick, National Archives; Sheila Biles, West Point Archives and Special Collections staff; Michael J. Winey, Curator of the Military History Institute; John Swantek, Curator of the Watervliet Museum; Lilla Vekerdy and Philip Skroska, Becker Medical Library; Ron Bolte, Carondelet Historical Society; Noel Holobeck, St. Louis Public Library; and family members and friends who have helped in countless ways: Marilyn McGuire, Andrew McGuire, Charles Hewitt, Lee Larkin, Gary Asher, and Bobbie Iasigi.

Randy R. McGuire, Ph.D.
Saint Louis University.